Document Formatting and Typesetting on the UNIX^{TM} System

Document Formatting and Typesetting on the UNIX™ System

Narain Gehani

AT&T Bell Laboratories
Murray Hill, N. J. 07974

Silicon Press
25 Beverly Road
Summit, N. J. 07901

Printed in the United States of America

Silicon Press
25 Beverly Road
Summit, N.J. 07901

First Edition
Printing 9 8 7 6 5 4 3 2 1 Year 90 89 88 87 86

UNIX is a trademark of AT&T
Cover by Nina Uppaluru

Library of Congress Cataloging in Publication Data

Gehani, Narain 1947-
Document Formatting and Typesetting on the UNIX System

Includes bibliography and index
1. Document Formatting 2. Computerized Typesetting
3. Document Preparation 4. UNIX System I. Title

Library of Congress Catalog Card Number: 85-61997
ISBN 0-9615336-0-9

To Indu and Neel

Contents

Preface

Computer document preparation can be divided into three parts: editing, formatting and viewing [Furuta, Scofield and Shaw 1982]. In the *editing* part, the document to be formatted is entered into the computer, or an existing document is modified; at this time, formatting instructions are also entered along with the document text. In the *formatting* part, the document is processed as specified by the formatting instructions. In the *viewing* part, the processed document is viewed on a display or printed on an appropriate device.

Document preparation tools have revolutionized the way people write and prepare documents. For example, documents are typed directly into the computer using text editors, spelling errors are detected mechanically, a document is automatically printed in the appropriate style, and two-dimensional equations and figures are specified using a one-dimensional notation. Moreover, the ease with which some document preparation tools, such as the UNIX document preparation tools, can be used has lead people to "compose" at the terminal while typing the document.

The UNIX system provides excellent document preparation tools. This is not surprising because one of the first uses of the UNIX system was to support document preparation (for the patent department of AT&T Bell Laboratories, circa 1971). It was the success of this project that established credibility of the UNIX system and provided the impetus for further development of the UNIX system [Ritchie 1979].

The UNIX system document preparation facilities are not only powerful and versatile, they are also easy to use. Most UNIX system users, sooner or later, gravitate towards using the UNIX document preparation facilities. The number of UNIX users is increasing rapidly because the UNIX system is being accepted as a *de facto* standard operating system; a rapidly increasing number of computer manufacturers and software houses are now offering the UNIX system.

1. Document Preparation on the UNIX System

The UNIX system provides extensive facilities for all three parts of the document preparation process. Several text editors are available on the UNIX system for entering documents into the computer, for example, `ed` (the standard UNIX editor), `vi` and `emacs`. `ed` represents the older generation of editors, called *line* editors, where editing is done on a line-by-line basis; `ed` is likely to be available on most UNIX systems. The newer generation of editors are the *screen* editors that allow file editing to be done directly on the portion of a file being viewed on the terminal screen or display. Two of the most popular screen editors on UNIX systems are `vi` and `emacs`.

The UNIX document formatting facilities, called the DOCUMENTER'S WORKBENCH[1] software [DWB 1984a-c], consist of tools such as the

- formatters `troff` and `nroff`,
- macro packages,[2] such as `mm` and `mv`, that are high-level alternatives to the formatters, and
- preprocessors, such as `tbl` for specifying tables, `eqn` and `neqn` for specifying two-dimensional equations, `pic` for specifying figures and `grap` for drawing graphs.

The DOCUMENTER'S WORKBENCH software also includes a variety of postprocessors with which the formatted document can be viewed or printed on several kinds of devices such as typesetters, laser and line printers, typewriters and bitmap displays.

In addition to the document preparation tools, the UNIX system also provides *writing tools* to help the writer find errors and improve the writing quality. These tools, which automate mechanical aspects of the copy editor's job, are collectively called the WRITER'S WORKBENCH[3] software [Macdonald 1982].

2. About This Book

In this book, I will focus on the formatting part of the document preparation. This is the most complicated part of the document preparation. The reader interested in finding out more about editing should refer to a book on the UNIX system ([AT&T UNIX 1983a, 1983b; Bourne 1982]). Information about viewing formatted documents is implementation dependent and may be found in documents describing the local commands on your UNIX system.

I will discuss the document formatting tools in detail and give many illustrative examples. Specifically, I will discuss the `mm` macro package and the preprocessors `tbl`, `eqn`, and `pic`; I will give a concise description of the

---

1. DOCUMENTER'S WORKBENCH is a trademark of AT&T.
2. Each instruction of the macro packages is actually a call to a formatter macro. Informally, a macro combines several instructions, and every macro call is replaced by the instructions in the corresponding macro.
3. WRITER'S WORKBENCH is a trademark of AT&T.

troff facilities that a mm user might need to fine tune a document; and I will briefly mention some of the other UNIX document fomatting tools. Finally, I will briefly discuss the writing tools.

Although this book is written especially for readers with little or no experience with the UNIX system document formatting facilities,[4] other readers will also find this book helpful. The novice is gradually introduced to the document formatting/typesetting facilities starting with the high-level mm (page-layout) macros. The reader already somewhat familiar with these facilities will learn about their advanced aspects. Both novices and experienced readers should find the examples beneficial.

Occasionally, the UNIX system provides more than one tool for doing the same task. For example, both pic and ideal are used for specifying figures; both mm and ms macro packages provide the user with high-level formatting capabilities. In such cases I have described only one of the tools; in particular, I have chosen to describe pic and mm because they are used by more people than ideal and ms, respectively;[5] moreover, they are standard components of the DOCUMENTER'S WORKBENCH software.

2.1 Organization of the Book

Each chapter is followed by exercises that complement the material presented in the chapter. There are many examples in this book; I have taken most of them from a variety of real documents such as letters, technical articles and books that were prepared using UNIX system document preparation facilities. A small glossary is given to provide the reader with a quick reference to some of the commonly used terms in document formatting and typesetting.

An extensive bibliography of articles on document formatting and on relevant topics is given at the end of the book. Many of the items in the bibliography are annotated to highlight their main points. The reader is urged to read the bibliography because it lists many interesting items, not all of which have been cited in the text.

---

4. However, I am assuming that the reader has some familiarity with the basics of the UNIX system [Bourne 1982; Kernighan and Pike 1984], for example, logging on, creation and manipulation of files and so on.

5. mm offers more facilities than ms, for example, automatically numbered lists, a variety of document types, definitions of page headers and footers, figure-, table- and equation-caption instructions and table-of-contents instruction. ideal has some facilities that are not provided by pic, for example, ideal allows dashed circles to be drawn and has facilities for shading objects.

2.2 Preparation of the Book

This book was prepared using the document formatting tools described in it.

Murray Hill, N. J. Narain Gehani
September 1985

Acknowledgment

I am grateful to AT&T Bell Laboratories for giving me the opportunity to write this book.

Many friends and colleagues have helped improve this book by giving constructive comments and suggestions on earlier versions of the book; for this I am grateful to A. V. Aho, R. B. Allen, R. F. Cmelik, R. Crabtree, F. Dalrymple, M. J. Harvey, C. L'Hommedieu, W. J. Letendre, J. P. Linderman, A. W. Nagle, D. E. Perry, M. A. Plotnick, W. D. Roome, K. K. Sabnani, J. Schwarz, R. K. TeVault, C. S. Wetherell and V. A. Vyssotsky.

Nancy Bock and Fred Dalrymple have, over the past several years, answered numerous questions about the UNIX document formatting facilities. I am grateful for this help.

Bill Letendre, Mike Harvey and Andy Nagle updated me on the latest changes to the DOCUMENTER'S WORKBENCH software and they provided me with appropriate documents and software. I appreciate their help.

I must also thank Phyllis Policastro and Mildred E. Stepney of Reprographic Services at AT&T Bell Laboratories for their help.

I am grateful to MummyD and Daddy, and MummyK and Papa for relieving me of many of the daily household chores which gave me time to write the book.

Chapter 1
Introduction

Writing good and readable documents is an important and often difficult task that requires good writing skills, creativity and a thorough knowledge of the appropriate subject matter. It also involves tedious and mechanical activity such as formatting the document, checking for spelling errors, improving writing style, writing equations and tables, and drawing figures. Fortunately, computers can be used to eliminate many of the tedious and mechanical aspects of document preparation. Though computer document preparation cannot replace the creativity, imagination or knowledge of the writer, such assistance can let the writer focus on the quality of the writing.

Some economic justifications for using computers to prepare documents [Furuta, Scofield and Shaw 1982] are the

- high cost of manual production of documents,
- decreasing cost of computers and
- availability and decreasing costs of high-quality computer-controlled printers and typesetters.

Making changes to a typed document requires a lot of work. Even small changes may require retyping the whole document, especially if the changes affect the document layout. But if the document has been stored in a computer, then only the changes to the document need to be made. Once this has been done, the computer can then produce a fresh copy of the document with all the changes incorporated.

Not only are computer-prepared documents cheaper, but they can be produced faster and are generally of a better quality than manually prepared documents. For example,

- informal experiments have shown that using the UNIX system to prepare technical articles is 2.4 times as fast as using typewriter composition and costs about one third as much [Lesk and Kernighan 1977].
- according to a Boston University study, "typeset business documents are more credible and can be read 27% faster than those turned out on a typewriter" [Business Week 1984].

Measured by any standards, the UNIX document formatting facilities have been and continue to be very successful [Furuta, Scofield and Shaw 1982]. Despite the fact that many of these facilities were designed several years ago, only a few other document formatting systems, for example, *TeX* [Knuth 1979] and `scribe` [Reid 1980], come close to providing capabilities similar to those provided by the UNIX document formatting tools. Moreover, these other formatting systems do not provide all the capabilities provided by the UNIX document formatting facilities. For example, *TeX* does not generate the table of contents automatically, number equations automatically [Spivak 1982] or provide facilities for drawing figures; `scribe` does not have facilities for describing figures, complex tables or complicated mathematical equations.

1. Document Format

A document prepared on the UNIX system has two forms: *raw* (unformatted input) and *formatted*. The *raw* document consists of two components: *text* that is to be printed and *document formatting instructions* specifying the text format and the layout of equations, tables and figures. The text and the document formatting instructions are intermixed. Document formatting instructions can be easily distinguished from text because they begin with the characters "`.`" or "`'`" at the beginning of a line, or they begin with the character "\".

The formatted document is produced by processing the raw document first with programs called *preprocessors* and then with a computer program called the *formatter*; each preprocessor translates formatting instructions meant for it into formatter instructions. Instructions that format text and lay out equations, tables and figures are not printed in the formatted document. Using appropriate programs, called *postprocessors*, the formatted document can be printed on devices such as a phototypesetter, a laser printer or a typewriter, or viewed on devices such as a bitmap display.

1.1 `troff` Example

Before we proceed further, let me give you a flavor of document formatting using the UNIX system formatter `troff`. Suppose you have entered (using some text editor) the following text [Carroll] in a file called `alice`:

```
"It sounds like a horse," Alice thought
to herself. And an extremely small voice,
close to her ear, said "you might make a
joke on that-something about horse and
hoarse, you know."
```

To format this file with `troff`, you may have to type a command that looks something like `troff alice | `*send*

where *send* is the command that will take the output of `troff` and send it to an appropriate printing device such as a phototypesetter or a laser printer or that will allow you to view the formatted document on your terminal.

Here is what the formatted version of the above document may look like:

> "It sounds like a horse," Alice thought to herself. And an extremely small voice, close to her ear, said "you might make a joke on that-something about horse and hoarse, you know."

Notice that there is no one-to-one correspondence between the raw text lines and the formatted text lines. By default, `troff` operates in *fill* mode; that is, it reads input and uses as much of it as possible to assemble an output line. `troff` then justifies the line, that is, inserts spaces between the words so the lines are right justified (i.e., flush with the right margin). After that, `troff` prints each line.

Suppose a document is to be formatted in the *no-fill* mode in which input lines are not combined or right justified. No-fill mode is specified with the `troff` instruction `.nf`; the fill mode is restored with the `troff` instruction `.fi`.

If file `alice` is formatted in no-fill mode, then it will be printed as

```
"It sounds like a horse," Alice thought
to herself. And an extremely small voice,
close to her ear, said "you might make a
joke on that-something about horse and
hoarse, you know."
```

It was not really appropriate to format this text in no-fill mode. But it is necessary and even desirable to use the no-fill mode for text such as poems:

```
Humpty Dumpty sat on a wall:
Humpty Dumpty had a great fall.
All the King's horses and all the King's men
Couldn't put Humpty Dumpty in his place again.
```

Let us now go back to our previous example and take a closer look at the output produced by formatting the file `alice`. The double quotes are not very pleasing. They are not like the nice looking quotes, “ and ”, that we are accustomed to seeing in high-quality documents. Most keyboards do not have keys for such quotes. Fortunately, `troff`, which is a very powerful and versatile formatter, provides ways of specifying quotes and other characters for which there are no keys, and a host of other things, such as characters in different styles (*fonts*) and in different sizes that we cannot type directly from a keyboard. For example, it interprets the character sequences ` `` ` and `''`, which we can enter from the keyboard, as the double quotes “ and ”, respectively.

Our example text has been printed in Times Roman font. This is the default font used by `troff`. Suppose we want to use another font to print some or all of the text. For example, let us say that we would like to print the words “extremely small” using italic font (i.e., *slanted letters*). All we have to do is to tell `troff` to use the italic font for these words. We do this by using a sequence of characters, called an *escape sequence*, which is interpreted by `troff` as instructions and not as part of the input text. Escape sequences begin with the backslash character, which is called the *escape* character. The escape sequence for specifying italic font is `\fI` in which the letter `f` indicates the action to be taken, that is, a font change, and the letter `I` specifies the new font, that is, italic. We must also tell `troff` when to stop using the italic font. The escape sequence for specifying this is `\fP` which instructs `troff` to resume using the previous font (in this case, Times Roman).

By default, `troff` prints text using a font of size 10 points (a point is 1/72 inch). You can instruct `troff` to use a smaller or larger point size. For example, the escape sequence `\s-4` instructs `troff` to use a point size that is 4 points smaller than the current point size. We will use this escape sequence to print the last part of the example text in a smaller point size. The escape sequence `\s0` instructs `troff` to go back to using the previous point size.

`troff` also recognizes an input line (a line in the raw document) that ends with a period, a question mark or an exclamation mark, as the end of a sentence. It automatically inserts an extra space between sentences.

The character “`-`” in the raw document was intended to be the dash character “—” and not the character “-” as printed in the formatted document; to print a dash, the escape sequence `\(em` must be used. This longer dash character does appear on most typewriter keyboards, but `troff` has the name `\(em` (meaning “em dash”) for it and will do the substitution.

Incorporating these changes, the raw document contained in file `alice` now looks like:

```
``It sounds like a horse,'' Alice thought
to herself.
And an \fIextremely small\fP voice,
close to her ear, said \s-4``you might make a
joke on that\(emsomething about horse and
hoarse, you know.''\s0
```

As you can see, the reason for mixing formatting instructions with the raw text is to change and control the default behavior of `troff` as the document is being processed.

The formatted form of the above raw text is

> "It sounds like a horse," Alice thought to herself. And an *extremely small* voice, close to her ear, said "you might make a joke on that—something about horse and hoarse, you know."

Let me show one more example before we move to another topic. Consider the input text:

```
Thank you for your letter dated 8th December
and the interest shown in our product.
The name/model number of the trouser press is

Colby Trouser Press 110-50
```

The formatted version of this text is

> Thank you for your letter dated 8th December and the interest shown in our product. The name/model number of the trouser press is
>
> Colby Trouser Press 110-50

Notice that there is one blank line in the raw text. A blank line does two things. First it causes a blank line to appear in the output. Second, it interrupts `troff` which is in the process of assembling an output line; this interruption is called a *break*. `troff` responds by printing the partially assembled output line, without right justifying it. Breaks are also caused by text lines that begin with a blank space or by the `troff` instruction `.br`.

Now suppose we want to center the last line. We can do this by putting an appropriate number of blanks at the beginning of the line; this number will require some effort to compute. We need to know the line length, the length of the text in the formatted output and the width of a blank. Even this may not lead to the line being centered exactly because we may need to specify "fractional blanks". Fortunately, we do not have to go through all this detail because we can use the `troff` instruction `.ce` to center an output line. The line to be centered is preceded by the `.ce` instruction:

`.ce`
line to be centered

Let me now tell you a little bit about `troff` instructions in general. They all have the form

`.`*xy parameters*

where the period must be in column one and *xy* is a two-letter lower-case instruction name. Some `troff` instructions cause a break in the output. This can be suppressed by using the acute accent ´ instead of the period at the beginning of the instruction.

Let us explore `troff` a bit more. Suppose we also want to reduce the line length to 3.75 inches (from the 4.5 inches that I have been using to show you the formatted output), increase the text indentation by 0.4 inches and leave 0.35 inches of blank vertical space (instead of one blank line) before the last line. These three changes can be specified easily using the line-length instruction `.ll`, the indentation instruction `.in`, and the vertical-space instruction `.sp`:

```
.ll 3.75i
.in +0.4i
Thank you for your letter dated 8th December
and the interest shown in our product.
The name/model number of the trouser press is
.sp 0.35i
.ce
Colby Trouser Press 110-50
```

The formatted output is

> Thank you for your letter dated 8th December and the interest shown in our product. The name/model number of the trouser press is
>
> Colby Trouser Press 110-50

As I have shown you, document formatting is simple and straightforward for many documents; all you have to do is give the text and appropriate formatting instructions. However, document formatting with raw `troff` can get complicated especially when documents contain lists, footnotes, tables, figures and equations.

1.2 UNIX Document Preparation Approach Versus the Visual Approach

UNIX document preparation facilities operate in "batch mode", that is, the user first types in the document and then formats and prints it. Other computer systems, such as the Apple Macintosh[4] computer, provide an interactive facility with graphical aids (referred to as the *visual* or the *what-you-see-is-what-you-get* approach) for typing in documents. On such systems there is no distinction between the raw and formatted document forms—they are the same. Essentially, the formatted document is the document typed in by the user—"what you see is what you get"; menus are used to specify appropriate fonts, point sizes, indentation and so on.

The visual approach has the advantages that it can be easy to learn and that the user can see the formatted document immediately. On the other hand, the visual approach requires a sophisticated user-interface, and a sophisticated and expensive display, for example, a bitmap display; moreover, such a document cannot be viewed on different types of terminals. On the other hand, the UNIX approach allows the document to be input from any kind of terminal, and to be viewed and printed on a variety of devices.

Other disadvantages with the visual approach are that some formatting decisions cannot be easily stated and that formatting decisions are not preserved. For example, how does one state the relationship between the placement of several graphical objects? In the interactive systems, the objects are placed visually and there is no record of the placement relationship. Similarly, there is no record of things such as the point size or indentation being used and their relationship to previous point sizes and indentation (of course, the point size and indentation can be measured explicitly). Moreover, it may be tedious to do repetitive things such as printing a large number of form letters with customized addresses.

2. The UNIX Document Formatting and Writing Tools

The UNIX document formatting facilities, collectively called the DOCUMENTER'S WORKBENCH software, are based on the formatters

4. Macintosh is a trademark licensed to Apple Computer, Inc.

troff and nroff. These formatters are difficult to use directly because they provide low-level instructions, appropriate for typesetters but often not nice for humans. To facilitate the use of these formatters, the UNIX system provides high-level extensions of these tools. For example, it provides the mm macro package to describe documents; mm provides instructions for specifying items such as headings, lists and footnotes. The UNIX system also provides preprocessing tools such as eqn, tbl and pic for describing two-dimensional equations, tables and figures in documents.

In addition to the document formatting tools, the UNIX system also provides *writing tools* to assist the writer. The writing tools, collectively called the WRITER'S WORKBENCH software [Macdonald 1982], provide facilities for checking word spelling, writing style and diction.

The document formatting tools take a raw document as input and produce a formatted document. The writing tools take the raw document as input and produce an analysis of the document text.

2.1 Differences between troff and nroff

Facilities provided by nroff are a subset of those provided by troff. nroff is designed to be used with simple printing devices that usually have few fonts and one point size, for example, typewriters, character-oriented display terminals such as the Hewlett-Packard HP2621 and impact-line printers. On the other hand, troff is designed to be used with sophisticated devices that have several fonts and point sizes, for example, typesetters, bitmap displays and laser printers. A raw document containing formatter instructions can be processed either by troff or nroff.[5] nroff ignores instructions that are specific to troff (which it cannot obey). For example, it treats troff instructions to change to unsupported fonts and instructions to change point sizes as null instructions.

I will base the discussion in this book on troff because, compared to nroff, it is the more powerful formatter. The reader can assume that, in general, the discussion also applies to nroff. I will mention nroff explicitly only when it is necessary to point out differences with respect to troff.

---

5. nroff and troff are highly compatible with each other and it is almost always possible to prepare input that can be processed by both these two formatters. Formatter specific input can be specified by using conditional instructions [DWB 1984a; Ossanna 1977].

   neqn (instead of eqn) should be used with nroff. The output is adequate for proof reading; the output quality depends upon the capabilities of the printing device used.

   Note that nroff does not support pic.

3. Using `mm` in Preference to `troff`

I will use the following text to illustrate the differences between `troff` and `mm` and to explain why I will use `mm`, instead of using `troff` directly, to format documents.

> Here is a summary of methods used for teaching sailing successfully:
>
> 1. Stress safety at all times.
> 2. Maintain strict discipline when on the water; do not let students fool around.
> 3. Praise frequently, go over mistakes publicly, but criticize the student only on rare occasions.
>
> Instructors disregarding these guidelines have only themselves to blame for producing incompetent sailors.

First I will show you how to specify this text using `troff`. Of particular interest is specification of the numbered-item list. `troff` does not know about lists; therefore, item numbers and the layout of the list must be explicitly specified by the user.

A list, such as the one shown above, can be constructed as follows: for each item, leave some vertical space before the item, place the item number at the appropriate position, specify the indentation for the item text, move to the starting position for the item text, give the item text, and then restore the original text indentation.

In terms of `troff` instructions, the paradigm for specifying a list item is as follows:

```
.sp 0.5v
   n.
.in +0.3i
.sp -1.0v
list item text
.in
```

The first line instructs `troff` to leave half a blank line. Line 2 specifies the placement of the item number. The indentation instruction `.in` on line 3 increases the item text indentation by 0.3 inches; this instruction also causes a break. Line 4 instructs `troff` to back up one line so that the initial portion of the item text is printed on the same line as the item number. Line 5 specifies the item text; this can, of course, span several lines. Finally, line 6 specifies that the original indentation is to be restored. (Note that this paradigm does not handle the situation when the break caused by the `.in` instruction results in a skip to a new page).

Using `troff` instructions, the example text shown above can be specified as

```
Here is a summary of methods used for
teaching sailing successfully:
.sp 0.5v
   1.
.in +0.3i
.sp -1.0v
Stress safety at all times.
.in
.sp 0.5v
   2.
.in +0.3i
.sp -1.0v
Maintain strict discipline when on the
water; do not let students fool around.
.in
.sp 0.5v
   3.
.in +0.3i
.sp -1.0v
Praise frequently, go over mistakes
publicly, but criticize the student
only on rare occasions.
.in
.sp 0.5v
Instructors disregarding these guidelines
have only themselves to blame for
producing incompetent sailors.
```

It would be convenient for the user if the paradigm for specifying list items could be encapsulated and provided as one instruction. The mm macro package does exactly this. Each mm instruction represents a sequence of `troff` instructions.[6] The general form of an mm instruction, with some minor

6. For the technically inclined, each mm instruction is really a call to a macro defined with the `troff` macro definition facility. This facility allows a symbolic name to be associated with a group of instructions and/or text. A *macro call* is replaced by the group of instructions (i.e., the macro body) associated with the macro name specified in the call.

exceptions, is

. *name parameters*

where *name* is a one- or two-letter upper-case instruction name.

The paradigm for specifying a list item using mm instructions is

```
.LI
list item text
```

In addition, the user has to also specify the beginning and end of a list with the `.AL` and `.LE` instructions. In return for this, mm automatically numbers the list items, does some error checking and offers the user a selection of list styles.

Using mm, the list shown earlier can be specified as

```
Here is a summary of methods used for
teaching sailing successfully:
.AL
.LI
Stress safety at all times.
.LI
Maintain strict discipline when on the
water; do not let students fool around.
.LI
Praise frequently, go over mistakes
publicly, but criticize the student
only on rare occasions.
.LE
.P
Instructors disregarding these guidelines
have only themselves to blame for
producing incompetent sailors.
```

The `.P` instruction specifies the beginning of a new paragraph.

The reason for this example was to show you the difference in specifying text format using `troff` and mm instructions. Compared to `troff` instructions, mm instructions are higher level. `troff` instructions are essentially assembly language instructions for text formatting, much like assembly language instructions of computers.

In addition to providing high-level document formatting instructions, mm knows the layout of objects, such as lists and footnotes, that are commonly used in documents and the layout of several document types such as letters and technical papers. The user does not have to explicitly specify the layout of these objects and document types as must be done in case of `troff`.

I will use mm, and not `troff` directly, for document formatting because, unlike `troff`, mm provides high-level document preparation facilities. At this point, let me quote B. W. Kernighan, a colleague at AT&T Bell Laboratories, who has been responsible for the design and implementation of a substantial portion of the UNIX document preparation facilities:

> The single most important rule of using `troff` is *not* to use it directly, but through some intermediary [Kernighan 1978].

Ideally, there should be no need to use `troff` instructions when using mm. Unfortunately, it is necessary in some cases to use `troff` because the facilities provided by mm are not complete. Consequently, even though we will be using mm most of the time, it is important to remember that mm instructions are expanded into a sequence of `troff` instructions and that it is `troff` that is doing the formatting.

4. Using the Document Formatting and Writing Tools

To format a document containing mm, `tbl`, `eqn` and `pic` instructions, the document formatting tools are used in the following order:

Typesetting a document with figures, tables and equations

If some of the above tools are not used in a document, then it is unnecessary (and wasteful of computer resources) to process the document with them. For example, if the document does not contain any `tbl` instructions, then the output from `pic` may be sent directly to `eqn`.

On some UNIX systems, a special command `mmt` is provided that invokes `troff` with the mm macro package. With appropriate options, it can be made to invoke the preprocessors `pic`, `tbl` and `eqn`, and send the output (the formatted document) directly to the typesetter:

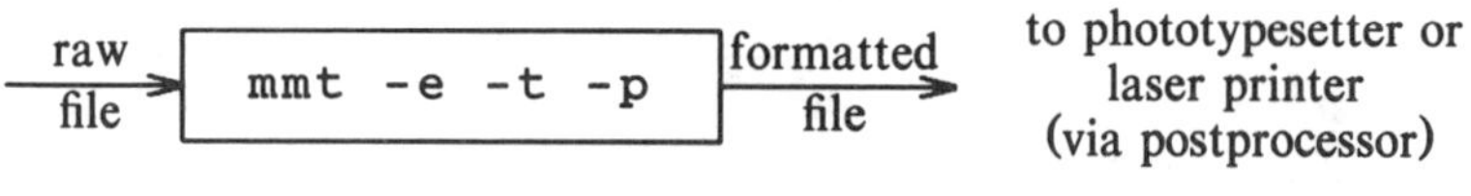

Typesetting a document with figures, tables and equations

Options `-e`, `-t` and `-p` of the `mmt` command invoke the tools `eqn`, `tbl` and `pic`, respectively.

The UNIX system also provides a tool, `checkmm`, that may be used to find `mm` and `eqn` errors

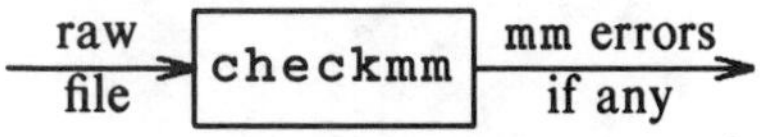

Check for `mm` errors

Writing tools take the raw document as input and produce an analysis of the document text. For example, `spell` examines the document for spelling errors, `double` checks the document for pairs of consecutive words that are identical and `style` checks the writing style used in the document. These tools, which are part of the WRITER'S WORKBENCH software, may be used collectively by invoking the command `wwb` or individually by specifying the appropriate tool, for example, `spell` or `double`.

5. The Typesetting Commands

Either of the following two commands may be used to typeset a document:

`pic` *files*`|tbl|eqn|troff -mm` *options*

or

`mmt -t -e -p` *options files*

files is a list of one or more UNIX files containing the document that is being typeset.

The output of these commands is then sent to the printing device using an appropriate command provided by your UNIX system. The `mmt` command automatically sends its output, by default, to the phototypesetter; optionally, the output can also be sent to other printing devices.

Of course, if the formatted document is to be printed on a typewriter, then the commands `nroff` and `mm` should be used instead of the commands `troff` and `mmt`, respectively.

Chapter 2
Specifying The Document Format

The mm macro package [DWB 1984b] is a set of `troff` macros for specifying the format of a document. mm is a versatile high-level formatting tool that provides facilities such as those for specifying

1. the document title and abstract, date and author(s),
2. automatic numbering of pages, sections and list items,
3. different kinds of lists, paragraphs, and section headings,
4. automatic numbering and placement of footnotes, and
5. different formats for different types of documents such as letters and papers for general distribution.

mm has been used to produce a wide variety of documents, such as letters, papers, viewgraphs, programming manuals and books (including this one). mm has built-in knowledge of some basic document types, such as memorandums and letters, and it knows their page layouts. In case of other documents, such as books, the users must explicitly specify their page layouts.

Despite the versatility of mm, the sophisticated user will find that it is occasionally necessary to use the low-level `troff` instructions with mm, for reasons such as "fine tuning" the document format, referring to special characters such as •, ¼, and ÷, and convenience. Only some `troff` instructions can be used safely with mm; other `troff` instructions may interfere with mm instructions and they should be used only after fully understanding their interaction with mm. Wherever it is necessary or appropriate, I will discuss the use of `troff` instructions in conjunction with mm instructions

1. An Example of Document Formatting

To give you a flavor of how documents are specified using mm, I will show you an example letter that was produced using mm. I will first show you the formatted letter and then its specification. Although I will discuss the specification of the letter line-by-line, I must warn you that I will not discuss each aspect of formatting or each formatting instruction in detail here—that is the purpose of the rest of the book. So please do not worry if you do not fully understand all the formatting details.

The example letter, shown below, was printed on a sheet of stationery preprinted with the company name and address, that is, on *letterhead*.

Transcendental Transportation Inc.
Three Wheel Drive, Busted Axle, Wyoming

April 1, 1985

Mr. A. L. Psmith
113 Niagara Falls Boulevard
Wheeling, West Virginia

Dear Mr. Psmith:

We are in receipt of your letter dated March 23 inquiring about the various types of tires manufactured and sold by us. We make three kinds of tires: the conventional circular tire and the revolutionary fuel-efficient square and elliptic tires.

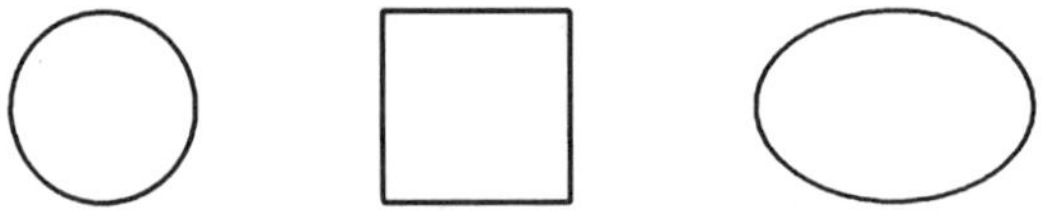

Sample prices for these tires are listed in the following table:

Tire Design	**Size**	**Price**
circular	medium	$55.00
square	medium	$88.00
elliptic	medium	$99.00

The square and elliptic tires are more expensive because of higher manufacturing costs.

Sincerely,

M. M. Yogi
President

The products of Transcendental Transportation are very interesting because they allow me to show you how to specify figures and tables, in addition to plain text, in a document.

The default page and line lengths used by mm are 11.00 and 6.50 inches, respectively. For ease of presentation, I have reduced the line width of the example letter to 4.5 inches. When specifying the page length of a document, space for the top and bottom margins must be included; but space for the left and right margins should not be included in the line length; these margins are independent of the line length and are specified separately.

I will now show you, in two parts, the raw document used to produce this letter, that is, the letter *specification.* The first part is

```
.ND "April 1, 1985"
.AU "M. M. Yogi"
.AT "President"
.MT 5
.DS
Mr. A. L. Psmith
113 Niagara Falls Boulevard
Wheeling, West Virginia
.SP 3
Dear Mr. Psmith:
.DE
.P
We are in receipt of
your letter dated March 23 inquiring
about the various types of tires
manufactured and sold by us.
We make three kinds of tires:
the conventional circular tire and
the revolutionary fuel-efficient square
and elliptic tires.
```

Notice the intermixing of the text and formatting instructions. Lines that begin with a period in column one are formatting instructions; in our example, they are all mm instructions. All other lines are text lines.

First is the new-date instruction `.ND` which is used to specify a date explicitly. If this instruction is not given, then mm will, by default, print the current date. The argument of the `.ND` instruction, the date, is enclosed within double quotes because mm requires arguments with embedded blanks to be enclosed within double quotes.

The second and third instructions are used to specify information about the author. The author-information instruction `.AU` is used to specify the author's name (as illustrated) and, when appropriate, give other pertinent information, such as the room number and the telephone extension. The author-title instruction `.AT` is used to specify the author's title. This information about the author will be used later for printing the signature line information at the bottom of the letter. The quotes around "`President`" are not strictly necessary, but they do no harm.

The fourth instruction, the document-type instruction `.MT`, is used to specify that this document is a letter (indicated by the argument value 5).

Next is the letter receiver's address and the line addressing the receiver:

.DS
address of receiver
and the salutation
.DE

Instruction `.DS` signals the beginning of a display and instruction `.DE` signals its end. Material within a display is treated as a block and is not split across pages; if it is not possible to place the displayed material on the current page, then the rest of the current page is left blank and the displayed material is printed on the next page. In addition to treating the displayed material as a block, the displayed material is, by default, processed in *no-fill* mode in which text is formatted without any rearrangement. Input lines are not combined to *fill* (construct) output lines and each input line is formatted, without any line justification, as one output line.

Within the display is the vertical-space instruction `.SP`, which instructs `mm` to leave three blank lines; these lines separate the receiver's address from the salutation. Following the display-end instruction is the begin-paragraph instruction `.P` which is followed by several lines of text.

Now let us take a look at the second part of the letter specification:

```
.DS CB
.PS
circle; move
box height 0.5 width 0.5; move
ellipse
.PE
.DE
.P
Sample prices for these tires are
listed in the following table:
```

```
.DS
.TS
center;
cb cb cb
a a a.
Tire Design☛Size☛Price

circular☛medium☛$55.00
square☛medium☛$88.00
elliptic☛medium☛$99.00
.TE
.DE
.P
The square and elliptic tires
are more expensive because of
higher manufacturing costs.
.SP
.FC Sincerely,
.SG
```

First there is a picture (figure) specification enclosed within a display:

`.DS CB`
figure specification
`.DE`

Argument `CB` of the display instruction `.DS` specifies that the displayed material, the figures of the three tires, is to be centered as a block. The figure specification has the form

`.PS`
instructions to draw the figure
`.PE`

The picture-start instruction `.PS` and the picture-end instruction `.PE` delimit the instructions to be preprocessed by `pic`. The first line of the figure instructions specifies a circle and then tells `pic` to move a bit without drawing anything. The next two lines contain instructions to draw a box and an ellipse.

After the display is a begin-paragraph instruction `.P` followed by two lines of text. Then there is another display enclosing a table specification of the form

`.TS`
table format and data
`.TE`

Instruction `.TS` signals the beginning of a table specification and `.TE` signals its end. The first line of the table specification indicates that the table is to be centered. The next two lines specify that the table will have three columns and the format of the table entries; the first line specifies the format of the first table row and the second line specifies the format of the remaining rows. Following these lines are the data lines that make up the contents of the table. Entries for different columns in a data line are separated by the tab character (which I have denoted by the symbol ☛ so that it will be visible as you read).

The table and figure specifications are processed by the `pic` and `tbl` preprocessors before the document is processed by `troff`; both `pic` and `tbl` generate `troff` instructions that specify how the figures and the table are to be drawn, respectively.

After the second display, is another begin-paragraph instruction and three more lines of text. Then comes the `.SP` instruction which specifies that one blank line is to be left.

The final two instructions, `.FC` and `.SG`, generate the end lines of a letter. The formal-letter-closing instruction `.FC` places its argument "`Sincerely`" at an appropriate place at the bottom of the letter. The signature instruction `.SG` prints the author's name and title at an appropriate place below the formal letter closing; it leaves enough space for the author to sign the letter.

2. Basics

In this section, I will discuss the basic concepts and details of mm necessary to use mm effectively.

2.1 Document Types

The mm macro package has built-in knowledge of the format of three types of documents: memorandums, external papers and external letters.

document type	**used for**
memorandum	Intra-company documents such as letters, papers, and notes for engineers and programmers.
external letter	Ordinary letter.
external paper	Paper prepared for publication or for general distribution.

mm can also be used to construct other types of documents, for example, books such as this one which was prepared camera-ready for publication. However, the format of these documents must be explicitly specified by the user.

2.2 Formatting Instructions—Stand-Alone and Embedded

As mentioned earlier, a raw document consists of text and formatting instructions. There are two kinds of formatting instructions: stand-alone and embedded. Each *stand-alone* formatting instructions occupies one complete line of the raw document; they begin with a period or an acute accent in column one and are terminated by the end of the line. Stand-alone instructions can be `mm` or `troff` instructions. By convention, upper-case letters are used for names of `mm` instructions and lower-case letters are used for names of `troff` instructions.

Embedded formatting instructions can be intermixed with the raw document text; there are two types of embedded formatting instructions:

1. `troff` *escape* sequences which begin with the backslash character `\`, and

2. in-line `eqn` instructions which begin and end with special characters designated as `eqn` delimiters. Often the delimiter used both to begin and end embedded `eqn` instructions is the dollar character **$**.

2.3 String and Integer Variables

I will often refer to *registers* and *strings*, which are `troff` integer and string variables, respectively. Variables are used for storing values for later use. String variables are often used as convenient abbreviations for long character strings. Integer variables are used as flags and counters, and for integer arithmetic.

`mm` does not have any variables of its own and it substitutes `troff` strings and registers. I will now describe strings and registers briefly; see Chapter 6 titled `troff/nroff`—*The Formatters* for additional details.

2.3.1 String Variables: String variables are defined by using the `troff` define-string instruction `.ds` which has the form

`.ds` *name string*

where *name* is a one- or two-character variable name. The effect of the `.ds` instruction is to associate the string with the variable. Long strings can be continued on to the next line by ending the line to be continued with a backslash. Values of string variables with one- and two-character names *x* and *xx* are obtained by referencing them as `\*`*x* and `\*(`*xx*, respectively. Some examples of string variable definitions are

```
.ds uN UNIX System
.ds tR \f(CWtroff\fP
```

A reference to the string variable `uN`; i.e., `\*(uN`, is replaced by the words "`UNIX System`"; similarly, `\*(tR` is replaced by the string

"`\f(CWtroff\fP`"

2.3.2 Registers: Registers (integer variables) are defined and assigned values with the number-register instruction `.nr`; this instruction has the form

`.nr` *name e*

where *name* is a one- or two-character register name. The effect of this instruction is to assign the value *e* to register *name*. Values of registers with one- and two-character names *x* and *xx* are obtained by referencing them as `\n`*x* and `\n(`*xx*, respectively. When a register is *interpolated* (that is, when the value is inserted into the text), the register value is, by default, output as a decimal string (i.e., in arabic numerals). Output in other formats such as upper- and lower-case letters, and Roman numerals can be specified by using the `troff` assign-format instruction `.af`. For more details, see Section 1.8 in Chapter 6.

2.4 Formatting

The basic operating mode of the formatter `troff` is to read input (raw document) lines, assemble output lines and then print the output lines. We must be able to change the formatter's operating mode to do things such as print lists, center input lines, skip pages and print footnotes. The operating mode of `troff` can be controlled and modified by using `mm` and `troff` instructions. `troff` replaces `mm` instructions by the corresponding `troff` instruction sequences before execution.

`troff` takes as input the raw document (after it has been preprocessed by appropriate tools such as `pic`, `tbl` and `eqn`) and constructs the formatted document by collecting words from the text input lines (in the raw document) and using these words to construct (fill) output lines (of the formatted document). This mode of formatting is called the *fill* mode. A new output line is started when the next word cannot be fitted onto the current output line. If both left and right justification are in effect (as with text on this page), then the spaces between the words in an output line are increased to justify the line on both ends.

2.5 New Sentences

An input text line ending with a period ("`.`"), question mark ("`?`"), or an exclamation mark ("`!`") is recognized by `troff` as the end of sentence. An extra space is automatically inserted between sentences. To take advantage of this feature, the user should begin each new sentence in the raw document on a new line.

2.6 Distance Units

Distances are specified by using *unscaled* (ordinary) numbers or *scaled* numbers. A *scaled* number is an ordinary number followed by a scale indicator which specifies the units associated with the number. Scale indicators that can be used are

scale indicator	meaning
`i`	inch
`c`	centimeter
`P`	Pica (1/6 inch)
`m`	em (approximately, the width of the letter *m* in the current point size)
`n`	en (em/2)
`p`	point (1/72 inch)
`u`	basic formatter unit
`v`	vertical line space

If the scale indicator is not specified, then the scale used is context dependent; for example, the scale is assumed to be ems (`m`) for horizontally oriented requests and vertical line spaces (`v`) for vertically oriented requests.

2.7 Page Dimensions

The default page and line lengths used by `mm` are 11.00 and 6.50 inches, respectively. The *page length* refers to the physical length of a page and it includes space for the upper and lower margins. The *page width* is the sum of the line length plus the left margin, which is called the *page offset* (default value is 1.0 inches for `troff` and 0.75 inches for `nroff`). The page width must be less than or equal to the physical page width. The line length is divided into two parts: indent (text is indented to the right from the page offset by this distance) and centering length (the *centering length* is the actual line length; items are centered with respect to this length).

These relationships can be summarized by the two equations:

page width = page offset (*po*) + line length (*ll*)
line length (*ll*) = indent (*in*) + centering length (*ce*)

These relationships can be depicted as follows [Bourne 1982]:

<table>
<tr><td rowspan="2">po</td><td colspan="2">ll</td></tr>
<tr><td>in</td><td>ce</td></tr>
</table>

The page length, line length and page offset can be changed by using `mm` command line options `-rL`, `-rW` and `-rO`, respectively. See Section 13 for more details. `mm` does not provide instructions for specifying the page length, line length and page offset within the document itself. However, values for these items can be specified within the document by using the following `troff` instructions:

instruction name	instruction format	explanation and comments
page length	`.pl` *n* `.pl` ±*n*	Set the current page length to *n* or to current length ± *n*; default page length is 11.0 inches. Note that the top and bottom margins are not provided automatically; they must be accounted for in the page length.
page offset	`.po` *n* `.po` ±*n*	Set the next page offset to *n* or to current page offset ± *n*; default offset used by mm is 0.75 inches.
line length	`.ll` *n* `.ll` ±*n*	Line length is set to *n* or to current length ± *n*; default line length is 6.5 inches.
line indent	`.in` *n* `.in` ±*n*	Indent all subsequent output lines by *n* or by current line indent ± *n*; default line indent is 0.0 inches.

For more details about `troff` instructions, see Chapter 6. It is important to note that the effect of `.ll` and `.in` instructions does not carry over the different mm environments such as document text and footnotes (discussed in Section 8.8.1).

2.8 Spaces

There are two kinds of spaces: *paddable* and *unpaddable*. Paddable spaces are spaces that can be padded with other spaces when right justifying a line. Normal spaces are paddable spaces. Padding may sometimes destroy the desired alignment or placement of text. In such cases unpaddable spaces should be used because spaces cannot be appended to unpaddable spaces. The spacing between two words separated only by unpaddable spaces will not be changed nor will these words be placed on different lines. An unpaddable space is specified by prefixing an ordinary space by the escape character "\".

As an example of the use of unpaddable spaces, consider the following three lines of a raw document:

```
The assignment statement ``X = 1''
causes the variable X to be assigned
the value one.
```

Right justification of the output may cause extra spaces to be inserted between words as in

> The assignment statement "X = 1" causes the variable X to be assigned the value one.

Suppose the phrase ``X = 1'' is to be kept intact, that is, no extra spaces are to be inserted within it (and it is not to be split across output lines); then the two spaces in this phrase must be made unpaddable by prefixing them with backslashes, for example, ``X\ =\ 1''. After this change, the text will be printed as

> The assignment statement "X = 1" causes the variable X to be assigned the value one.

Multiple spaces between words are not discarded; however, trailing spaces on an input line are discarded. As mentioned before, an input line beginning with a space causes a break. Thus, you must be careful not insert extraneous spaces in the raw document.

In most fonts, the width of a character depends upon the character itself. In such fonts, spaces are generally smaller than spaces in a font where each character has the same width. For example, consider the line, printed in constant-width font, that begins with ten spaces:

```
          Alice in Wonderland
```

The Times Roman font version of this line is

          Alice in Wonderland

The Times Roman font version is closer to the left margin than the constant-width font version because Times Roman font spaces are smaller than the constant-width font spaces.

2.9 Special Characters, Symbols and Strings

`troff` and mm extend the keyboard character set by predefining a large number of special characters, symbols and strings that have names made up of characters available on most keyboards.

2.9.1 Special Characters Defined by `troff`: `troff` allows the user to refer to a large number of non-ASCII special characters. These characters have names of the form "`\(`*xy*" where *x* and *y* are ASCII characters. Some examples of the special characters and their names are

character	denotation	name	character	denotation	name
□	`\(sq`	square	†	`\(dg`	dagger
~	`\(ap`	approximates	○	`\(ci`	circle
σ	`\(*s`	sigma	Σ	`\(*S`	Sigma

For a complete list of the special characters, see Chapter 6.

2.9.2 Special Symbols and Strings Defined by mm*:* The mm macro package predefines some commonly used symbols as strings:

symbol	string	meaning/effect
bullet	`\*(BU`	Automatically produces a bullet for both `troff` (•) and `nroff` (⊕) versions of a document.
date	`\*(DT`	Current date in the form "month, day, year".
dash	`\*(EM`	Automatically produces a dash for both `troff` (—) and `nroff` (--) versions of a document.
trademark	`\*(Tm`	Places the letters "TM" half a line above the preceding text and in a smaller point size (`troff` only).
grave accent	`` \*` ``	E.g., è is printed by the string `` e\*` ``.
acute accent	`\*'`	E.g., é is printed by the string `e\*'`.
circumflex accent	`\*^`	E.g., ô is printed by the string `o\*^`.
tilde accent	`\*~`	E.g., ñ is printed by the string `n\*~`.
cedilla	`\*,`	E.g., ç is printed by the string `c\*,`.
lower-case umlaut	`\*:`	E.g., ü is printed by the string `u\*:`.
upper-case umlaut	`\*;`	E.g., Ü is printed by the string `U\*;`.

2.9.3 Dashes, Hyphens and Minus Signs: The dash (—), hyphen (-) and the minus sign (−) are denoted in `troff` as `\(em`, `-` and `\-`, respectively. `nroff` prints all three of these characters as -; it would be preferable to print the dash as two minus signs to distinguish it from a hyphen. Normally, this would require changing the document appropriately depending on whether mm is being used with `troff` or `nroff`. Anticipating this, mm provides the predefined string "`\*(EM`" which is automatically translated into a dash for `troff` and two minus signs for `nroff`.

2.10 Some Characteristics of mm Instructions

To conclude this section on the basics of mm and before discussing mm in-depth, I will describe some characteristics of mm instructions.

1. An mm instruction has the form

   .name arguments

   name is a one- or two-character instruction name; names are usually constructed from upper-case letters, but there are some exceptions, e.g., `1C` and `2C`.

2. Each `mm` instruction starts on a new line and begins with a period (`.`) in column one.
3. Spaces are used to separate the `mm` instruction arguments; arguments containing spaces are enclosed within double quotes.
4. The double quotes character `"` is not permitted as part of a `mm` instruction argument; if necessary, the character pairs ` `` ` (grave accents) `''` (acute accents) should be substituted for double quotes at the left and right ends of a string, respectively. The character pair ` `` ` is printed as " and the character pair `''` is printed as ".
5. Special characters, `troff` escape sequences and in-line `eqn` expressions can be given as `mm` instruction arguments (or as parts of arguments).
6. Some `mm` instructions cause a break in the output (in the formatted document); output is then continued on a new line.
7. Some `troff` instructions can be intermingled with `mm` instructions.
8. A null argument is denoted by a pair of double quotes (`""`).

3. Fonts

A *font* is a complete collection of alphanumeric characters and other commonly used special characters such as the comma, exclamation and question marks, all of the same style and size. Here is the same set of characters in five different fonts:

font	**sample characters**
Times Roman	abcdefg ABCDEFG 0123456789 +−,;!?
Times Italic	*abcdefg ABCDEFG 0123456789 +−,;!?*
Times Bold	**abcdefg ABCDEFG 0123456789 +−,;!?**
`Constant-Width`	`abcdefg ABCDEFG 0123456789 +−,;!?`
Helvetica	abcdefg ABCDEFG 0123456789 +−,;!?

Times Roman, Helvetica and Constant-Width are commonly used fonts. Fonts come in many sizes. Informally, all the different sizes of the same font style are called one font. Strictly speaking, it is more accurate to say that these fonts belong to the same font family. Font families also include closely related fonts that are used for variety or emphasis; for example, the Times Roman font family includes the Italic and Bold versions of Times Roman. Font families are aesthetically harmonious and look pleasing together. There are literally hundreds of different fonts and font families available; a few are shown in Appendix C.

By default, mm prints a document in Times Roman font (this font). The default italic and bold fonts used by mm are Times Italic and Times Bold fonts, respectively.

Different fonts are used within the same document for reasons such as tradition, style, emphasis and differentiation. For example mm, by default, prints headings in italic font for emphasis. I am using bold font for the level-one and level-two headings in this book. Also, I am using the constant-width font for fragments of raw documents to differentiate them from the rest of the text; Use of a constant-width font makes the raw document examples look like the text entered at computer terminals.

The user can change fonts at will in mm, printing different portions of documents in different fonts. There are three ways of changing fonts: troff escape sequences, mm instructions or troff instructions. In the remainder of this section I will discuss in detail how fonts can be changed, but first I will give you a list of different fonts available on a typical typesetter. This will give you an idea of the fonts you can expect to find on your typesetter or laser printer.

3.1 Fonts Available on a Typical Typesetter

Here is a list of some fonts that are available on my typesetter:

font	name	font	name
Times Roman	R	Times Italic	I
Times Bold	B	Constant Width	CW
Helvetica	H	Helvetica Italic	HI
Helvetica Black	HB	Palatino	PA
Palatino Italic	PI	Palatino Bold	PB
Century Expanded	CE	Century Bold Italic	CI
Techno Bold	TB	Stymie Medium	SM
Script	SC	German Script	GS

For example text printed using these fonts, see Appendix C.

3.2 Using the Available Fonts

You can use all the available fonts in your document; the list of available fonts is implementation-dependent. By default, troff mounts a standard set of fonts. For example, the `troff` on my UNIX system mounts the following fonts for the Autologic APS-5 phototypesetter:

font position	**font**	**name**
1	Times Roman	`R`
2	*Times Italic*	`I`
3	**Times Bold**	`B`
4	Helvetica	`H`
5	`Constant-Width`	`CW`
6	Special	`S`
7	Special 1	`S1`
8	Greek	`GR`

Special fonts `S` and `S1` contains characters such as ☛, ○ and •. If a character is not available in the current font, then the special fonts are searched, for the character, in an order specified by the implementation.

If you use an unmounted font, then this font is automatically mounted on the special font position 0. Such use of font position 0 facilitates the occasional use of non-standard fonts (the user cannot mount a font on position 0). There are limitations to using unmounted fonts; e.g., use of two unmounted fonts in one output line leads to incorrect computation of character widths. Fonts are mounted with `troff` instruction `.fp` which has the form

`.fp` *n f*

where *f* is a one- or two-character name for the font to be mounted at position *n*; *n* must be in the range 1 to 8 for my `troff`. For example,

```
.ft 5 SM
```

replaces the Constant-Width font by Stymie Medium font on position 5.

3.3 In-Line Font Changes Using `troff` Escape Sequences

The following `troff` escape sequences can be embedded in the text to change fonts:

escape sequence	**effect**
`\f`*x*	Change to font *x*, where *x* is a one-character font name.
`\f(`*xy*	Change to font *xy*, where *xy* is a two-character font name.
`\fP`	Change back to the previous font.

Here is some sample text that uses escape sequences to change fonts:

```
The UNIX system document macro packages, such
as \f(CWmm\fP and \f(CWms\fP, preprocessors ...
In addition to the
\fIdocument formatting tools\fP ...
```

This text is printed as

> The UNIX system document macro packages, such as `mm` and `ms`, preprocessors ... In addition to the *document formatting tools* ...

3.4 Changing Fonts Using `mm` Instructions

`mm` provides instructions for switching to Roman, bold and italic fonts only:

instruction name	format	explanation and comments
bold font	`.B` `.B` a_1 a_2 ... a_n	The first form is used to switch to the bold font; the bold font is then used until another font change instruction is encountered. The second form is used to print the odd-numbered arguments in bold font and even-numbered arguments in the font in use before this instruction was encountered. The maximum number of arguments allowed is 6. All arguments are concatenated. The font in use before this instruction was encountered is restored after the instruction. For example, the instruction `.B for " and " while " loops"` is printed as "**for** and **while** loops". Notice that blanks are used in the second and fourth arguments to separate the four words in the output.
italic font	`.I` `.I` a_1 a_2 ... a_n	Similar to the `.B` instruction.
roman font	`.R`	Switch to the roman font.
italic-bold bold-italic italic-roman roman-italic roman-bold bold-roman	`.IB` a_1 a_2 ... a_n `.BI` a_1 a_2 ... a_n `.IR` a_1 a_2 ... a_n `.RI` a_1 a_2 ... a_n `.RB` a_1 a_2 ... a_n `.BR` a_1 a_2 ... a_n	Print odd-numbered arguments in the font specified by the first letter and the even-numbered arguments in the font specified by the second letter (`I` = italic, `B` = bold and `R` = roman). Maximum number of arguments allowed is 6.

As an example illustrating the use of `mm` font instructions, consider the text

Predicted Reliability. New model. No data; similar to *Ford Fairmont*.

This text was specified as

```
.B "Predicted Reliability" .
New model.
No data;
similar to
.I "Ford Fairmont" .
```

3.5 Using `troff` Instructions to Change Fonts

The `troff` instruction `.ft` can be used to switch to another font. This instruction has the form[7]

`.ft` [*f*]

where *f* is a font name; the `.ft` instruction results in a switch to this font. If the font name is omitted or if the font name used is `P`, then the `.ft` instruction causes a switch to the previous font.

3.6 Changing Fonts—My Preference

In general, I prefer to use the in-line `troff` escape sequences for switching to another font because they

- are more general than the mm font instructions; they can be used to switch to any font while the mm font-change instructions allow switching only between Roman, bold and italic fonts.
- can be used to specify the fonts of mm instruction arguments.
- can be used in conjunction with other formatting tools such as `tbl` and `pic` (eqn provides its own facility for changing fonts). For example, the mm font-change instructions and the `troff` font-change instruction `.ft` cannot be used for specifying fonts of individual items in `pic` and `tbl` instructions.

---

7. In describing the syntax of the formatting instructions, I will use square brackets ([and]) and the vertical bar (|) as follows:
   - [a] specifies the optional occurrence of item a
   - a | b specifies either item a or item b

I use the `troff` instruction `.ft` occasionally for switching fonts. Using the `troff` escape sequence on a line by itself implies an empty input line and produces a blank output line. In such cases, I use the `.ft` instruction to change the font.[8]

4. Point Size and Vertical Spacing

The *point size* of a font is the size of the characters in the font.[9] Character sizes are usually measured in *points*, a printer's unit of measurement; one point is equal to 0.0138 inches (approximately 1/72 inch).

The *vertical spacing* (or *leading*) is the distance between the base lines of two consecutive lines in the formatted document. When the point size is increased, it is a good idea to increase the vertical spacing also; otherwise, consecutive lines will be too close to each other and they may even overlap. The default point size used is 10 points and the default vertical spacing used is 12 points. One rule of thumb is to use vertical spacing equal to the point size plus two points.

4.1 In-Line Point Size Changes Using `troff` Escape Sequences

The following `troff` escape sequences can be used to change the point size:

escape sequence	effect
`\s`*d* `\s(`*dd*	Switch to point size *d* or *dd* (*d* is a single digit); if the specified point size is not available, then switch to the closest available point size.
`\s±`*d* `\s±(`*dd*	Change point size by ±*d* or ±*dd*, if possible; otherwise, switch to the closest available point size.
`\s0`	Switch back to the previous point size.

Here is some sample text with escape sequences to change the point size:

---

8. For examples illustrating use of the `.ft` instruction, see definitions of the `.(P` and `.)P` macros in Section 12.6 titled *Macros*.

9. To be more precise, the point size of a font is the amount of vertical space between the lowest descender and the maximum ascender of the characters in a font (the point size does not describe the height of either upper- or lower-case letters). A *descender* is the part of a lower case letter that descends below its main body; an example of a descender is the bottom part of the letter "y". An *ascender* is the part of a lower case letter that rises above its main body; an example of a ascender is the top part of the letter "b".

```
The point size can be \s-3decreased\s0
or \s+3increased\s0 in-line just as
the fonts can be \fBchanged\fP in-line.
```

This text is printed as

> The point size can be decreased or increased in-line just as the fonts can be **changed** in-line.

4.2 Changing Point Size and Vertical Spacing Using mm Instructions

The mm instruction `.S` can be used to change both the point size and the vertical spacing. It has the form

`.S` *point-size* [*vertical-spacing*]

where arguments *point-size* and *vertical-spacing* may have the following values:

point-size or *vertical-spacing*	**effect**
C	Use current value as the new value.
P	Use previous value as the new value.
D	Use default value as the new value.
n	Use *n* (where *n* is an integer).
± *n*	Use current value ± *n* (where *n* is an integer).

If the second argument is omitted, then the default vertical spacing (new point size + 2) is used.

I will use the following limerick from Lear [1964] to illustrate effects of changing the point size and vertical spacing (it is first printed in point size 10 with 12 point vertical spacing, both of which are default values):

> There was an Old Man of Peru,
> Who watched his wife making a stew;
> But once by mistake, in a stove she did bake,
> That unfortunate Man of Peru.

Instruction

`.S 8`

changes the point size to 8 points and vertical spacing to 10 points; sample text in this point size and vertical spacing is

> There was an Old Man of Peru,
> Who watched his wife making a stew;
> But once by mistake, in a stove she did bake,
> That unfortunate Man of Peru.

Instruction

```
.S +3
```

increases the point size in use by 3 to 13 points (default value is 10 points) and the vertical spacing to 15; sample text in this point size and vertical spacing is

> There was an Old Man of Peru,
> Who watched his wife making a stew;
> But once by mistake, in a stove she did bake,
> That unfortunate Man of Peru.

In these examples, mm uses the default vertical spacing, two points greater than the point size. If appropriate vertical spacing is not used, then the output may have too much or too little space between the lines; for example, after the instruction

```
.S +3 C
```

which increases the point size but not the vertical spacing, the limerick will be printed as

> There was an Old Man of Peru,
> Who watched his wife making a stew;
> But once by mistake, in a stove she did bake,
> That unfortunate Man of Peru.

4.3 Using `troff` Instructions to Change Point Size

The `troff` instruction `.ps` can be used to change the character point size. The `.ps` instruction has two forms. The first form of the `.ps` instruction

`.ps` [*n*]

causes a switch to point size *n*. If no argument is specified, then the `.ps` switches to point size that was being used before the last change.

The second form of the `.ps` instruction

`.ps ±n`

is used to increment or decrement the current point size by ± *n* points. If the requested font size is not available, then the closest valid point size available is used.

4.4 Changing Vertical Spacing Using `troff`

The `troff` instruction `.vs` used to change the vertical spacing has two forms. The first form

`.vs [n]`

changes the vertical spacing to *n* points. If no argument is specified, then `.vs` restores the previous vertical spacing.

The second form of the `.vs` instruction

`.vs ±n`

is used to increment or decrement the current vertical spacing by ± *n* points.

4.5 Changing Point Size and Vertical Spacing—My Preference

I use in-line `troff` escape sequences when I have to embed point size changes within the text, for example, to specify the point size

1. of arguments to `mm` instructions,
2. of items and arguments in other formatting tools, for example, `pic` and `tbl` and
3. small portions of input text where it is not necessary to change the vertical spacing.

For changing the point size of major portions of an input document, I prefer to use the `.S` instruction because it automatically adjusts the vertical spacing.

5. Document Structure

A raw document consists of four logical components or parts:

Definitions, Style and Appearance Parameters:
: Macro and string definitions and `eqn` definitions used in the document are given here along with parameters that specify style and appearance of the document; examples of parameters set here are page length and width, margin justification and heading style.

Prelude:
: Items that occur only at the beginning of a document, for example, date, author name, and document title.

Body:
: The document text along with formatting instructions, figures, tables and equations.

Postlude:
: Items that occur only at the end of a document, for example, formal closing in a letter, signature and approval lines in letters and in internal versions of technical papers, indication of the persons who will receive copies of the letters, documents enclosed or attached with this document and so on; also given here are instructions to produce summary pages such as the table of contents, list of tables and the cover sheet of a document.

The formatted document consists of three components: an optional cover sheet, the body, and an optional table of contents along with a list of figures, equations and tables.

In the ensuing sections, I will discuss in detail each of the four logical components of a raw document.

6. Document Definitions, Style and Appearance Parameters

The first component of a raw document contains definitions that will be used in the document and instructions specifying the style and appearance of the document. Some items that can be included at the head of the document are

- `eqn` definitions (shorthand notation for frequently used mathematical symbols and expressions),
- macro and string definitions (using the `troff` macro and string definition facilities),
- heading style specification,
- footnote style specification,
- page headers and footers,
- specification of right justification,
- double spacing instruction and

- a request to perform hyphenation.

I will discuss some of these items here and leave discussion of the rest for later.

6.1 Right Justification

The `.SA` instruction is used to set the right justification for the main body of a document. It has the form

`.SA` *0-or-1*

Calling the `.SA` instruction with 0 as an argument turns off right justification and calling it with 1 turns on right justification.

The following text is an example of text that is not right justified:

> C is a flexible programming language that gives a great deal
> of freedom to the programmer. This is one of the main
> strengths of C.

When right justification is turned on, the text is printed as

> C is a flexible programming language that gives a great deal
> of freedom to the programmer. This is one of the main
> strengths of C.

6.2 Hyphenation

Hyphenation is done by the formatter `troff`; it is not done by `mm`. By default, `troff` does not do hyphenation; however, `troff` will hyphenate words containing hyphens or dashes (i.e., the character "`\(em`"), after the hyphen or dash, even if hyphenation is turned off. Hyphenation can be turned on by setting register `Hy` to 1 at the beginning of the document. (This does not turn on hyphenation in footnotes; for information on hyphenation in footnotes, see Section 8.8.)

As an illustration of hyphenation, consider the following text which was formatted without allowing hyphenation:

> The *raga* is a melodic scheme. It is a nucleus based on certain traditionally accepted rules which in actual performance are improvised upon, expanded and embellished, thus drawing out possibilities inherent in the melodic embryo. This simple idea has been made unnecessarily complicated by the pedant.

If hyphenation is turned on, then this text will be printed as

> The *raga* is a melodic scheme. It is a nucleus based on certain traditionally accepted rules which in actual performance are im-provised upon, expanded and embellished, thus drawing out possi-bilities inherent in the melodic embryo. This simple idea has been made unnecessarily complicated by the pedant.

The algorithm used for hyphenating words is not perfect; therefore, `troff` provides facilities for suppressing hyphenation of specific words and the explicit specification of hyphenation points in words. To prevent a word from being hyphenated, it is prefixed by the hyphenation indicator `\%`. Normally, `troff` automatically determines appropriate hyphenation points in a word; the user can specify alternative hyphenation points in a word by inserting the hyphenation indicator at these points. The hyphenation indicator is not printed in the output. For example, the correct hyphenation of embryos could be specified as " `em\%bry\%os`".

7. Document Prelude

The document prelude, the second logical component of a raw document, consists of items specified only once in the document:

1. document date,
2. document title,
3. author information,
4. abstract,
5. specification of attachments,
6. keywords and
7. document type.

In the rest of this section, I will first discuss the order which items in the document prelude are specified and then discuss instructions for specifying each item.

7.1 Order of Specifications of the Document Prelude Items

A document prelude need not have all the items that were listed above. However, all prelude items actually used in a document must appear in the following order:

```
.ND new-date (date to be printed on the document)
.TL charging-number filing-number (document title)
lines specifying the title text
.AF company-name (alternate first-page format)
.AU name initials location dept extension room ... (author info.)
.AT author-title (author title)
.TM memo-number
.AS abstract-style indent (abstract begin)
abstract input lines
.AE (abstract end)
.NS notation-style (specification of attachments, enclosures, etc.)
input lines specifying an attachment, enclosure, etc.
.NE (end of specification)

  :

.NS notation style
input lines specifying an attachment, enclosure, etc.
.NE
.OK keyword1 keyword2 ... keywordn (for memorandums)
.MT memo-type addressee (document type)
```

Trailing arguments of an `mm` instruction can be omitted, if appropriate; however, some arguments cannot be ommited. Omitting an argument is the same as supplying the null string (`""`) for the argument.

The following information must be given for memorandums and external papers:

- title (`.TL` instruction)
- author information (`.AU` instruction)
- document type (`.MT` instruction)

7.2 Date

The current date is automatically printed in the "date" field of a memorandum and at the appropriate place in an external letter. Automatically printed dates have the form

month day, year

for example, June 28, 1985. Although automatic date printing is convenient, the user should remember that a different date will be printed if the document is printed on a later date. Also, it is sometimes necessary to use a date other than the current date.

The new-date instruction `.ND` can be used to specify a specific date to be printed on a memorandum or an external letter; this instruction has the form

`.ND` *new-date*

where *new-date* is a user-supplied date. The date may be specified in any format; remember, quotes must be used if the specified date contains embedded blanks. Here are two examples of dates:

```
.ND 12-1-84
.ND "December 1, 1984"
```

By default, the date is printed in bold font (Roman font in case of `nroff`); command-line option `-E` can be used to specify whether the date is to be printed in Roman or bold font (see Section 13).

7.3 Document Title

The subject of a memorandum and of an external paper is specified by using the title instruction `.TL`; this instruction has the form

`.TL` *charging-number filing-number*
lines specifying the title text

Text lines following the `.TL` instruction up to the next `mm` instruction are considered to be part of the title. In the case of memorandums, the title is prefixed by "subject:" and is printed on the top left hand of the first page. In the case of external papers, the title is centered and printed in bold. The title is also automatically printed on the cover sheets of memorandums and external papers. Arguments *charging-number* and *filing-number*[10] are used for identifying memorandums (only). If these arguments are identical, then they are printed after the title along with a prefix "Charging and Filing Case:"; otherwise, they are printed on separate lines with the prefixes "Charging Case:" and "Filing Case:".

A multiple-line title of the form

line 1 of title
line 2 of title
line 3 of title
...

is printed by specifying it as [DWB 1984b]

10. These arguments are artifacts of the AT&T Bell Laboratories method of filing memorandums and may be omitted, if you wish.

```
.TL charging-number filing-number
lines specifying the text of line 1 of title
.br
\!.br
lines specifying the text of line 2 of title
.br
\!.br
lines specifying the text of line 3 of title
  :
```

Each part of the title that is to be printed on a separate line is separated from the other parts of the title by the two lines

```
.br
\!.br
```

7.4 Author Firm

The company name is automatically printed on top of the first page of a memorandum or an external paper. The author-firm instruction **.AF** can be used to change or to suppress printing of the company name; this instruction has the form

.AF "*company-name*"

where *company-name* is the name to be printed instead of the default company name. When using preprinted stationery the author-firm instruction **.AF** with a null argument, that is,

.AF ""

can be used to suppress printing of the company name.

7.5 Author Information

Author information is specified by using the **.AU** instruction

.AU *name initials location department extension room* a_1 a_2 a_3

where the *location* is a code indicating the geographical location of the author's office; location codes will vary from one installation to another. Arguments a_1, a_2 and a_3 can be used to specify additional information that may be appropriate (e.g author's electronic mailing address); each of these arguments will be printed on a separate line after the other author information. Several **.AU** instructions may be given, one for each author.

Author information specified in the **.AU** instruction or derived from this information is printed on the cover sheet, on the first page of a memorandum or an external paper, and at the end of a document.

The following is an example of the use of the `.AU` instruction:

```
.AU "N. Gehani" NG MH 11382 4461 3D-414 allegra!nhg
```

`MH` is a code that represents "Murray Hill", the AT&T Bell Laboratories location where I work. For an external paper, this prints the complete company address. Specifying the address of an author associated with another company is a little complicated; see Chapter 8 for an example.

7.6 Author Title

The title of an author is specified by using the `.AT` instruction, which must be given immediately after the `.AU` instruction associated with the same author. The `.AT` instruction has the form

`.AT` $title_1$ $title_2$ `...` $title_n$

where $title_i$ is the ith part of the title and $n \leqslant 9$. Presence of the signature instruction `.SG` will cause each of these title parts to be printed on a separate line, following the author's signature, in the signature portion of a memorandum or an external letter.

As an example, assume that the following `.AU` and `.AT` instructions have been given:

```
.AU "E. Pushy"
.AT "Executive Vice President" "Sales Division"
```

The signature instruction `.SG` will cause the following to be printed:

E. Pushy
Executive Vice President
Sales Division

7.7 Memorandum Numbers

Up to nine numbers may be associated with a memorandum by means of the `.TM` instruction which has the form

`.TM` n_1 n_2 `...` n_k

where $k \leqslant 9$. The letters "TM" followed by the specified memorandum numbers are printed on the cover sheet and the first page of a memorandum.[11] This instruction is ignored in the case of external papers and letters.

11. This information is specified for the AT&T Bell Laboratories filing system.

7.8 Abstract

An abstract can be specified for a memorandum or an external paper (abstracts are not allowed for external letters) by using the abstract-start `.AS` and the abstract-end `.AE` instructions. An abstract specification has the form

`.AS` *abstract-style indent*
abstract input lines
`.AE`

where the effect of different *abstract-style* values is as follows:

abstract-style	**effect**
0	Abstract is printed on the cover sheet requested using the `.CS` instruction and on the first page of a memorandum or an external paper.
1	Abstract is printed on the cover sheet requested using the `.CS` instruction of a memorandum or an external paper.
2	Abstract is printed on the cover sheet and the first page. A cover sheet is produced automatically (without using the `.CS` instruction).

Headings and displays (discussed later) are not permitted within abstracts.

7.9 Specification of Attachments, Enclosures, Persons Receiving Copies, etc.

Information such as attachments, enclosures and persons receiving copies specified by using the `.NS/.NE` instruction pair, can be printed on the memorandum cover sheet. This information is specified in the prelude only if `.AS 2` is used. See Section 9 for the use of `.NS/.NE`.

7.10 Specification of Keywords

Keywords (up to 9) may be printed on the cover sheet of a memorandum by using the keyword instruction `.OK` which has the form

`.OK` $keyword_1$ $keyword_2$ ... $keyword_k$

7.11 Document Type

The document type is specified with the `.MT` instruction which has the form

`.MT` [*type* [*addressee*]]

Argument *type* specifies the nature and style of the document:

type	**document specified**
`0 or ""`	Memorandum; this form is also used for writing intra-company letters.
1 or *unspecified*	Memorandum; header "MEMORANDUM FOR FILE" is printed on the first page of the memorandum.
2	Memorandum; header "PROGRAMMER'S NOTES" is printed on the first page of the memorandum.
3	Memorandum; header "ENGINEER'S NOTES" is printed on the first page of the memorandum.
4	External paper, that is, a paper prepared for publication or for general distribution.
5	Ordinary letter.
"*string*"	Memorandum; header "*string*" is printed on the first page of the memorandum, for example, "CONFERENCE NOTES".

The second argument of the `.MT` instruction, *addressee*, is the name of the addressee of the letter or memorandum (not appropriate for an external paper).[12] The normal page header is replaced by the name of the addressee followed by the page number. For example,

```
.MT 5 "Narain Gehani"
```

will produce the header

`Narain Gehani` — *i*

on page *i* of a letter; no header is printed on page 1.

In the case of external papers (`.MT 4`), the document title is printed at the top of the page; it is centered and printed in bold and is followed by the authors' names and their affiliations. By default, only the company location of the last author is printed after the authors' names. However, if 1 is given as the second argument to the `.MT` instruction, then the appropriate company name and location are printed after each author's name.

mm assumes that letterheads will be used for the first page of external letters.

---

12. If the first argument of the `.MT` instruction is 4, then the second argument is not used for specifying the addressee; it is used for changing the author affiliation style, as discussed later.

Example templates of several different types of documents and the outputs produced by them are given in Chapter 8. These examples also illustrate how to specify the addresses of co-authors affiliated with another company.

8. Document Body

The portion of a raw document corresponding to the document body consists of text intermixed with `mm` instructions specifying items such as headings, paragraphs, text that is to be displayed, lists, footnotes, preprocessor instructions specifying tables, equations and figures, and perhaps `troff` instructions.

In this section, I will discuss the `mm` instructions used in specifying the document body. Wherever appropriate or necessary, I will also discuss the use of `troff` instructions.

8.1 Paragraphs

Paragraphs can be of two types: left-justified (default style) or indented. In a left-justified paragraph, the first line (like the other lines) begins at the left margin. In an indented paragraph, the first line is indented five spaces (default indentation), but the other lines still begin at the left margin.

A new paragraph is specified by using the begin-paragraph instruction `.P` which has the form

`.P` [*para-type*]

The effect of different values of argument *para-type* on the paragraph that follows is

para-type	**paragraph style**
omitted	default style
0	left-justified
1	indented

The `.P` instruction tries to ensure that the first two lines of a paragraph will fit on a page; otherwise, it begins the paragraph on a new page. The default paragraph style can be changed by setting register `Pt` to one of the following values:

value of register `Pt`	paragraph style
0 *(default value)*	left-justified
1	indented (all paragraphs)
2	paragraphs after headings, lists or displays are left-justified while others are indented

The default indentation is 3 ens (5 spaces in `nroff`); this can be changed to another value, say *i*, by setting register `Pi` to *i*.

Paragraphs may be numbered with respect to level-one headings (level-one headings are used to indicate sections in a document; headings are discussed later). Suppose we are in section *n*, that is, in the text after the nth level-one heading. Paragraphs in this section are to be prefixed with the numbers *n*.01, *n*.02, *n*.03 and so on. Paragraph numbering is specified by setting register `Np` to 1. Paragraph numbering works for both left-justified and indented paragraphs.

Now an example (with a rather strange layout):

> 1. **The Himalayas**
>
> Some years ago I flew from Delhi to Moscow.
>
> A few minutes after take-off, I glanced out of the window. The Himalayas were piercing the clouds. It was a gripping sight.
>
>   I had never seen them before.
>
> 2. **Cooking of India**
>
> 2.01 Continental India is divided into twenty-two states.
>
> 2.02 Each state has its own and distinct cuisine.
>
>   2.03 The variety, combination and the uses of spices distinguish Indian cooking from other cuisines.

This text consists of two sections (labeled "1." and "2."). Each section contains three paragraphs; the first two are left justified and the third one is indented. Paragraphs in the first section are unnumbered while those in the second section are numbered.

The above text was specified as

```
.H 1 "The Himalayas"
.P
Some years ago I flew from Delhi
to Moscow.
.P
A few minutes after take-off,
I glanced out of the window.
The Himalayas were piercing the clouds.
It was a gripping sight.
.P 1
I had never seen them before.
.nr Np 1
.H 1 "Cooking of India"
.P
Continental India is divided into
twenty-two states.
.P
Each state has its own and distinct
cuisine.
.P 1
The variety, combination and
the uses of spices distinguish Indian
cooking from other cuisines.
```

Setting register `Np` to 1 (with the instruction `.nr Np 1`) specifies the use of numbered paragraph style.

8.2 Vertical Space

Vertical space (blank lines) is specified by using the `mm` instruction `.SP` which has the forms

instruction	effect
`.SP`	Leave one blank line.
`.SP` *n*	If *n* is an unscaled number, then leave *n* blank lines; otherwise leave blank space equal to *n*.

Vertical space requests made by the `.SP` instruction are ignored at the top of the page; `troff` can be instructed not to ignore such requests by preceding them with the restore-spacing instruction `.rs`. Vertical space can also be specified by using the `troff` instruction `.sp`. The only difference between `.SP` and `.sp` instructions is that in the case of consecutive `.SP` instructions, the `.SP` instruction specifying the maximum vertical space is selected; other `.SP` instructions are ignored. In the case of consecutive `.sp` instructions, the result is the sum of the spaces specified by the `.sp` instructions.

8.3 Skipping Pages

The `.SK` instruction is used to skip pages; its effect is described in the following table:

instruction	effect
`.SK` `.SK 0`	If the current output position is at the top of a page, then do nothing; otherwise, skip to the top of the next page.
`.SK` *n*	Leave *n* blank pages and skip to the top of the next page.

8.4 Displays

Displays are used to specify blocks of text and other items, such as tables and equations, that are to be kept intact. The displayed material is not split across pages even though this might result in some blank space being left on the current page. Of course, if the displayed material is too big to fit in one page, then it is split across pages. By default, the displayed text is processed in no-fill mode; that is, each line inside a display is printed on a separate line.

There are two kinds of displays: static and floating. A *static* display ensures its contents have the same relative position in the formatted document as in the raw document. If the displayed material cannot fit on the current page, then rest of the current page is left blank and the displayed material is printed on the next page.

A *floating* display does not guarantee that the displayed material will have the same relative position in the formatted document as it had in the raw document. If a floating display cannot fit on the current page, then it is printed as soon as possible after the top of the next page. However, the remainder of the current page is not left blank; it is filled with items that follow the floating display in the raw document. The relative position between two floating displays is always preserved. Of course, there may be several floating displays waiting to be printed a the next page change; if they all cannot fit there, then the remaining ones will flow onto the following page, and so on.

A static display specification has the form

`.DS` [*format* [*fill* [*rindent*]]]
material to be displayed
`.DE`

and a floating display specification has the form

.DF [*format* [*fill* [*rindent*]]]
material to be displayed
.DE

The third argument *rindent* specifies the indentation from the right margin; effectively, this argument reduces the line length by the specified value. The effect of different values of *format* and *fill* is explained in the following two tables:

format	**display style**
"", L or omitted	Do not indent the displayed material.
I	Indent the displayed material; the default indentation is 3 ens (five spaces in nroff); this can be changed to another value, say *i*, by setting register Si to *i*.
C	Center each line of the displayed material individually.
CB	Center the displayed material together as a block.

fill	**display style**
"", N or omitted	Process display in no-fill mode.
F	Process display in fill mode.

By default, a ½ vertical space (a blank line in nroff) is left before and after a display. Output of this vertical space can be suppressed by setting register Ds to 0.

To print each input line of a display on a separate line, the text is enclosed in a no-fill mode display; for example, enclosing the following limerick [Lear 1964] within a .DS/.DE instruction pair,

```
.DS
There was a Young Lady of Welling
Whose praise all the world was a telling;
She played on a harp, and caught several carp,
That accomplished Young Lady of Welling.
.DE
```

will cause it to print as

There was a Young Lady of Welling
Whose praise all the world was a telling;
She played on a harp, and caught several carp,
That accomplished Young Lady of Welling.

If this limerick is enclosed in a display with the fill mode on (for example, by using the instruction `.DS L F`), then it will be printed as

There was a Young Lady of Welling Whose praise all the world was a telling; She played on a harp, and caught several carp, That accomplished Young Lady of Welling.

As an example of the various display formats, consider the following portion of a poem:

```
Outside his realm a king
Has no reputation:
But the fame of the scholar
Goes with him everywhere.
```

If the poem is displayed without any indentation (e.g., `.DS`), then it will be printed as

Outside his realm a king
Has no reputation:
But the fame of the scholar
Goes with him everywhere.

If the poem is displayed with the standard indent (e.g., `.DS I`), then it will be printed as

    Outside his realm a king
    Has no reputation:
    But the fame of the scholar
    Goes with him everywhere.

If each line of the poem is centered (e.g., `.DS C`), then it will be printed as

```
            Outside his realm a king
               Has no reputation:
           But the fame of the scholar
            Goes with him everywhere.
```

If the poem is centered as a block (e.g., `.DS CB`), then it will be printed as

```
            Outside his realm a king
            Has no reputation:
            But the fame of the scholar
            Goes with him everywhere.
```

8.5 Centering Output Lines

mm provides no instruction specifically for centering output lines (displays can be used to center output lines in the document text, but they cannot be used everywhere, for example, in footnotes and abstracts). Fortunately, the `troff` center instruction `.ce` can be used, without any untoward effects, to center output lines. The `.ce` instruction has the form

`.ce` *n*

where *n* indicates the number of lines in the raw document that are to be centered; a break occurs after each of the *n* input lines.

As an example, consider the following two centered lines:

```
            AT&T Bell Laboratories
                Murray Hill, NJ
```

These two lines were specified as

```
.ce 2
AT&T Bell Laboratories
Murray Hill, NJ
```

8.6 Headings

A *heading* consists of text printed at the head of a document section or subsection; the heading text is used to identify or introduce the material in the section. The heading is normally made to stand out from the rest of the text by printing it in a different font, point size or style. Headings in mm are classified into seven levels, from level 1 to level 7. Level-one headings are used to indicate major sections in a document. Other heading levels are used for specifying subsections in a major section. Headings are specified by using the `.H` instruction. For example, the following headings in this chapter

> **8. Document Body**
> **8.6 Headings**
> *8.6.1 Starting Headings on a New Page:*
> *8.6.2 Space After Headings:*

were printed with the heading instructions:

```
.H 1 "Document Body"
.H 2 "Headings"
.H 3 "Starting Headings on a New Page:"
.H 3 "Space After Headings:"
```

The first argument indicates the heading level number. (Section numbers are automatically printed for numbered headings.)

The heading instruction `.H` has the form

`.H` *level* [*text* [*suffix*]]

where *level* is the heading level and *text* is the heading text; *suffix* is appended to the heading text in the document body but not in the table of contents. For example, a heading suffix might be used to specify a footnote mark.

The default heading style for various heading levels is described in the following table:

heading level	default font	default heading style
1	italic (underlined in `nroff`)	Heading is preceded by one vertical space and followed by a ½ vertical space (in `nroff`, it is two blank lines and one blank line, respectively). Text after the heading is indented according to the current paragraph style.
2	italic (underlined in `nroff`)	Heading is preceded and followed by a ½ vertical space (one blank line in `nroff`). Text after the heading is indented according to the current paragraph style.
3 to 7	italic (underlined in `nroff`)	Heading is preceded by a ½ vertical space (one blank line in `nroff`); text after the heading is printed on the same line as the heading.

By default, headings are printed using the current point size with one exception: bold stand-alone headings are printed using a point size equal to the current point size minus one. In older versions of the `mm` macro package, level-one and level-two headings are, by default, printed in bold and all other headings are printed in italics.

8.6.1 Starting Headings on a New Page: All headings with level numbers less than or equal to *n* can be started on a new page by setting register `Ej` to *n*. The default value of this register is zero.

8.6.2 Space After Headings: Space left after the headings can be controlled by assigning appropriate values to the following registers:

register	**used for setting**	**default value**	**effect**
`Hb`	heading break level	2	Text after all headings with a level ⩽ `Hb` begins on a new line.
`Hs`	heading space level	2	½ vertical space (one blank line in `nroff`) is inserted after each heading with level ⩽ `Hs`.
`Hi`	post-heading indent	1	**value of `Hi`** — **indentation** 0 — Text is left justified. 1 — Current paragraph style is used for the text following the heading. 2 — Text is indented up to the first word of the heading.

Note that if a heading level is greater than the values of both `Hb` and `Hs`, then the text will be continued on the same line as the heading; otherwise the text is continued on a new line. Headings that are printed on a line by themselves are called *stand-alone* headings; other headings are called *run-in* headings. It is good style to end run-in headings with a "`.`" or "`:`" so that it is easy to notice the end of the heading text.

8.6.3 Centered Headings: Headings are left justified by default. All level-one through level-*n* headings can be centered by setting register `Hc` to *n*.

8.6.4 Unnumbered Headings: The `.HU` heading instruction is similar to the `.H` instruction except that the section number is not printed. Each unnumbered heading is considered to be a heading of level 2 (default value of register `Hu`). Even though section numbers are not printed by the `.HU` instruction, `mm` keeps track of the current section number. The `.H` and `.HU` heading instructions can be intermixed.

8.6.5 Fonts Used For the Headings: By default, all headings are printed in italic font (underlined in `nroff`). A user can explicitly specify alternative fonts for headings by setting the string `HF` as follows:

`.ds HF` *level-1-font-position level-2-font-position ... level-n-font-position*

where $n \leqslant 7$; the default font is used for heading levels $n+1$ to 7.

For example, in this book, level-one and level-two headings are printed in bold and all other headings in italic. To do this, I defined the string `HF` as

```
.ds HF 3 3 2 2 2 2 2
```

because bold and italic fonts are mounted on positions 3 and 2, respectively (see section 3.2).

8.6.6 Point Size Used For the Headings: As mentioned earlier, headings are printed using the current point size with one exception: bold stand-alone headings are printed using a point size equal to the current point size minus one. By default, all headings are printed in italic font, and level-one and level-two headings are stand-alone headings while all other headings are run-in headings.

Alternative point sizes for headings are specified by setting the string `HP` as follows:

`.ds HP` *level-1-point-size level-2-point-size ... level-n-point-size*

where $n \leqslant 7$; the default point-size is used for heading levels $n+1$ to 7. If *level-i-point-size* is a unsigned integer, then it represents the point size to be used for a level-*i* heading; if it is a signed integer, then it specifies that the current point size, plus or minus this integer, should be used as the point size for level-*i* headings.

For example, in this book, level-one headings are printed in point size 12 and all other headings are printed in point size 10. To do this, I defined the string `HP` as follows:

```
.ds HP 12 10 10 10 10 10 10
```

8.6.7 Heading Numbering Style: Section numbers in headings are printed, by default, in arabic numerals. An example of a heading number is

2.3.1

which refers to section 2.3.1 (subsection one of the third subsection of section two). The heading mark instruction `.HM` is used to alter the heading number style; for example, instead of arabic numerals, lower-case letters may be used to mark sections. The `.HM` instruction has the form

`.HM` *level-1-style level-2-style . . . level-n-style*

where $n \leqslant 7$. Values that can be used for arguments *level-i-style* ($i \leqslant n$) and their effects are described in the following table:

level-i style	**comments**	**heading numbers printed**
1	arabic numerals (default)	1, 2, 3, ...
0001	arabic numerals with leading zeroes to match the number of digits specified	0001, 0002, 0003, ...
a	lower-case letters	a, b, ..., z, aa, ab, ...
A	upper-case letters	A, B, ..., Z, AA, AB, ...
i	lower-case Roman numerals	i, ii, iii, ...
I	upper-case Roman numerals	I, II, III, ...

As mentioned earlier, the subsection numbers are concatenated to the section number. This concatenation can be suppressed by setting register `Ht` to 1. Then just the subsection number will be printed; for example, instead of heading number 3.1.4, only 4 will be printed.

8.6.8 Level-One Headings and Page Numbering Style: Level-one heading numbers can be printed along with the page number in the page header by using the `mm` command line options `-rN3` or `-rN5` (see Section 13).

8.6.9 Paragraphs After Stand-Alone Headings: I normally omit the `.P` instruction after stand-alone headings because `mm` automatically prints the text after the headings using the default paragraph style as specified by register `Pt`.

8.7 Lists

`mm` defines several kinds of itemized lists: lists with automatically numbered items, lists whose items are tagged with identical marks or with different marks supplied by the user, and so on. List specifications are of the form

begin-list instruction (`.AL`, `.BL`, `.DL`, `.ML`, `.RL` or `.VL`)
`.LI` [*item-mark*]
input lines describing list item
`.LI` [*item-mark*]
⋮
`.LI` [*item-mark*]
input lines describing list item
`.LE` [`1`]

A begin-list instruction indicates the beginning of a list and its type, and the list-end instruction `.LE` signals the end of a list. Each list item must be preceded by a list-item instruction `.LI`; a list item is terminated either by the next `.LI` instruction, a `.LE` instruction or by a nested begin-list instruction.

The different types of begin-list instructions available in `mm` are listed in the following table:

begin-list instruction	**type of list specified**
`.AL`	Automatically-sequenced list—items are tagged by an automatically maintained sequence of labels that can be numbers or letters.
`.BL`	Bullet list—each item is tagged by a bullet symbol • (in case of `nroff`, the bullet symbol is produced by overstriking the letter o with +).
`.DL`	Dash list—each item is tagged by a dash (—).
`.ML`	Marked list—same as bullet and dash lists except the items are tagged with a single user-supplied mark.
`.RL`	Reference list—automatically numbered lists in which the numbers labeling the items are enclosed in square brackets.
`.VL`	Variable-mark list—a mark is supplied (as an argument of the `.LI` instruction) for each item.

The list-end instruction `.LE` can be used without an argument or with the integer 1 as its argument; the effect of this argument is to print a ½ vertical space (a blank line for `nroff`) at the end of the list. Generally, the extra half vertical space makes the list look more attractive.

8.7.1 Automatically-Sequenced Lists: An *automatically-sequenced list* is a list with items tagged by an automatically maintained sequence of labels. Automatically-sequenced lists are specified by using the begin-list instruction `.AL` which has the form

`.AL` [*list-type* [*text-indent* [1]]]

Argument *list-type* is used to specify different types of marks:

list-type	**comments**	**item mark sequence**
1	arabic numerals (default list type)	1, 2, 3, ...
0001	arabic numerals with leading zeroes to match the number of digits specified	0001, 0002, 0003, ...
a	lower-case letters	a, b, ..., z, aa, ab, ...
A	upper-case letters	A, B, ..., Z, AA, AB, ...
i	lower-case Roman numerals	i, ii, iii, ...
I	upper-case Roman numerals	I, II, III, ...

The item text is indented 5 ens (6 character positions in the case of `nroff`) from the current indent, that is, from the indent in effect just before the begin-list instruction was encountered. Argument *text-indent* can be used explicitly to specify the indentation for the item text; if *text-indent* value supplied is unscaled, then it is assumed to be in ens (character positions in `nroff`). The value of *text-indent* affects only the space between the current indent and the item text; the item mark is printed in this space. The default text indentation (5 ens) is used if the text indentation is not specified or if a null argument is supplied.

Normally, a ½ vertical space (one blank line in `nroff`) is printed before the list and between the list items. Printing of the ½ vertical space before each list item can be suppressed by specifying 1 as the third argument of the begin-list instruction `.AL`.

Here is an example of an automatically-sequenced list with items marked by arabic numerals:

> A good programming methodology should
>
> 1. help the programmer master the complexity of the problem to be solved.
>
> 2. require the programmer to keep a written record of the program design process.
>
> 3. create programs that are understandable.
>
> 4. be generally applicable.

This list was specified as

```
A good programming methodology should
.AL 1
.LI
help the programmer master the
complexity of the problem to be
solved.
.LI
require the programmer to keep a
written record of the program
design process.
.LI
create programs that are understandable.
.LI
be generally applicable.
.LE
```

The item marks in the list can be changed to upper-case Roman numerals by changing the argument in the begin-list instruction `.AL` from `1` to `I`. The list will then be printed as

> A good programming methodology should
>
> I. help the programmer master the complexity of the problem to be solved.
>
> II. require the programmer to keep a written record of the program design process.
>
> III. create programs that are understandable.
>
> IV. be generally applicable.

8.7.2 Bullet Lists: A *bullet list* is a list with each item tagged by a bullet symbol •. Bullet lists are specified by using the begin-list instruction `.BL` which has the form

`.BL` [*text-indent* [`1`]]

As in the case of automatically-sequenced lists, argument *text-indent* specifies the distance that the item text is to be indented from the current indent. Specifying the second argument, the integer 1, suppresses printing of the ½ vertical space before each list item.

Using the begin-list instruction

`.BL`

the example list is printed as

> A good programming methodology should
>
> - help the programmer master the complexity of the problem to be solved.
> - require the programmer to keep a written record of the program design process.
> - create programs that are understandable.
> - be generally applicable.

8.7.3 Dash Lists: A *dash list* is a list with each item tagged by a dash (—). Dash lists are specified by using the begin-list instruction `.DL` which has the form

`.DL` [*text-indent* [1]]

Except for the different item marks, dash lists are identical to bullet lists.

8.7.4 Marked Lists: A *marked list* is a list with each item tagged by a user-supplied mark. Marked lists are specified by using the begin-list instruction `.ML` which has the form

`.ML` *item-mark* [*text-indent* [1]]

where *item-mark* is any user-supplied symbol such as ☛ (denoted by the string `\(rh)`. Except for the difference in the item mark, a marked list is similar to bullet and dash lists.

8.7.5 Reference Lists: A *reference list* is similar to an automatically-sequenced list with arabic numeral marks except that the marks are enclosed in square brackets. It is called a reference list because such a list is often used to specify a bibliography. Reference lists are specified using the begin-list instruction `.RL` which has the form

`.RL` [*text-indent* [1]]

8.7.6 Variable-Mark Lists: A *variable-mark list* is similar to a marked list except that a different mark can be specified for each list item. A variable-mark list has the form

```
.VL text-indent [mark-indent [1]]
.LI m1
input lines describing list item
.LI m2
  :
.LI mn
input lines describing list item
.LE [1]
```

As before, argument *text-indent* specifies the indentation of the item text with respect to the indent in effect at the beginning of the list. Argument *mark-indent* is the distance from the current indent to the item mark. Specifying the third argument, the integer 1, suppresses printing of the ½ vertical space before each list item. Item marks m_i can be strings of characters; however, the marks *must not* contain ordinary (paddable) spaces because they cause alignment problems if the text is being right justified.

Here is an example of a list with variable marks:

T′POS(X)	The position number of X in its definition. For example COLOR′POS(BLUE) = 2 POSITIVE′POS(3) = 3
(1, 2, 3, 4, 5)	is a one-dimensional array value with 5 elements; the ith element has value i.

The variable-mark list was specified as

```
.VL 2.1i .5i
.LI T$app$POS(X)
The position number of X in its definition.
For example
.DS
    COLOR$app$POS(BLUE) = 2
    POSITIVE$app$POS(3) = 3
.DE
.LI "(1,\ 2,\ 3,\ 4,\ 5)"
is a one-dimensional array value with 5
elements; the $i sup th$ element has value i.
.LE
```

There are several interesting things about this list specification:

1. Displays and other `mm` instructions can be given in the list items; for example, the `.DS/.DE` instruction pair has been used to specify a display in a list item.
2. Unpaddable spaces (spaces preceded by a backslash) have been used in the second item mark to avoid alignment problems that would otherwise be caused by right justification.
3. List items and item marks can both contain `eqn` expressions; strings enclosed by the dollar character `$` are `eqn` expressions (see Chapter 5).

8.7.7 Hanging-Indent Lists: A *hanging-indent* list is a list with items whose first line hangs out on the left as illustrated by the following example:

> Gehani, Narain 1983. *Ada: An Advanced Introduction with the Ada Reference Manual.* Prentice-Hall.
>
> Lear, E. 1964. *The Nonsense Books of Edward Lear.* The New American Library.

The list items have no marks associated with them; the text indent used is 5 ens. Hanging-indent lists are specified as variable-mark lists but without supplying any item marks. For example, this hanging-indent list was specified as

```
.VL 5
.LI
Gehani, Narain 1983.
\fIAda: An Advanced Introduction with
the Ada Reference Manual\fP.
Prentice-Hall.
.LI
Lear, E. 1964.
\fIThe Nonsense Books of Edward Lear\fP.
The New American Library.
.LE
```

8.7.8 Nested Lists Example: Lists can be nested; the maximum list-nesting level allowed is 6. Here is an example of two bullet lists nested inside an automatically-sequenced list:

There are several kinds of high-level languages:

1. *Sequential*
    - Pascal
    - Fortran
    - C
2. *Concurrent*
    - Concurrent Pascal
    - Concurrent C

The nested lists were specified as

```
There are several kinds of high-level
languages:
.AL
.LI
\fISequential\fP
.BL
.LI
Pascal
.LI
Fortran
.LI
C
.LE
.LI
\fIConcurrent\fP
.BL
.LI
Concurrent Pascal
.LI
Concurrent C
.LE
.LE
```

8.8 Footnotes

A *footnote* is a note of reference, explanation or comment that is printed at the bottom of a page, below the main text. mm separates footnotes from the main text by drawing a short line (one inch long). The point size used for footnotes is 2 points less than that used in the main text (in the case of `nroff` there is no change in the point size).

There are two kinds of footnotes: automatically-numbered and user-labeled. In the case of automatically-numbered footnotes, `mm` automatically generates the next footnote number. In the case of user-labeled footnotes, the user must supply a footnote label; it is the user's responsibility to ensure that two footnotes on the same page do not have the same label. Automatically-numbered and user-labeled footnotes can be intermixed.

Automatically-numbered footnotes are specified as

```
...\*F
.FS
the footnote text (can contain some formatting instructions
such as paragraphs and lists, but not displays)
.FE
...
```

where "`...`" denotes the input text. `mm` will automatically replace the escape sequence `\*F` with the next footnote number. The first footnote is numbered one. The footnote number is printed in a smaller font size and is printed half a line above the text to be footnoted.

User-labeled footnotes are specified as

```
...label
.FS label
the footnote text (can contain some formatting instructions
such as paragraphs and lists, but not displays)
.FE
...
```

where the character sequence *label* is the user-supplied footnote label and "`...`" denotes input text.

This example illustrates both automatically-numbered and user-labeled footnotes:

Ada* is the first major general purpose programming language† to provide high-level concurrent programming facilities[1] based on the rendezvous concept.[2] Although these facilities seem to be elegant and easy to use, they are as yet essentially untried and untested in the field.

---

* Ada is a registered trademark of the U. S. Government—Ada Joint Program Office.

† Examples of other major languages are C and COBOL.

1. PL/I and Algol 68 have low-level concurrent programming facilities.
2. Hoare's CSP notation is also based on the rendezvous concept.

The text and footnotes were specified as follows:

```
Ada*
.FS *
Ada is a registered trademark of the
U. S.  Government\*(EMAda Joint
Program Office.
.FE
is the first major general purpose
programming language\(dg
.FS \(dg
Examples of other major languages
are C and COBOL.
.FE
to provide high-level concurrent
programming facilities\*F
.FS
PL/I and Algol 68 have low-level
concurrent programming facilities.
.FE
based
on the rendezvous concept.\*F
.FS
Hoare's CSP notation is also
based on the rendezvous concept.
.FE
Although these facilities
seem to be elegant and easy to use,
they are as yet essentially untried
and untested in the field.
```

Unlike the automatically generated footnote numbers, user-supplied footnote labels (e.g., the asterisk * and dagger †), are not printed as superscripts nor are they printed in a smaller point size. The footnote label asterisk * looks like a superscript because that is the way an asterisk is printed in the Times Roman font. To print a user-supplied footnote label *label* in the text as a superscript and in a smaller point size, the following paradigm may be used:

```
 ...\u\s-2label\s+2\d
.FS label
the footnote text
.FE
 ...
```

The `troff` escape sequences `\u` (up) and `\d` (down) raise and lower the printing position by half an em.

8.8.1 Footnote Style: By default, footnote labels are left justified, and the text is indented and right justified; moreover, hyphenation is not used for the footnote text. The footnote style can be changed by using the `.FD` instruction which has the form

`.FD` [*style* [1]]

Different values of the argument *style* have the following effect:

style	**hyphenation**	**right margin justification**	**text indent**	**label justification**
0	no	yes	yes	left
1	yes	yes	yes	left
2	no	no	yes	left
3	yes	no	yes	left
4	no	yes	no	left
5	yes	yes	no	left
6	no	no	no	left
7	yes	no	no	left
8	no	yes	yes	right
9	yes	yes	yes	right
10	no	no	yes	right
11	yes	no	yes	right

If argument *style* is not specified, then by default it is assumed to be 0 (10 for `nroff`). Presence of the second argument makes automatically-numbered footnotes start with 1 after every level-one heading.

Multiple footnotes on a page are separated by a three-point vertical space (one blank line in `nroff`). Separation between footnotes can be increased by a factor *n* by just setting the register `Fs` to *n*. For example, setting register `Fs` to 2 will cause footnotes to be separated by a six-point vertical space (two blank lines in `nroff`).

8.8.2 Restrictions on Footnotes: There are some restrictions on the use of footnotes:

1. Displays are not permitted within footnotes.

2. Footnotes cannot be nested; that is, a footnote cannot contain another footnote.

3. Automatically-numbered footnotes cannot be used for information that is placed on the cover sheet of a paper, for example, they cannot be used in document titles; however, user-labeled footnotes can be used.

8.9 References

Automatically-numbered references are specified as

```
...\*(Rf
.RS xy
the reference text
.RF
...
```

where "`...`" denotes the input text. mm will automatically replace the escape sequence `\*(Rf` with the next reference number. The first reference is numbered one. The two character string-name *xy* can be used subsequently to refer to this reference text; mm will automatically generate a correct citation. The citation consists of the reference number printed in square brackets, in a smaller point size and half a line above the associated text. In the case of `nroff`, the reference number is printed in the regular point size and it is placed on the same line as the associated text if the printing device does not allow half-line vertical motions.

A page with the default title "REFERENCES" and all the references specified in the document will be automatically generated at the end of the document (before the cover sheet page). The reference page is also listed in the table of contents. The default title can be changed by defining the string `Rp` as follows:

`.ds Rp "`*new-title*`"`

Here is an example illustrating the use of automatically-numbered references:

> Concurrent C[1] is an upward-compatible superset of C[2] that provides parallel programming facilities. In this paper, I will show that Concurrent C[1] can be used for programming robots.

> -7-
>
> REFERENCES
>
> 1. Gehani, N. H. and W. D. Roome. Concurrent C. AT&T Bell Labs, 1984.
> 2. Kernighan, B. W. and D. M. Ritchie. *The C Programming Language*. Prentice-Hall, 1978.

The above example was specified as

```
Concurrent C\*(Rf
.RS gR
Gehani, N. H. and W. D. Roome.
Concurrent C.
AT&T Bell Labs, 1984.
.RF
is an upward-compatible superset of C\*(Rf
.RS kR
Kernighan, B. W. and D. M. Ritchie.
\fIThe C Programming Language\fP.
Prentice-Hall, 1978.
.RF
that provides
parallel programming facilities.
In this paper, I will show that
Concurrent C\*(gR can be used for
programming robots.
```

Note the use of string name `gR` to refer to a citation given previously.

8.10 Two-Column Output

mm provides facilities for printing documents in two-column format. The two-column instruction `.2C` turns on two-column formatting and the one-column instruction `.1C` reverts to a single full-width column format. The portion of the document that is to be formatted in two-column format is enclosed by the `.2C` and `.1C` instructions:

`.2C`
text to be formatted in two-column format
`.1C`

Just putting the `.2C` instruction at the beginning of a document will cause everything to be printed in two-column format; for example, the document title and the table of contents will all be printed in two-column format. To avoid this, put the `.2C` instruction before the text you want to print in two-column format and turn off the two-column format with the `.1C` instruction immediately after the text.

Here is a two-column output sample (produced with page length and width equal to 5.5 and 3.5 inches, respectively):

The high level
programming language Ada
is named in honor of
Augusta Ada Byron, the
Countess of Lovelace and
the daughter of the English
poet Lord Byron. She was
the assistant, associate and
supporter of Charles
Babbage, the
mathematician and inventor
of a calculating machine
called the Analytical
Engine. With the help of
Babbage she wrote a nearly
complete program for the
Analytical Engine to
compute the Bernoulli
numbers circa 1830.
Because of this effort, the
Countess may be said to
have been the world's first
computer programmer.

Because of the shorter lines in two-column format, ugly-looking spaces may appear in the lines if it is not possible to fill them with words. Hyphenation may be turned on to allow more text to fit on each line:

The high level program-
ming language Ada is
named in honor of Augusta
Ada Byron, the Countess of
Lovelace and the daughter
of the English poet Lord
Byron. She was the assis-
tant, associate and supporter of Charles Babbage, the
mathematician and inventor
of a calculating machine
called the Analytical En-
gine. With the help of
Babbage she wrote a nearly
complete program for the
Analytical Engine to com-
pute the Bernoulli numbers
circa 1830. Because of this
effort, the Countess may be
said to have been the
world's first computer programmer.

The footnote and display format used with two-column output can be controlled using the width-control instruction `.WC`; this instruction has the form

`.WC` *arguments*

where the possible *arguments* are listed in the following table along with their effects:

argument	effect
`N`	Default mode: implies `-WF`, `-FF`, `-WD` and `FB`.
`WF`	Wide footnotes even in two-column output.
`-WF`	Footnotes are printed in the output style in effect, that is, one- or two-column output.
`FF`	All footnotes have the same width as the first footnote on the page.
`-FF`	Footnotes are printed according to `WF` or `-WF`, whichever option is set.
`WD`	Wide displays even in two-column output style.
`-WD`	Displays are printed in the output style in effect, that is, one- or two-column output.
`FB`	Floating displays cause a break when output on the current page.
`-FB`	Opposite of `FB`.

8.11 Convenient `troff` Instructions

I find the following `troff` instructions convenient to use with `mm` instructions when specifying the body of a document:

`troff` instruction	explanation
`.ce` *n*	Center the next *n* input lines; if *n* is missing, then it is assumed to be 1.
`.br`	Skip to the next output line.
`.ll` [[±]*n*]	If a plus or minus sign is not specified, then the line length is set to *n*; otherwise it is set to the current length ± *n*. If no argument is specified, then the previous line length is restored.
`.in` [±*n*]	Increase or decrease the current indent by ± *n*; if no argument is specified, then the previous indent is restored.

9. Document Postlude

The last part of the raw document, the document postlude, contains instructions for items that appear at the end of a document such as signature lines, a list of attachments and a list of persons who will be sent copies of the document. Instructions to generate a table of contents and a cover sheet are also given here, even though these items logically appear at the beginning of the document. The table of contents, reference page, lists of tables and figures, and the cover sheet are generated at the end of a document because they contain summary information about the whole document.

9.1 Order of Specifications of the Document Postlude Items

A document postlude is organized as follows:

```
.FC [closing] (formal letter closing)
.SG [typist-initials] (signature instruction)
.NS notation-style (specification of attachments, enclosures, etc.)
input lines specifying an attachment, enclosure, etc.
.NE

 ⋮

.NS notation style
input lines specifying an attachment, enclosure, etc.
.NE (end of notation lists)
.AV "approver-name" (approval instruction)
.TC arguments (table-of-contents instruction)
.CS (cover-sheet instruction)
```

All the above instructions need not be used in a document postlude; however, if they are used, then they should be given in the above order. Except for the table-of-contents instruction `.TC` and the cover-sheet instruction `.CS`, none of the other instructions in this section apply to external papers; they are just ignored in external papers [DWB 1984b].

9.2 Formal Letter Closing

The formal closing in a letter such as "Sincerely," is specified by using the formal-letter-closing instruction `.FC`; this instruction has the form

`.FC` [*closing*]

If no argument is specified, then the `.FC` instruction prints

Yours very truly,

as a formal closing of a letter. A user may explicitly specify a different closing, for example, the `.FC` instruction

```
.FC Sincerely,
```

will produce the line

Sincerely,

9.3 Signature

Letters and memorandums are signed by the authors at the end of the document; the signature is usually placed just above the author's printed name. Names and titles of authors, with sufficient space for signatures, are printed by using the signature instruction `.SG`; it prints the name and title of each author specified using the `.AU` and `.AT` instructions, respectively. Each name is printed beginning at the center of a line and is preceded by three blank lines for the actual signature. The signature instruction has the form

`.SG` [*typist-initials*]

If the argument *typist-initials* is present, then the `.SG` instruction also prints reference information such as the last author's initials, organization number (specified in the `.AU` instruction) and the typist's initials on the same line as the name of the last author.

9.4 Specification of Attachments, Enclosures, Persons Receiving Copies, etc.

Information such as items attached to a document, items enclosed with a document, a list of persons who will be sent copies of the document and items related to a document but which are being sent separately is often listed at the end of the document. mm provides the `.NS` and `.NE` instructions for specifying such information:

`.NS` [*style* [`1`]]
information corresponding to argument "style"
`.NE`

Argument *style* specifies the different items that are to be printed on the document:

style	**prints**
absent	Copy to
0	Copy to
1	Copy (with att.) to
2	Copy (without att.) to
3	Att.
4	Atts.
5	Enc.
6	Encs.
7	U. S. C.
8	Letter to
9	Memorandum to
10	Copy (with atts.) to
11	Copy (without atts.) to
12	Abstract Only to
13	Complete Memorandum to
"*string*"	Copy (*string*) to
"*string*" with the second argument equal to 1	*string*

Older versions of the mm macros do not support styles 10 through 13 nor the last style with the second argument.

Here is an example showing the use of the `.NS/.NE` instruction pair:

```
.NS
E. Hedrick
C. Wetherell
.NE
.NS 6
Memo titled \fIConcurrent C\fP
.NE
```

will cause the following information to be printed:

> Copy to
> E. Hedrick
> C. Wetherell
>
> Encs.
> Memo titled *Concurrent C*

9.5 Approval Line

If a document requires signature(s) for approval, then the approval instruction `.AV` can be used to print the approver's name and to leave sufficient space for the approver's signature. The `.AV` instruction has the form

`.AV` "*approver-name*" [1]

and it causes the approver's name and the date captions to be printed in the document as follows:

> ⋮
>
> APPROVED
>
> ______________________________   ____________
>
> *approver-name*   Date

The optional second argument is used to suppress the printing of the string "APPROVED" that is printed automatically by the `.AV` instruction.

9.6 Table of Contents

The table of contents, which is printed by the `.TC` instruction, consists of the document headings and the numbers of the pages where these headings appear. The `.TC` instruction has the form

`.TC` l_1 *n* l_2 *separator-char-code* a_1 ... a_5

Its arguments are explained in the following table:

argument	default value	explanation
l_1	1	Headings with level $\leqslant l_1$ will be separated by *n* ½ vertical spaces (*n* blank lines in `nroff`); *n* is the second argument of the `.TC` instruction.
n	1	Related to the first argument l_1
l_2	2	Page numbers of headings with level $\leqslant l_2$ are right justified and are separated from the headings, which are left justified, by the character specified by *separator-char-code*. Page numbers of other headings are separated from the headings by two blank spaces.
separator-char-code	0	If *separator-char-code* is 0, then periods (leaders) are used to separate the page numbers from the heading text; alternative leader characters can be specified using the `troff` instruction `.lc`. If *separator-char-code* is greater than 0, then spaces are used.
a_1 ... a_5		These arguments are centered and printed on separate lines preceding the table of contents.

Trailing arguments of the `.TC` instruction can be omitted; typically, all arguments of the `.TC` instruction are omitted. Only headings with level less than or equal to the contents of the `Cl` register are saved for the table of contents. The default value of `Cl` is 2; this value can be changed by the user.

9.6.1 List of Tables: The `.TC` instruction prints a list of tables whose captions have been specified with the `.TB` instruction (see Chapter 3). Production of this list can be suppressed by setting register `Lt`, whose default value is 1, to 0.

9.6.2 List of Figures: The `.TC` instruction prints a list of figures whose captions have been specified with the `.FG` instruction (see Chapter 4). Production of this list can be suppressed by setting register `Lf`, whose default value is 1, to 0.

9.6.3 List of Equations: The `.TC` instruction can print a list of equations whose captions have been specified with the `.EC` instruction (see Chapter 5); for `.TC` to print the equation list, register `Le` must be set to 1 (default value of `Le` is 0);

9.7 Cover Sheet

The cover sheet of a document contains information such as the name and affiliation of the author, and an abstract. A cover sheet for a memorandum or an external paper is printed with the cover-sheet instruction `.CS`:

`.CS` *text-pages other-pages total-pages #figures #tables #references*

The `.CS` instruction arguments, which are self explanatory, are used only for the cover sheet of an internal paper. Trailing arguments can be omitted. Values for these arguments will be automatically computed (values for the number of figures and tables are computed by counting the number of `.TB` and `.FG` instructions.

`mm` produces cover sheets in three different styles:

1. External paper style
2. Internal paper style
3. *Memorandum for File* style (this cover sheet is printed by the abstract instruction `.AS 2`; there is no need for the `.CS` instruction).

10. Advanced Aspects of `mm`

In this section, I will discuss the concept of an environment in `mm`, double-spaced output, interactive input, the generation of form letters, printing page headers and footers, and forcing printing to resume on an odd-numbered page.

10.1 Environments

The document text, displays, and footnotes are formatted in their own environments. An *environment* consists of the current font, point size, line length, mode (fill or no-fill), indentation, hyphenation status and so forth. Each environment has its own set of default values. Making changes to one environment does not lead to changes in the other environments. For example, a font or point size change inside a display will not affect text following the display, but this change will remain in effect for all subsequent displays. This is because all displays are processed in the same environment.

Initially, the default environments of the document text, displays and footnotes are essentially similar. One difference between the footnote environments and the default text and display environments is that the default point size used for footnotes is two points smaller than the default point size used for the document text or displayed text.

10.2 Double-Spaced Output

There are two ways of printing a document in double-spaced format: by using the `troff` instruction `.ls` or by using the mm command-line option `-rC4`.

10.2.1 The `.ls` *Instruction:* The `troff` instruction `.ls` (with argument equal to 2) can be used to double space a document. A `.ls` instruction must be given inside a display or a footnote to turn on double spacing in displays or footnotes, respectively. Double spacing is turned off by using the `.ls 1` (or just `.ls`) instruction.

10.2.2 mm *Command-Line Option* `-rC4`*:* mm option `-rC4` can also be used to double space a document. However, this option also causes a page footer with the word DRAFT and the current date to be printed on the bottom of every page. Displays and footnotes are not double spaced by this option; the `.ls` instruction must be used to double space displays and footnotes.

10.3 Interactive Text Insertion

Text can be read interactively from the standard input (terminal or a redirected file) by using the read instruction `.RD`. The `.RD` instruction is useful for producing, from a template (form letter), documents that differ slightly from each other. For example, customized letters can be produced from a form letter by reading the name and address of the person and other appropriate items when formatting the template. Execution of the `.RD` instruction causes output of the formatted document to be suspended; text is then read from the standard input until two consecutive new-line characters are read or until an end-of-file is signaled by entering control-D as the first character of a line; after this, output of the formatted document is resumed.

The `.RD` instruction has the form

`.RD` *prompt diversion string*

The three arguments *prompt*, *diversion* and *string* are described below:

`.RD` **argument**	**explanation**
prompt	Input prompt string which is printed on the terminal; if *prompt* is the null string (`""`), then the user is prompted for input by printing the character `bel` at the terminal (this character rings the terminal bell).
diversion	Name of the macro where input is stored; input can be referenced by calling this macro. For example, if *diversion* is `aA`, then each subsequent macro call `.aA` is replaced by the input supplied for the `.RD` instruction.
string-name	Name of the string in which the input first line is stored. This input line can be referenced using the escape sequence used for accessing string values. For example, if *string-name* is `aS`, then its contents are referenced as `\*(aS`. Being able to access the first line of the input can be convenient. For example, suppose that the input consists of a person's name and address, with the first input line being the person's name; *string-name* can be used to reference the person's name.

The `.RD` instruction is not designed to read input from a file other than standard input; this limits its utility for mass producing customized letters; for example, instruction `.RD` cannot be used to read a list of names and addresses from a file. (Moreover, the `.RD` does not work if the formatting command "pipes" the input to the formatter.) It is best to use the `.RD` instruction with simple formatting commands, for example,

`nroff -mm` *form-letter*
`troff -mm` *form-letter*

where *form-letter* is the file containing the `.RD` instruction. As an example of the use of the `.RD` instruction, consider the following form letter:

```
.PH ""
.AU "Narain Gehani"
.AT "Editor"
.MT 5
.DS
.RD "" aA aN
.aA
.SP 3
Dear \*(aN:
.DE
.SP 1
This is to acknowledge receipt
of your paper
.RD "" aP
.ft I
.aP
.ft P
submitted by you for publication in
\fIThe Journal of Document Formatting\fP.
We will contact you as soon as the
review process has been completed.
.SP 2
.FC Sincerely
.SG
```

Note that the first `.RD` instruction is executed in the no-fill mode to keep the input lines separate so that the name and address can be printed just as they were input.

Here is an example of a letter produced using the form letter:

Journal Name and Logo
Address and Phone number

month, day, year

D. K. Smith
New York

Dear D. K. Smith:

This is to acknowledge receipt of your paper *New Formatting Style* submitted by you for publication in *The Journal of Document Formatting.* We will contact you as soon as the review process has been completed.

Sincerely,

Narain Gehani
Editor

The following input was used for the example:

```
D. K. Smith
New York

New Formatting Style
```

Customized letters can be mass produced from the form letter by using the UNIX command language, called the *shell*, to execute the formatting and printing commands repeatedly. For example, the *shell* script

```
read n
while test $n -ne 0
do
mm form-letter-template | letter-quality-printer
n=`expr $n - 1`
done
```

will cause the command

mm *form-letter-template* | *letter-quality-printer*

to be executed *n* times where *n* is a user-supplied value; command *letter-quality-printer* prints its output on the printer. (The mm command is similar to the `mmt` command, but it invokes `nroff` instead of `troff`; see Appendix B for more details).

10.4 Halting After Printing Each Page

The mm command-line option `-s`*n* can be used to stop printing of the formatted document after every *n* pages (default value is 1) to allow the paper to be reloaded or changed. Printing is resumed by typing a new-line.

10.5 Page Headers and Footers

A *page header* is text that appears at the top of a page. It consists of two lines that are printed in the following order:

- a one-line *main* header that is printed on all pages and
- a one-line *even-* or *odd-page header* that is printed on even or odd pages, respectively.

By default, only a one-line main header is printed; it is of the form

- *n* -

where *n* is the page number. Even- and odd-page headers are left as blank lines.

A *page footer* is text that appears at the bottom of a page. Like a page header, a page footer consists of two lines that are printed in the following order:

- a one-line *even-* or *odd-page footer* that is printed on even or odd pages, respectively, and
- a one-line *main footer* that is printed on all pages.

By default, the page footers are all blank lines.

Page footers and headers are specified by instructions of the form

.*ab* "'*left-part*'*center-part*'*right-part*'"

where .*ab* is a page-header or page-footer instruction as described in the table given below. The three arguments *left-part*, *center-part* and *right-part* are left-justified, centered and right-justified, respectively. Any other character may be used as a delimiter instead of the apostrophe '; however, the delimiter character must not occur within the arguments.

The following instructions are used for specifying page headers and footers:

instruction	name	comments
`.PH`	main header	Default value is a line with the page number *n* in the format "-*n*-"; the page number is printed in arabic numerals; the first page header is not printed in a memorandum or an external paper or letter.
`.EH`	even-page header	Default value is a blank line.
`.OH`	odd-page header	Default value is a blank line.
`.PF`	main footer	Default value is a blank line.
`.EF`	even-page footer	Default value is a blank line.
`.OF`	odd-page footer	Default value is a blank line.

Strings and register names may be referenced in the page-header and -footer instruction arguments. If string and register references in page-header or -footer instructions are to be evaluated when printing the header or footer instead of when the instructions are encountered, then these references must be preceded by three extra backslashes.[13]

As examples of page headers, here are the page-header instructions used for this chapter:

```
.PH ""
.EH "'x''y'"
.OH "'y''x'"
```

13. This is a consequence of using macros and of mm implementation details; for a more elaborate explanation, please see [DWB 1984b; Ossanna 1977; Kernighan 1982c].

where *x* is the character sequence

```
\\\\nP
```

and *y* is the character sequence

```
\fB\s-1Chapter 2: Specifying The Document Format\s0\fP
```

Printing of the default main header is effectively suppressed by setting it to the null string. The reference to the page-number register `\nP` had to be prefixed by three extra backslashes so that its current value was printed as each page was printed.

10.6 Proprietary Marks

The `.PM` instruction may be used to print a proprietary message that is appended to the page footer. This instruction has the form

`.PM` [*code*]

where the effect of different values of argument *code* is as follows:

code	**effect**
omitted	Stop printing a proprietary message.
`P`	Print "PRIVATE".
`N`	Print "NOTICE".
`BP`	Print "*company* PROPRIETARY"; value of *company* is implementation dependent.
`BR`	Print "*company* RESTRICTED"; value of *company* is implementation dependent.
`ILL`	Print message indicating that the document must be rendered illegible before discarding.
`PM1, PM2, PM3` `PM4, PM5, PM6`	Implementation dependent.

The word "PRIVATE" can be printed at the top of the page (before the page header) by setting the register `Pv` to an appropriate value; this word is centered and underlined:

value of register `Pv`	effect
0	Do not print "PRIVATE" (default).
1	Print "PRIVATE" on first page only.
2	Print "PRIVATE" on all pages.

10.7 Bottom Blocks

Arbitrary text can be printed at the bottom of every page (after the footnotes, but before the page footer) by using bottom blocks which have the form

```
.BS
text to be printed at the bottom
of every page
.BE
```

where `.BS` and `.BE` are the bottom-block start and end instructions. The bottom block can be erased by specifying a null bottom block:

```
.BS
.BE
```

10.8 Top and Bottom Margins

The top margin (space before the page header) and the bottom margin (space after the page footer) can be increased by using the vertical-margin instruction `.VM`;[14] this instruction has the form

`.VM` *top bottom*

where the arguments *top* and *bottom* specify the number of lines by which the top and bottom margins, respectively, are to be increased. These arguments must not be negative and must be unscaled (i.e., ordinary numbers).

10.9 Forcing Output to Begin on an Odd Page

Components of some documents, such as chapters of a book (including this one), must begin on an odd-numbered page. The odd-page instruction `.OP` is used to force a skip to an odd-numbered page; this may result in a blank (even-numbered) page.

---

14. mm does not provide a corresponding instruction for decreasing the top and bottom margin space; the top margin can be decreased by redefining the top-of-page processing; for more details, see the mm reference manual [DWB 1984b].

11. Interfacing with `troff` Preprocessors

mm provides instructions for delimiting `pic`, `tbl` and `eqn` specifications from the rest of the document; moreover, these instructions also allow mm to position the specified items properly. (These instructions are also recognized by the corresponding preprocessors.)

Interfaces for the preprocessors mentioned above are as follows:

- `pic` (figure) specifications must be bracketed by the `.PS` and the `.PE` instructions.
- `tbl` (table) specifications must be bracketed by the `.TS` and the `.TE` instructions.
- `eqn` (equation) specifications must be bracketed by the `.EQ` and the `.EN` instructions; these instructions must normally be enclosed in `.DS/.DE` displays. `eqn` specifications can also be embedded in the text by using in-line `eqn` expressions.

11.1 Figure, Table and Equation Caption Instructions

Automatically-numbered captions for figures, tables and equations can be generated by the `.FG`, `.TB` and `.EC` instructions, respectively (see appropriate chapters for details). These captions are printed using the table-of-contents instruction `.TC`.

12. Interaction of `troff` with mm

`troff` facilities are used in conjunction with mm for reasons such as fine tuning a document format, referring to special characters provided by `troff`, to make up for facilities missing in mm or for convenience. Some examples of facilities missing in mm that are available in `troff` are

1. facilities for defining string and integer variables,
2. a mechanism for defining macros,
3. instructions for changing the default behavior of some mm instructions and
4. instructions for changing to a font other than Times Roman, Times Bold or Times Italic.

In this section, I will discuss the harmonious use of `troff` with mm.

12.1 Convention for User-Defined Names

To avoid collisions with names used by `troff` and its preprocessors, mm recommends the following convention for constructing macro, string and register (integer variable) names:

Construct names that consist of a single lower-case letter or a lower-case letter followed by a character *other* than a lower-case letter (note that names `c2` and `nP` are already in use).

Register names may be the same as macro or string names. For more details about the naming convention used by `troff`, `mm` and other document formatting tools, the user should see the document describing `mm` [DWB 1984b].

12.2 Some Useful `troff` Instructions

We have already discussed and used some `troff` instructions in conjunction with `mm` instructions, for example, the font and point size instructions. Here is a list of `troff` instructions that can be useful:

`troff` **instruction**	**use**
`.af`	assign output format to registers
`.br`	move to next line
`.bp`	skip to next page
`.ce`	center lines
`.de`	define/redefine a macro
`.fi`	turn on fill mode
`.in`	change indentation
`.ll`	change line length
`.nf`	turn off fill mode
`.ns`	turn on no-space mode
`.nx`	switch input file
`.rd`	read from standard input
`.rm`	remove macro or string
`.rr`	remove register
`.rs`	turn off no-space mode
`.so`	include specified file
`.ta`	set tabs
`.ti`	temporary indent
`.tl`	three-part title
`.tr`	translate characters

For details about these instructions, see Chapter 6.

12.3 Explicit Specification of the First-Page Number

Suppose that you format a book one chapter at a time. By default, the first page of a document is numbered one. This is fine for the first chapter, but for the other chapters you would like to start with an appropriate page number (e.g., last page of last chapter plus one) The user can explicitly specify an alternative first page number in one of several ways including

1. The `troff` page-number instruction `.pn` can be used to specify an alternative first page number; this instruction has the form

   `.pn` *n*

   where *n* is the desired first page number. This instruction must be given at the beginning of the raw document.

2. The first page number can also be specified by using the `mm` command-line option `-rP`*n*, where *n* is the desired first page number.

12.4 Explicit Specification of the First Footnote and Reference Number

By default, the first automatically-numbered footnote is numbered one. As in the case of the first page numbers, it may be desirable or necessary to start a document with a footnote number other than one. `mm` keeps the number of the last automatically-numbered footnote processed in register `:p`. By default, the initial value of this register is 0 (i.e., the first footnote is numbered one). The first footnote number can be changed by setting register `:p` to an appropriate value. For example, if *n* is the desired first footnote number, then register `:p` should be set to $n-1$.

Explicit specification of the reference numbers is similar to that of footnote numbers. The last reference number is kept in register `:R`.

12.5 Explicit Specification of the First Level-One Heading Number

By default, the first level-one heading is numbered one. As in the case of first page numbers, it may be necessary to start with a level-one heading that has a number other than one. `mm` keeps the last level-one heading number used in register `H1`. By default, the initial value of this register is 0. The first level-one heading number can be changed by setting register `H1` to an appropriate value. For example, if *n* is the desired first level-one heading number, then register `H1` should be set to $n-1$.

12.6 Macros

A *macro* facility allows a group of instructions or text to be given a symbolic name called the *macro name*; the group of instructions or text is called the *macro body*. When the instructions or text in the macro body are needed, mention of the macro name (a *macro call*) causes `troff` to replace the name with these instructions or text.

Macros are a convenient mechanism for referring to frequently used groups of instructions or text by symbolic names; they can be used to reduce the raw document size. Macros can also make document modifications easier: only the macro definition needs be changed rather than all the places where the macro is used.

12.6.1 Macro Definitions: Although `mm` does not have a macro definition facility, the `troff` facility can be used. `troff` macro definitions have the form

```
.de xx
instructions and/or text; that is, the macro body
..
```

where *xx* is the name of the macro to be defined or redefined. The body of the macro begins on the next line and is terminated by a line beginning with the characters "`..`". Macros can be parameterized with up to 9 parameters; these parameters are referenced in the macro body as `\\$`i $(1 \leqslant i \leqslant 9)$.

12.6.2 Macro Calls: Macro calls have the form

`.`*xx* arguments

where *xx* is a macro name. Arguments must be separated by spaces; moreover, arguments with embedded blanks must be enclosed within double quotes. If all the arguments do not fit on one line, then they can be continued on the next line provided the line being continued is ended with a backslash.

12.6.3 Examples of Macros: As examples, consider the two macros "`.(P`" and "`.)P`" that I use for beginning and ending constant-width font displays. These macros are defined as

```
.de (P
.DS
.ft CW
..
.de )P
.ft P
.DE
..
```

A call to the macro `.(P` is replaced by the two instructions

```
.DS
.ft CW
```

which start a display and change the current font to the constant-width font. Similarly, a call to the macro `.)P` is replaced by the two instructions

```
.ft P
.DE
```

to restore the font in effect before the `.(P` macro call and to end the display.

There is one disadvantage to using these two macros instead of using the instructions in their bodies directly. `checkmm` does not replace macro calls by the corresponding macro bodies; consequently, it will not be able to detect any mismatched `.DS/.DE` pairs caused by mismatched `.(P/.)P` pairs.

12.7 Space-Width Problem When Changing Fonts

There is a minor problem with `troff` that becomes obvious when changing to a font whose space character has a noticeably different width than the space character of the previous font. The problem is due to the fact that `troff` prints the space preceding an in-line font change request using the new font instead of the old font. The resulting output can look a bit ugly because `troff` leaves a little more or a little less space than expected. For example, consider the following line with a font change request (I will use the constant-width font `CW` for illustration):

```
Transaction \f(CWdata\fP is called by one process.
```

This will be printed as

Transaction `data` is called by one process.

Notice the little extra space before the word `data` in the above line. This does not look good. Fortunately, when changing between most of the other commonly used fonts, the effect of this `troff` problem is usually not noticeable.

One way of bypassing this problem is to use the escape sequence "`\&\f(CW`"; the zero-width non-printing character `\&` forces `troff` to output the space before the font change takes effect (this solution was suggested by B. W. Kernighan). Using the escape sequence with the zero-width character, the example line given above is printed as

Transaction `data` is called by one process.

I use the escape sequence "`\*(cW`" to change to constant-width font; this escape sequence refers to the string `cW` which I predefine as

```
.ds cW \&\f(CW
```

Each reference to the string `cW`, i.e., `*\(cW`, is replaced by the string `\&\f(CW`.

13. mm Command-Line Options

Document characteristics such as the style, format, page width and page length can usually be specified as options in the command-line used to format the document. These options are specified along with commands that invoke the mm macro package; the raw document itself is not changed. For example, an appropriate command-line option can be used to produce the draft version of a document with the word "DRAFT" and the current date printed at the bottom of each page.

Options that can be set from the command line are described below:

-o*list* Print only pages whose page numbers appear in the comma-separated *list* of numbers and ranges. A range *n*-*m* means pages *n* through *m*; an initial -*n* means from the beginning to page *n*; and a final *n*- means from page *n* to the end.

-rA*n* Specification of alternative formats for the "*Subject/Date/From*" block:

n	**effect**
1	Equivalent to invoking the .AF instruction without an argument; suppresses printing of the company name and the "*Subject/Date/From*" headings.
2	Allows printing of the company logo if available on a printing device (for use with nroff).

-rC*n* Produces different versions of the formatted document:

n	**effect**
1	Print "OFFICIAL FILE COPY" at the bottom of each page.
2	Print "DATE FILE COPY" at the bottom of each page.
3	Print "DRAFT" at the bottom of each page.
4	Print "DRAFT" at the bottom of each page, double space the document and indent each paragraph by 10 spaces.

-rD1 Set the debugging mode. In this mode, mm continues processing even if it detects an error; some debugging information, such as the current line number of the input file, is given in the default page header.

-rE*n* Change the font used for the "*Subject/Date/From*" fields:

n	***Subject/Date/From*** **field font**
1	bold (default for `troff`)
2	Roman (default for `nroff`)

`-rL`*k* Set the page length to *k*; for `troff` the value of *k* is specified as a scaled number representing the page length while for `nroff` it is an integer representing the number of lines in the page. Default page length is 11.00 inches for `troff` and 66 lines for `nroff`.

`-rN`*n* Change the style used for the page headers:

n	**effect on page 1**	**effect on other pages**
0	Header is printed.	Header is printed.
1	Current header replaces footer.	Header is printed.
2	No header is printed.	Header is printed.
3	Page numbers are printed at the bottom of the page (as page footers) using the style "section no-page no" where *section no* refers to the current level-one heading number. Each level-one heading starts on a new page.	Same as page 1.
4	No header.	No header is printed unless one has been explicitly specified by using the `.PH` instruction.
5	Same as *n* = 3; moreover "section no-figure no" numbering style is used for the figure captions specified with the `.FG` instruction (*section no* refers to the current level-one heading number). Each level-one heading starts on a new page.	Same as page 1.

`-rO`*k* Offset the output to the right by (i.e., set left margin to) *k*; for `troff` *k* must be a scaled number (default offset value is 1.0

inches for `troff` and 0.75 inches for `nroff`).

`-rP`*n* The document page numbers are to start with *n*.

`-rS`*n* Use point size *n* (default is 10) and *n*+2 point vertical spacing (default is 12); this option applies only to `troff`.

`-rW`*k* set the page width (line length) to *k*; for `troff` *k* is a *scaled* number (6.0 inches) representing the page width while for `nroff` it is a unscaled number representing the number of characters in the line.

`-s`*n* In the case of `nroff`, this option stops printing the formatted document after every *n* pages (default value is 1) to allow reloading or changing of paper). Printing is resumed by typing a new-line.

With this option `troff` generates instructions for the post-processor to stop the typesetter every *n* pages. It is a bad idea to use this option with `troff` unless you operate the typesetter yourself.

14. Hints for Managing Large Documents

Here are some hints for formatting large documents:

1. Break up the document into small components and typeset these components separately. It is easier to manipulate small documents. This reduces the cost of making a mistake because the cost is often proportional to the size of the document. For a book, the natural components are chapters; for large chapters or larger papers the natural components are sections with level-one headings.

2. Keep figures, tables, large equations and programs in separate files. Figures can be included in the main document by using the `.PS` or `include pic` instructions, equations with the `include eqn` or the `.PS pic` instructions, tables with the `.PS pic` instruction, and text with the `troff` instruction `.so`.

3. Only the first part of a large document is likely to start with page number one. Remember to typeset the other parts with the starting page numbers explicitly specified. You might have to do the same for the footnotes, reference numbers and level-one headings.

4. Write UNIX shell scripts to format documents, especially multi-file documents, using the desired commands with appropriate options.

15. Checking for Errors: `checkmm`

`checkmm` detects `mm` errors such as instructions used in the wrong order, unbalanced `.DS/.DE` instructions and so on. The UNIX `checkmm` command has the form

`checkmm` *files*

If no files are specified, then `checkmm` reads from standard input. `checkmm` will not check for `troff` errors; it does not replace macro calls by the corresponding bodies when checking for errors even though the macro bodies may consist only of `mm` instructions. `checkmm` does not check for misspelled instructions.

`checkmm` also checks for `eqn` errors.

16. A Final Example

In this example, I will show you the complete specification of an article (paper) that was produced using `mm`. The example paper, which is shown below along with its specification, is a radically shortened version of a paper titled *Concurrent C* [Gehani and Roome 1984]. For ease of presentation, I will discuss the example paper, one page at a time. First, I will show you a page of the paper in its formatted form, commenting when necessary. Then I will show you how this page was specified.

A paper consists of two parts: a cover sheet and the body of the paper. The cover sheet, which comes before the paper body, consists of the title of the paper, the names of the authors and their affiliations, and the abstract of the paper. The cover sheet of our example paper is[15]

---

15. The page and line lengths used to produce the sample output are 5.50 and 3.50 inches, respectively.

Concurrent C

N. H. Gehani
W. D. Roome

AT&T Bell Laboratories
Murray Hill, New Jersey 07974

ABSTRACT

Concurrent C is a superset of C that provides concurrent programming facilities.

Cover Sheet of an External Paper

The cover sheet was produced by using the information supplied in the initial portion of the raw document:

```
.TL
Concurrent C
.AU "N. H. Gehani" "" MH
.AU "W. D. Roome" "" MH
.AS 1
Concurrent C is a superset of C that
provides concurrent programming facilities.
.AE
.MT 4
```

Raw Document Corresponding to the Cover Sheet

Notice that each author's name in the `.AU` instruction is enclosed within a pair of double quotes; mm instruction arguments are enclosed within double quotes if they contain embedded blanks. The authors' affiliation was, by default, assumed to be "AT&T Bell Laboratories" because that is where the paper was formatted and printed. The geographical location is specified by the predefined location code `MH` in the `.AU` instruction. In this case `MH` is defined as the string "Murray Hill, New Jersey 07974". The address associated with the location code is printed after the company name. Each mm implementation defines the default author affiliation along with location codes specifying company locations.

The cover sheet is generated by using the cover-sheet instruction `.CS`. The cover-sheet instruction must be given at the end of the raw document to allow collection of summary information, such as the number of pages, that is printed on cover sheets of some documents.

Now it is time to look at the first page of the paper:

Concurrent C

N. H. Gehani
W. D. Roome

AT&T Bell Laboratories
Murray Hill, New Jersey 07974

1. Introduction

Concurrent programming is becoming increasingly important because multicomputers are becoming attractive alternatives to maxicomputers.

Concurrent programming has many advantages:

1. Concurrent programming facilities can lead to notational convenience and conceptual elegance.

2. Concurrent programming can reduce program execution time.

First Page of an External Paper

The paper title, authors' names, affiliation and company address are printed again, just as they were printed on the cover sheet. Next, we see the initial part of the paper's body. As much of the paper body as possible is printed, subject to the formatting instructions given, in the space remaining on the first page.

Here is the raw document for page one:

```
.H 1 "Introduction"
Concurrent programming is becoming
increasingly important because
multicomputers are becoming attractive
alternatives to maxicomputers.
.P
Concurrent programming has many
advantages:
.AL
.LI
Concurrent programming facilities can lead to
notational convenience and conceptual elegance.
.LI
Concurrent programming can reduce program
execution time.
.LE
```

Raw Document Corresponding to the First Page

Notice that the author name, affiliation and location information was not specified again for page one, even though this information is printed on page one. As in the case of the cover sheet, this information was printed using the information supplied in the `.AU` instructions given earlier.

Now let us take a look at the second page of the paper:

-2-

2. Concurrent Programming

Few major programming languages offer concurrent programming facilities:

language	concurrent programming
Fortran	No
PL/I	Yes (low-level)
Pascal	No
C	No
Ada	Yes

3. Concurrent C

The concurrency model in Concurrent C is based on the *rendezvous* concept. A Concurrent C program consists of one or more processes cooperating to accomplish a common objective.

A *process* is an instantiation of a process type. A process has its own flow-of-control; it executes in parallel with other processes.

Page 2 of External Paper

Page numbers are automatically printed by `mm`.

The portion of the raw paper corresponding to page two is

```
.H 1 "Concurrent Programming"
Few major programming languages
offer concurrent programming facilities:
.DS
.TS
box, center;
c | c
a | a.
language☛concurrent programming
=
Fortran☛No
PL/I☛Yes (low-level)
Pascal☛No
C☛No
Ada☛Yes
.TE
.DE
.H 1 "Concurrent C"
The concurrency model in Concurrent C is
based on the \fIrendezvous\fP concept.
A Concurrent C program consists of one or more
processes cooperating to
accomplish a common objective.
.P
A \fIprocess\fP is an instantiation of a
process type.
A process has its own flow-of-control; it
executes in parallel with other processes.
```

Raw Document Corresponding to Page 2

The table specification (which will be processed by `tbl`) was enclosed within a display to ensure that the table was not split across pages:

```
.DS
.TS
```
table specification
```
.TE
.DE
```

The first line of the table specification indicates that the table is to be enclosed within a box and that it is to be centered. The next two lines specify that the table will have two columns; they also specify the format of the table entries. Following these lines are the data lines that make up the contents of the table.

As before, I have used the symbol ☛ to denote the tab character. The data line with only the character = specifies that a double horizontal line is to be drawn. See Chapter 3 for details about table specifications.

Let us now move on to the final page of the paper:

-3-

4. Conclusions

Concurrent C is a versatile language that can be used for a variety of applications.

Page 3 of External Paper

The final page was specified as

```
.H 1 "Conclusions"
Concurrent C is a versatile language that
can be used for a variety of applications.
.CS
```

Raw Document Corresponding to Page 3

The first line is a level-one heading instruction; this is followed by two lines of text and the cover sheet instruction `.CS`. The cover sheet, which I showed you at the beginning of the paper, is actually printed at the end of the paper.

17. Exercises

1. Define the following formatting terms:

   i. point

   ii. em

   iii. point size

   iv. font

   v. leading

2. Explain the difference between the following two forms of the `.SK` instruction:

   ```
   .SK
   .SK 1
   ```

3. Documents are printed in an "outline" style by using the heading style specified by the instructions

   ```
   .HM I A 1 a i
   .nr Ht 1
   ```

   What is the effect of these instructions? Verify your answer by formatting and printing some example text.

4. In-line font changes are used to print parts of the document in fonts other than the default fonts. What are the pros and cons of undoing the font changes with the escape sequence "`\fP`", which restores the previous font or the escape sequence "`\fR`", which specifies a switch to the Roman font?

5. User-defined macros `.(P` and `.)P` are used to define constant-width displays. Under what circumstances will the `.)P` macro call not correctly restore the font in effect just before the macro call `.(P`? State an assumption about the use of these two macros that can be used to change the definition of the `.(P` macro to make it robust. What change

will you make?

6. Give the text and formatting instructions to print the text

procedure SWAP(X, Y: **in out** FLOAT) **is**
   T: FLOAT;   ––temporary variable
begin
   T := X;
   X := Y;
   Y := T;
end SWAP;

7. The keyword instruction `.OK` is ignored for external papers. How will you print keywords on the cover sheet of an external paper?

8. Write a pair of macros (similar to the constant-width display macros `.(P` and `.)P`) to begin and end centered displays that print the displayed text in 8-point italic font.

Chapter 3

Specifying Tables

A *table* is a systematic arrangement of data organized in rows and columns. On the UNIX system, tables can be specified in a document by using `tbl`, a `troff/nroff` preprocessor designed by M. E. Lesk [DWB 1984c; Lesk 1976]. `tbl` provides a high-level declarative language for specifying tables in a simple and straightforward manner. A `tbl` table specification contains information such as

- the form of the table, for example, centered and boxed,
- format of the table entries, for example, left adjusted or centered, font and point size,
- headings to be repeated for multi-page tables and
- the table entries themselves.

1. An Example `tbl` Specification

As an example of a table specified using `tbl`, consider the table listing font positions that was given in Chapter 2:

font position	**font**
1	Times Roman
2	*Times Italic*
3	**Times Bold**
4	Helvetica
5	`Constant-Width`

This table was specified as follows:

```
.DS
.TS
box, center;
cb | cb
a | a.
font position☛font
=
1☛Times Roman
_
2☛\fITimes Italic\fP
_
3☛\fBTimes Bold\fP
_
4☛\fHHelvetica\fP
_
5☛\f(CWConstant-Width\fP
.TE
.DE
```

In this and subsequent table specifications, I have used the right-hand symbol ☛ to denote the tab character.

I will now explain the table specification in detail. The first and last lines of the specification are actually mm instructions specifying a display that contains the table specification. Tables are kept in mm displays to prevent them from being split across pages.

Table specifications begin with the table-start instruction `.TS` and end with the table-end instruction `.TE`. The `.TS` instruction is followed by an optional line containing global attributes, which specify the overall form of the table. This table has an attribute `box`, which specifies that the table is to be enclosed in a box, and an attribute `center`, which specifies that the table is to be centered across the page. Only a single line containing global attributes, optionally separated by commas, can be given and it must be terminated by a semicolon.

The format of the table entries, that is, the data format, is specified after the global table attributes. Lines 4 and 5 specify the data format. Line 4

```
cb | cb
```

specifies the format of the first line of data (the first row of the table). This table will have two columns; this is indicated by number of item formats. Each item format in this line, `cb`, specifies that the corresponding data item is to be centered (`c`) and printed in bold font (`b`). The vertical bar (`|`) between the two item formats specifies that a vertical line is to be drawn between the items.

The ith data format line specifies the format of the entries in the ith row of the table. The last data format line is special because it specifies the format of all the remaining lines of data. The period at the end of an item format line signals the end of the data format lines.

```
a | a.
```

which is the last data format line, specifies the format of the remaining rows. Item format `a` specifies that the corresponding entry will be alphabetic. Alphabetic entries are left justified with respect to the largest one of them; moreover, the largest entry is centered in the column.

The data format lines are followed by the data lines, that is, lines 6-16: Lines that contain just the character = or the character _ are special `tbl` control lines even though these lines appear in the data part of the table specification. They instruct `tbl` to draw single (_) or double (=) table-wide horizontal lines. The item format lines do not apply to these control lines.

Excluding the control lines, each data line corresponds to one row of the formatted table. Data for adjacent table entries is separated by tabs; the tab character is the default table-entry separator.

The first data line specifies the entries "font position" and "font" for the columns of the first row, which serves as the table heading. As specified in the first item format line (line 4), these entries will be centered and printed in bold font. The third data line specifies entries of the second row; entries of this row will, by default, be printed in the font that was being used just before the table specification was encountered—in this case, in Roman font. The fifth data line specifies entries of the third row. Notice that the second column entry in this row contains a `troff` escape sequence (`\fI`) that explicitly specifies the font to be used, that is, italic. This escape sequence overrides the font specification, if any, in the corresponding data format line. Explicit font (and point size) changes specified in data items should normally be undone (e.g., `\fP` restores the previous font) within the data items; otherwise `tbl` may get confused when calculating the table width.

The treatment of the remaining data lines (excluding the control lines) is similar to that of the fifth data line. The second data format line is used for formatting entries in these data lines.

If a data line contains more entries than specified in the corresponding item format line, the extra entries are ignored; if the data item contains fewer entries than specified, the missing entries are left blank.

Finally, the second last line (in the specification shown) is the `.TE` instruction that signals the end of the table specification.

2. Format of a Table Specification

A table specification has three components: an optional section describing the overall form of the table, a section describing the format of the table entries and a section containing the data. Most table specifications are of the form

```
.TS
Global Table Format (one line only)
Data Format Lines (i.e., Format of the Table Entries)
Table Data
.TE
```

If there is not enough space on a page, then a table is continued on the next page. Vertical lines separating columns and boxes enclosing a table are not drawn properly if a table is split across pages. Table specifications may be enclosed within mm displays to prevent the tables from being split across pages and to keep the text associated with them (e.g., captions) on the same page:

```
.DS
text that is to be printed above the table
.TS
table specification
.TE
text that is to be printed below the table
.DE
```

3. Specification of the Global Table Format

The optional global table format specification consists of one line of the form

attribute$_1$, *attribute*$_2$, . . . , *attribute*$_n$;

where each *attribute*$_i$ can be one of the keywords

attribute	explanation
`center`	Center the table; by default, the table is left adjusted.
`expand`	Expand the table to make it as wide as the current line length; if this attribute is not specified, then the table width will depend upon the width of the table data or, if specified, upon the column widths.
`box`	Enclose the table in a box.
`doublebox`	Enclose the table in a double-ruled box.
`allbox`	Enclose each table entry in a box; eliminates the need to specify the `box` attribute.
`tab(`*x*`)`	The data items will be separated by the character *x*; by default, `tbl` expects the data items to be separated by the tab character.
`delim(`*xy*`)`	Specifies that characters *x* and *y* will be used as `eqn` delimiters; `tbl` needs this information in some cases so that it can correctly format table entries containing in-line `eqn` expressions; for example, `tbl` needs this information when a numeric-column entry contains an `eqn` expression.

Global table attributes may be separated by spaces, tabs or commas; they must be terminated by a semicolon. The global table format can be changed easily by changing the global attributes. For example, if the global table attribute line in the table specification shown earlier was changed to

```
doublebox;
```

then this table will be printed using a double-ruled box and will not be centered:

font position	font
1	Times Roman
2	*Times Italic*
3	**Times Bold**
4	Helvetica
5	`Constant-Width`

4. Data Format Specification

The table data format is specified on one or more data format lines with the last line being terminated by a period. The ith data format line specifies the format of row *i*; in addition, the last data format line specifies the format of all the remaining table rows. Each data format line has the form

a_1 a_2 . . . a_n

where a_i is the format of the ith entry in the row whose format is being specified. Each item format a_i consists of a set of column attributes: a *key-letter* followed by zero or more key-letter qualifiers. The order of the qualifiers is immaterial. These item formats can be separated by a single or double vertical bar (`|` or `||`). Vertical bars between two item formats specify that the corresponding column entries are to be separated by vertical lines. Vertical bars given before (after) the first (last) item format specify vertical lines before (after) the first (last) entry.

To enhance readability of table specifications, spaces may be used to separate item formats from each other and from the single and double vertical bars.

4.1 Alignment of Column Entries—Key-Letters

The alignment of a column entry is specified with a *key-letter*. Some key-letters specify the alignment directly while others specify the alignment indirectly by specifying the data type. Valid key-letters are listed below:

key-Letter	explanation
`L` or `l`	Left adjust the column entry.
`R` or `r`	Right adjust the column entry.
`C` or `c`	Center the column entry.
`N` or `n`	Column entry will be numeric. Numeric entries are aligned with respect to their decimal points; if there is no decimal point, then one is assumed to exist at the right of the least significant digit. If an item has multiple decimal points, then the rightmost one is used. The non-printing character `\&` may be used in a data item to force alignment at that point. `\&` overrides all other implied alignments. A non-numeric item without a `\&` is centered.
`A` or `a`	Column entry will be alphabetic. The widest entry is centered and all other entries are left adjusted with respect to this entry.
`S` or `s`	Indicates a horizontally-spanning entry: entry from the previous column continues into this column.
`^`	Indicates a vertically-spanning entry: entry from the previous row continues into this row.

The number of columns in a table is equal to the number of item formats in the data format line with the largest number of item formats. Data format lines with fewer item formats than the number of columns are appropriately right extended with the key-letter `l`.

As mentioned earlier, if a data line has more items than the number of columns, then the extra items are ignored. And if a data line has fewer items than the number of columns, then blanks are printed for the missing items.

4.2 Example Illustrating Column Alignment

Column entry alignment depends upon the alignment specified or implied by the corresponding key-letter. In this example, I will illustrate some of the different types of alignment. The example table given below has four columns and each column has the elements

```
3
50
3.14
45.00
7.0
3.00.00
emp.name
radius
emp.name\&
\&3.14
\&radius
```

A different key-letter—one of `a`, `c`, `r` and `n`—is used to align entries in each column; the center of each column is indicated by a down arrow (↓):

a (alphabetic)	c (center)	r (right adjust)	n (numeric)
↓	↓	↓	↓
3	3	3	3
50	50	50	50
3.14	3.14	3.14	3.14
45.00	45.00	45.00	45.00
7.0	7.0	7.0	7.0
3.00.00	3.00.00	3.00.00	3.00.00
emp.name	emp.name	emp.name	emp.name
radius	radius	radius	radius
emp.name	emp.name	emp.name	emp.name
3.14	3.14	3.14	3.14
radius	radius	radius	radius

4.3 Spanning Table Entries

Spanning table entries are frequently used to position headings that extend over multiple columns or rows. A *spanning* table entry is specified by a non-spanning key-letter (`c`, `l` or `r`) followed by a sequence of item formats with a spanning key-letter `s` (horizontal spanning) and `^` (vertical spanning). Spanning key-letters allow entries to float horizontally across columns or vertically over rows.

Horizontally-spanning entries float to the position specified in the starting column. For example, if the starting key-letter is `c`, then the entry will float to the center of the starting column and the last spanning column. Vertically-spanning entries, by default, float to the center of the starting row and the last spanning row. They can be anchored to the top row by using the vertical-spanning qualifier `t` (discussed later).

4.3.1 Examples of Horizontally-Spanning Entries: The following example shows three horizontally-spanning entries, each of which spans four columns. The down arrows (↓) indicate the centers of these columns:

↓	↓	↓	↓
Centered Horizontally-Spanning Heading			
Left-Adjusted Horizontally-Spanning Heading			
Right-Adjusted Horizontally-Spanning Heading			

The data format lines used for the above spanning entries are

```
c s s s
l s s s
r s s s
```

Each spanning entry spans all the four table columns. The spanning entries are centered, left-adjusted and right-adjusted as specified by the corresponding first key-letters.

The data lines used for the spanning entries are

```
Centered Horizontally-Spanning Heading
Left-Adjusted Horizontally-Spanning Heading
Right-Adjusted Horizontally-Spanning Heading
```

Note that each data line consists of only one table entry (the words are not separated by tabs) because they correspond to spanned headings.

As another example of a horizontally-spanning entry, consider the table

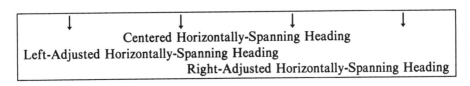

Multiplication Table										
a*b	1	2	3	4	5	6	7	8	9	10
1	1	2	3	4	5	6	7	8	9	10
2	2	4	6	8	10	12	14	16	18	20
3	3	6	9	12	15	18	21	24	27	30
4	4	8	12	16	20	24	28	32	36	40
5	5	10	15	20	25	30	35	40	45	50
6	6	12	18	24	30	36	42	48	54	60
7	7	14	21	28	35	42	49	56	63	70
8	8	16	24	32	40	48	56	64	72	80
9	9	18	27	36	45	54	63	72	81	90
10	10	20	30	40	50	60	70	80	90	100

The format lines and the first three data lines used in specifying the above table are

```
allbox, center;
cB s s s s s s s s s s
cBp+2 c c c c c c c c c c
c c c c c c c c c c c.
Multiplication Table
a\(**b☞1☞2☞3☞4☞5☞6☞7☞8☞9☞10
1☞1☞2☞3☞4☞5☞6☞7☞8☞9☞10
```

Notice the use of the `allbox` attribute to specify that all the table entries are to be enclosed in boxes. The "`B`" and "`p+2`" in the format of the first entry of the second row specify that the entry is to be printed in bold font and using a point size that is 2 points larger than the current point size.

4.3.2 Examples of Vertically-Spanning Entries: I will give two examples of vertically-spanning entries. As the first example, consider the table

instruction name	**format**
add	`add a, b`
subtract	`sub a, b`
shift	`sh r`

The second column heading was printed in the center of the first two rows of the second column by specifying it as a vertically-spanning data item.

This table was specified as

```
.TS
box, center;
cb ¦ cbw(2.0i)
cb ¦ ^
a ¦ afCW.
instruction☞format
name
=
add☞add a, b
subtract☞sub a, b
shift☞sh r
.TE
```

This example also illustrates the use of *key-letter qualifiers* (see next section for details) to specify additional item characteristics:

- The letter "`b`" specifies that the corresponding items are to be printed in bold font.
- The letter sequence "`fCW`" specifies that the corresponding items are to be printed in constant-width font.
- The character sequence "`w(2.0i)`" specifies that the corresponding column is to be 2.0 inches wide.

Notice that the second data line

```
name
```

has only one data item for column one; no entry is given for the second column because the second data item from the first row will span downwards into the second row as specified in the second data format line

```
cb ¦ ^
```

Here is the second example of a vertically-spanning entry in which the first column entry spans five rows:

	of a
	vertically-
Example	spanning
	entry
	in column 1

The data format specifications that were used in this example are

```
c a
^ a.
```

and the corresponding input data is

```
Example☛of a
☛vertically-
☛spanning
☛entry
☛in column 1
```

The second data format line represents the format for the last four data lines. The first data entry in the last four data lines is empty because the first entry of the first row is to float over the last four rows.

4.4 Extensions to the Key-Letters Scheme

A key-letter can be

- replaced by the characters _ or = to indicate single or double horizontal lines, respectively.
- followed by qualifiers that change the format and placement of the corresponding entry or change the size and shape of the columns.

4.4.1 Horizontal Lines: The underscore character (_) or the equal sign character (=) may be used instead of a key-letter to specify a single or double horizontal line, respectively.[16] Horizontal lines are extended to meet adjacent vertical or horizontal lines, if any.

Data entries should not be given if the corresponding item format is the character _ or =. Data given for these items will be ignored and warning messages will be printed.

As an example illustrating the use of horizontal and vertical lines, consider the figure that depicts a *tic-tac-toe* game:

×		
	o	
	×	o

The data format specifications used for the tic-tac-toe figure are

16. Horizontal lines can also be drawn by giving the characters _ and = as data items (see Section 5).

```
c | c | c

_   _   _
c | c | c

_   _   _
c | c | c.
```

and the data lines used are

```
\(mu
☛\(ci
☛\(mu☛\(ci
```

where `\(mu` and `\(ci` are `troff` escape sequences that denote the multiplication sign and a circle, respectively. Notice that there are only three data lines while there are five data format lines.

4.4.2 Column-Entry Font and Point Size Specification: The font and point size used for a table are the same as those in effect when the table-start instruction `.TS` is encountered. Alternative font and point sizes for table entries can be explicitly specified by using key-letter qualifiers.

4.4.2.1 Font: The font of a column entry can be explicitly specified by using a *font qualifier* which consists of the letter `f` followed by a one- or two-letter font name. Examples of font qualifiers are `fB` (bold font), `fI` (italic font) and `fCW` (constant-width font). The letters `B` and `b` are short forms of the font qualifier `fB` while the letters `I` and `i` are short forms of the font qualifier `fI`. A single-character font name should be separated from whatever follows by a space or a tab; however, this is not necessary for abbreviated font qualifiers such as `i` or `b`. Fonts can also be specified in the input data itself by using `troff` escape sequences; these font escape sequences override fonts specified with the font qualifiers.

4.4.2.2 Point Size: The point size of a column entry can be explicitly specified by using a *point-size qualifier* that consists of the letter `p` (or `P`) followed by an integer number. If the number is unsigned, then it specifies an absolute point size If the number is signed, then it specifies a relative point size, that is, the default point size is to be increased or decreased by this number, depending upon whether the number is positive or negative, respectively. Examples of point-size qualifiers are `p+1` (increase point size by one), `p-1` (decrease point size by one) and `p8` (use point size 8). Point sizes can also be specified in the data entry itself by using `troff` escape sequences; these point-size escape sequences override point sizes specified using point-size qualifiers.

4.4.2.3 Font and Point-Size Qualifier Example: As an example of the use of font and point-size key-letters, consider the table

Operator	`Operation`	*Operand Types*	*Result Type*
and	`conjunction`	*Boolean*	*same Boolean*
or	`disjunction`	*Boolean*	*same Boolean*
or else	**short circuit or**	Boolean	**same Boolean**

The global table format and the data format lines used for printing this table are

```
center, box;
abp+1 | afCWp+1 | aip+1 | aip+1
ab | afCW | ai | ai.
```

The second of the three format lines (the first data format line) specifies that the first entry of this row is to be printed in bold (specified by `b`), the second in constant-width font (specified by `fCW`) and the last two entries in italics (specified by `i`); each entry of first row is to be printed using the default point size plus one (specified by `p+1`). The second data format line specifies fonts for the entries in the remaining rows but, unlike in the first data format line, point sizes are not specified.

The input data used to produce the table was

```
Operator☛Operation☛Operand Types☛Result Type

and☛conjunction☛Boolean☛same Boolean
or☛disjunction☛Boolean☛same Boolean
\fIor else\fP☛\fBshort circuit or\fP☛\
\fRBoolean\fP☛\fBsame Boolean\fR
```

The last two lines represent one table data line because a data line terminating with a backslash continues on the next line.

`troff` font-change requests given in the data for the last row override the fonts specified in the data format line. Notice that the font in use prior to the font change is explicitly restored at the end of the entry. As mentioned earlier, all font and point changes specified within table entries must be undone within the table entries; otherwise `tbl` may not be able to compute table characteristics correctly.

4.4.3 Column Characteristics: Column characteristics such as the spacing between columns and the column width can be explicitly specified. In most cases, the default values used by `tbl` are satisfactory. However, in some cases it may be desirable to change the column characteristics, for example, to reduce the spacing between columns to make a table fit on a page, or to make two tables have identical column widths.

Here are the column characteristics that can be changed:

column characteristics	specification
spacing between columns	A key-letter may be followed by a *column-separation qualifier* which is just a number that specifies the separation between the columns in ens. The default separation is 3 ens. For example, the data format specification `a1 a` specifies that two alphabetic columns are to be separated by one en. If different column separations are specified for the same pairs of columns in different data format lines, then the largest separation will be used. Presence of the global table format attribute `expand` causes the column separation to be multiplied by a constant so as to widen the table to the current line length. If a column-separation qualifier follows a point-size qualifier, then these two qualifiers must be separated by a space to avoid ambiguity.
column width	A key-letter may be followed by a *column-width qualifier* which specifies the minimum width of a column. The column-width qualifier is of the form `w(`*x*`)` (or `W(`*x*`)`), where *x* is the minimum column width specified in `troff` units (e.g., `i` for inches, `c` for centimeters and `n` for ens). If no units are specified, then `tbl` assumes ens. Some examples of the column-width qualifier are `w(1.5i)`, `W(1.0c)` and `w(24)`. If multiple widths are specified for the same column, then the *last* width specified is used as the column width; if column data entries are wider than the specified column width, then the width of the largest element is used as the column width. Column widths are also used as the default line lengths of text blocks (discussed later).

column characteristics	specification
equal-width columns	Widths of two or more columns can be made equal by qualifying their key-letters with the *equal-width qualifier* `e` (or `E`).
staggered columns	A key-letter may be followed by a *staggered-column qualifier* `u` (or `U`) which indicates that the corresponding entry should be moved up half a line.
zero-width entry	A key-letter may be followed by the *zero-width qualifier* `z` (or `Z`) which instructs `tbl` to ignore the width of the corresponding data item in calculating the column width.

4.4.4 Vertical Spacing: A key-letter may be followed by a *vertical-spacing qualifier* that specifies the vertical spacing, that is, line separation, for multi-line table entries called text blocks (see Section 5). This qualifier consists of the letter `v` (or `V`) followed by a number specifying vertical spacing in *points*. An unsigned number is taken to be the new vertical spacing; a signed number is taken to be the current vertical spacing plus (or minus) this number. The vertical-spacing qualifier is ignored if the corresponding entry is not a text block.

4.4.5 Vertical Spanning: Vertically-spanning entries are, by default, vertically centered between the rows spanned by them; their horizontal alignment is specified by the key-letter in the starting column. Vertically-spanning entries can be forced to start at the first of the spanned rows by using the *vertical-spanning qualifier*, which is just the letter `t` (or `T`).

5. Table Data

The table data consists of lines containing table entries separated by the table-entry separator. Along with the table entries, a variety of other items can also be given in the data part of a table, for example, instructions to draw horizontal lines, `troff` instructions, requests to treat text blocks as multi-row table entries, requests to repeat the same character for the width of the column and specifications of vertically-spanning entries.

5.1 Simple Table Entries

For most tables, each line of data corresponds to one table row. Long data lines can be continued on successive lines by terminating the line to be continued with the escape character \; this character is not printed in the table.

5.2 Extending Table Entries to the End of the Column

Consider the following table in which the first column's entries are extended to the end of the column by a sequence of dots:

Name	Number
Narain Gehani	4461
John Fitzgerald Holmes	5234
Al Roy	3134
Jim Smith	2213

Extending the column entries manually will be a tedious trial-and-error process. Fortunately, `tbl` provides a mechanism for extending the column entries automatically by an appropriate amount:[17] if a column entry is followed by the `troff` escape sequence `\a`, then it will be extended with the *leader* character.[18] By default, the leader character is a dot; an alternative leader character can be specified by using the `troff` instruction `.lc` which has the form

`.lc` *alternative-leader-character*

The table with entries extended by dots was specified as

```
.TS
box, center;
cbw(3.0i) cb
a a.
Name☞Number
=
Narain Gehani\a☞4461
John Fitzgerald Holmes\a☞5234
Al Roy\a☞3134
Jim Smith\a☞2213
.TE
```

5.3 Horizontal Lines

The underscore character _ and the equals character = can be used in the table data to specify single and double table-wide, column-wide and entry-wide

17. I am grateful to Ravi Sethi, a colleague at AT&T Bell Laboratories, for pointing out the mechanism for extending table entries to the width of the column.

18. For more details about the leader character, see the `nroff/troff` *User's Manual* [DWB 1984a; Ossanna 1977];

horizontal lines:

line type	**specification**
table-wide lines	A data line containing only the character _ or the character = specifies a single or a double table-wide horizontal line.
column-wide lines	A column entry consisting of only the character _ or the character = specifies a single or a double column-wide horizontal line; this line is extended to meet adjacent horizontal or vertical lines, if any.
entry-wide lines	A column entry consisting of just the characters _ or the characters \= specifies a single or double horizontal line, respectively, whose width is equal to the width of the widest column entry. Unlike the column-wide lines, entry-wide lines are not extended to meet adjacent horizontal or vertical lines.

The special role of the characters _ and = as horizontal-line specifiers can be suppressed by prefixing them with the non-printing zero-width character \&.

As an illustration of entry-wide horizontal lines, here is a table representing a grocery bill:

Item	**Qnty.**	**Unit Price**	**Cost**
Dt. Coke	2	1.39	2.78
Crest	1	1.99	1.99
Kiwi Pol.	1	0.79	0.79
Selzer	6	0.25	1.50
		Subtotal	7.06
		6% Tax	0.42
		TOTAL	7.48

This table was specified as

```
.TS
center;
cb cb cb cb
cb cb cb cb
a n n n.
☞☞Unit
Item☞Qnty.☞Price☞Cost
=
.sp 0.5p
Dt. Coke☞2☞1.39☞2.78
Crest☞1☞1.99☞1.99
Kiwi Pol.☞1☞0.79☞0.79
Selzer☞6☞0.25☞1.50
☞☞☞\_
☞☞Subtotal☞7.06
☞☞6% Tax☞0.42
☞☞☞\_
☞☞TOTAL☞7.48
.sp 3p
☞☞☞\=
.TE
```

5.4 Character Repetition

A table entry of the form `\R`*x*, where *x* is a character, specifies a sequence of *x*'s whose length is equal to the width of the widest column entry; this sequence is not extended to meet adjacent horizontal or vertical lines.

5.5 Vertical Spanning

Vertically-spanning entries can also be specified in the input data (instead of specifying them in the data format lines). The character sequence `\^` specifies that the table entry immediately above this row will span downwards into this row.

5.6 Text Blocks (Multi-Row Entries)

Consider the following table in which columns 2-4 have blocks of text, each of which spans several rows in a column:

operator	**name**	**operand types**	**result type**
=	simple assignment	arithmetic, pointer, union or structure	if both operands have arithmetic types, then right operand value is converted to left operand type

`tbl` provides a facility especially for specifying text blocks. Text blocks are given as entries for the rows in which their first lines are to be placed. Text blocks are specified using the notation

`...☞T{`
text block
that can span
several lines
`T}☞...`

The character pair "`T{`" signals the beginning of a text block and the character pair "`T}`" (which must start in column 1) signals the end of a text block. Other table entries (including text blocks) can precede or follow a text block.

Text blocks are treated differently from other table entries; they are taken out of the table and processed separately as just another piece of text (outside `tbl`) by `troff`. Consequently, arbitrary `troff` instructions (and many mm instructions) can be given within text blocks. Text blocks can be used to specify figures within tables. However, they cannot be used to specify nested tables.

A text block is processed by `troff` using the environment in effect just before the table-start instruction `.TS` was encountered; this environment is modified to reflect the data format specifications and `troff` requests given inside the text block. However, environment changes made in other table entries (including other text blocks) have no effect on the processing of a text block.

Using text blocks, the table given at the beginning of this section is specified as:

```
.TS
center, box;
cb | cb | cb | cbw(1.5i)
^ | ^ | cb | cb
cfCW | l | l | l.
operator☛name☛operand☛result
☛☛types☛type
=
\&=☛T{
simple
assignment
T}☛T{
.na
arithmetic,
pointer,
union or
structure
.ad
T}☛T{
.na
if both operands have arithmetic
types, then right operand value is
converted to left operand type
.ad
T}
.TE
```

I specified the last column width and I turned off right justification (using `troff` instruction `.na`) for the last two text blocks because the width computed by `tbl` was too small and because right justification caused big gaps between the words. Here is the table that was produced by `tbl`:

operator	**name**	**operand types**	**result type**
=	simple assignment	arithmetic, pointer, union or structure	if both operands have arithmetic types, then right operand value is converted to left operand type

As another example of a table with text blocks, consider the following table that gives brief descriptions of the `mm` page footer instructions:

instruction	name	comments
`.PF`	main footer	default value is a blank line
`.EF`	even-page footer	default value is a blank line; the even-page footer is printed before the main footer
`.OF`	odd-page footer	default value is a blank line; the odd-page footer is printed before the main footer

This table was specified as

```
.DS L F
.TS
box, center;
cbw 1 | cbw(1.0i) 1 | cbw(2.7i) 1
afCW | a | a.
instruction☛name☛comments
=
\&.PF☛T{
main footer
T}☛T{
default value is a blank line
T}
_
\&.EF☛T{
even-page footer
T}☛T{
default value is a blank line;
the even-page footer is printed
before the main footer
T}
_
\&.OF☛T{
odd-page footer
T}☛T{
default value is a blank line;
the odd-page footer is printed
before the main footer
T}
.TE
.DE
```

Note the use of the non-printing zero-width character \& to suppress interpretation of lines beginning with a period as mm instructions.

6. Tables with Groups of Repeated Rows

The last data format line can be used to specify the format of a group of rows, with identical element types, at the end of the table. However, the last data format line cannot be used to specify the format of multiple groups of rows or the format of a single group if it is not at the end of the table.

As an example, consider the following table describing some financial figures:[19]

Financial Figures of the Week				
Stocks	**Latest week**	**Week ago**	**Month ago**	**Year ago**
Std. & Poors 500	**158.07**	158.97	157.30	161.81
P/E Ratio (S&P 500)	**11.22**	11.28	11.19	12.78
Dividend (S&P 500)	**4.61%**	4.59%	4.64%	4.32%
DJI Avg.	**1162.90**	1164.57	1154.31	1209.46
NYSE daily vol. (millions)	**80.2**	89.7	79.4	92.2
Money Markets	**Latest week**	**Week ago**	**Month ago**	**Year ago**
Federal Funds	**9.55%**	10.45%	9.62%	8.45%
Prime Rate	**12.00%**	12.00%	11.50%	10.50%
Cm. Paper, 3-month	**10.15%**	10.00%	10.00%	8.8%
T. Bills, 3-month	**9.66%**	9.76%	9.79%	8.14%
T. Bills, 6-month	**9.78%**	9.86%	9.90%	8.20%
Euro$ Rate, 3-month	**10.89%**	10.73%	10.61%	9.14%
CDs, 3-month	**10.47%**	10.50%	10.37%	8.45%
Monetary Indicator	**Latest week**	**Week ago**	**Month ago**	**Year ago**
Money Supply (M1)	**$536.4**	$533.4	$536.0	$496.2

Note that this table has groups of rows with identical element types, but these groups are not at the bottom of the table. The straightforward (and very tedious) way of specifying this table is

19. Adapted from *Business Week* dated May 7, 1984.

```
.DS
.EQ
delim off
.EN
.TS
box, center;
cb sb sb sb sb
lb rb rb rb rb
lb rb rb rb rb
lb rb r r r
lb rb r r r
lb rb r r r
lb rb r r r
lb rb r r r
lb rb rb rb rb
lb rb rb rb rb
lb rb r r r
lb rb r r r
lb rb r r r
lb rb r r r
lb rb r r r
lb rb r r r
lb rb r r r
lb rb rb rb rb
lb rb rb rb rb
lb rb r r r.
Financial Figures of the Week
=
Stocks☛Latest☛Week☛Month☛Year
\^☛week☛ago☛ago☛ago
_
Std. & Poors 500☛158.07☛158.97☛157.30☛161.81
P/E Ratio (S&P 500)☛11.22☛11.28☛11.19☛12.78
Dividend (S&P 500)☛4.61%☛4.59%☛4.64%☛4.32%
DJI Avg.☛1162.90☛1164.57☛1154.31☛1209.46
NYSE daily vol. (millions)☛80.2☛89.7☛79.4☛92.2
=
Money Markets☛Latest☛Week☛Month☛Year
\^☛week☛ago☛ago☛ago
_
Federal Funds☛9.55%☛10.45%☛9.62%☛8.45%
```

```
Prime Rate☛12.00%☛12.00%☛11.50%☛10.50%
Cm. Paper, 3-month☛10.15%☛10.00%☛10.00%☛8.8%
T. Bills, 3-month☛9.66%☛9.76%☛9.79%☛8.14%
T. Bills, 6-month☛9.78%☛9.86%☛9.90%☛8.20%
Euro$ Rate, 3-month☛10.89%☛10.73%☛10.61%☛9.14%
CDs, 3-month☛10.47%☛10.50%☛10.37%☛8.45%
=
Monetary Indicator☛Latest☛Week☛Month☛Year
\^☛week☛ago☛ago☛ago
_
Money Supply (M1)☛$536.4☛$533.4☛$536.0☛$496.2
.TE
.EQ
delim $$
.EN
.DE
```

Before I discuss the disadvantages of the above table specification, I would like to point out some of its interesting aspects:

1. **$**, which commonly used as an `eqn` delimiter, is deactivated as an `eqn` delimiter at the beginning of the table specification so that it can be used as an ordinary character in the data; **$** is reactivated as an `eqn` delimiter at the end of the table specification.

   Alternatively, instead of deactivating **$** as an `eqn` delimiter, identifier `dollar`, which is defined by `eqn` as **$**, could have been used to specify **$** in the table entries.

2. This table specification illustrates the use of the character pair "\^" to specify a vertically-spanning entry.

Now let us critically examine the table specification. In addition to being tedious and cumbersome, it suffers from several other disadvantages:

- a data format line must be given for each row of the table,
- increasing or decreasing the number of rows with the same format (except in the last group) requires a corresponding change in the data format specifications and
- the data lines are quite removed from their specifications; correspondence between the data format lines and the data lines is not immediately obvious.

`tbl` provides a facility for resetting column formats. This is useful for specifying tables with groups of rows that have identical element formats. Table specifications are split up into component specifications such that the last set of rows in each component contains rows that have matching element types. The last data format line in each component is used to specify the format of rows with identical element types.

A table specification that is split into components has the form

```
.TS
Global Table Format (one line only)
Data Format Lines
Table Data
.T&
Data Format Lines
Table Data
.T&
 :
.T&
Data Format Lines
Table Data
.TE
```

where table-continuation lines of the form

```
.T&
```

separate the different components of the table specification. The last data format line in each component specifies the format of the remaining data lines in the component. Using this facility to split up a table specification into components, the example table given above can now be specified as

```
.DS
.EQ
delim off
.EN
.TS
box, center;
cb sb sb sb sb
lb rb rb rb rb
lb rb rb rb rb
lb rb r r r.
```

```
Financial Figures of the Week
=
Stocks☛Latest☛Week☛Month☛Year
\^☛week☛ago☛ago☛ago
_
Std. & Poors 500☛158.07☛158.97☛157.30☛161.81
P/E Ratio (S&P 500)☛11.22☛11.28☛11.19☛12.78
Dividend (S&P 500)☛4.61%☛4.59%☛4.64%☛4.32%
DJI Avg.☛1162.90☛1164.57☛1154.31☛1209.46
NYSE daily vol. (millions)☛80.2☛89.7☛79.4☛92.2
.T&
lb rb rb rb rb
lb rb rb rb rb
lb rb r r r.
=
Money Markets☛Latest☛Week☛Month☛Year
\^☛week☛ago☛ago☛ago
_
Federal Funds☛9.55%☛10.45%☛9.62%☛8.45%
Prime Rate☛12.00%☛12.00%☛11.50%☛10.50%
Cm. Paper, 3-month☛10.15%☛10.00%☛10.00%☛8.8%
T. Bills, 3-month☛9.66%☛9.76%☛9.79%☛8.14%
T. Bills, 6-month☛9.78%☛9.86%☛9.90%☛8.20%
Euro$ Rate, 3-month☛10.89%☛10.73%☛10.61%☛9.14%
CDs, 3-month☛10.47%☛10.50%☛10.37%☛8.45%
.T&
lb rb rb rb rb
lb rb rb rb rb
lb rb r r r.
=
Monetary Indicator☛Latest☛Week☛Month☛Year
\^☛week☛ago☛ago☛ago
_
Money Supply (M1)☛$536.4☛$533.4☛$536.0☛$496.2
.TE
.EQ
delim $$
.EN
.DE
```

6.1 Limitations of Split `tbl` Specifications

The component specifications in a split table specification cannot be used to change the global table attributes; moreover, the data format lines in the component specifications cannot be used to

1. change the number of columns,
2. change the spacing between columns or
3. alter the set of equal-width columns.

7. `troff` Instructions

Lines beginning with a period are assumed to be `troff` instructions and they are output unchanged and without any interpretation by `tbl`. `troff` instructions may be used to fine tune tables. For example, the `troff` instruction `.sp` can be used to change the spacing between the table rows. `troff` instructions should, however, be used with care because they can confuse `tbl` (see Section 10 for more details).

As an example illustrating the use of `troff` instructions within `tbl` specifications, consider the table

item denotation	**item**
`sum`	Σ
`int`	$\int$
`prod`	Π
`union`	$\cup$
`inter`	$\cap$
`oppE`	$\exists$

`tbl` is unable to compute the vertical spacing required for the `eqn` expressions correctly. This table would look better if it is printed as

item denotation	**item**
`sum`	Σ
`int`	$\int$
`prod`	Π
`union`	$\cup$
`inter`	$\cap$
`oppE`	$\exists$

The table (with increased spacing between the rows) was specified as

```
.TS
center, box;
cb ¦ cb
cfCW ¦ a.
.sp 3p
item denotation☛item
.sp 3p
=
.sp 3p
sum☛$sum$
.sp 3p
_
.sp 3p
int☛$int$
.sp 3p
_
.sp 3p
prod☛$prod$
.sp 3p
_
.sp 3p
union☛$union$
.sp 3p
_
.sp 3p
inter☛$inter$
.sp 3p
_
.sp 3p
oppE☛$oppE$
.sp 3p
.TE
```

Notice the use of the `.sp` instruction to increase the spacing between the rows. In this case, it would have been easier to increase and decrease the vertical spacing between the rows by using the `troff` instruction `.vs` which is placed just before the `.TS` instruction and just after the `.TE` instruction:

```
.vs +3p
.TS
center, box;
cb ¦ cb
cfCW ¦ a.
item denotation☛item
=
sum☛$sum$
_
int☛$int$
_
prod☛$prod$
_
union☛$union$
_
inter☛$inter$
_
oppE☛$oppE$
.TE
.vs
```

If the first character of a data line is a period, then it should be prefixed by the zero-width non-printing character `\&` to prevent `tbl` from interpreting the line as a `troff` instruction.

8. Interface with mm

In general, a table should be placed within a display to prevent it from being split across pages and to keep the text associated with the table on same page as the table (I am assuming that the table and the associated text can fit on one page), that is,

```
.DS parameters
Text to be Placed Above the Table
.TS
Table Specification
.TE
Text to be Placed Below the Table
.DE
```

8.1 Multi-Page Tables

Multi-page tables can be specified with `tbl`.[20] Such tables *must not* be enclosed within displays. The format for specifying multi-page tables is

```
.TS H
Global Table Format (one line only)
Data Format Lines
Title Lines (Initial Part of Input Data)
.TH
Rest of the Data
.TE
```

where the title, that is, header, lines (input data lines before the `.TH` instruction) are repeated at the top of each new page. The `.TH` instruction must be given even if there are no title lines. The `H` parameter ensures that boxed tables and columns will be drawn properly and that titles will not be printed on the portion of the table continued on succeeding pages.

Giving `N` as a `.TH` instruction argument specifies that the title lines are to be printed only if they are the first title lines on the page. For example, consider the two tables specified one after the other:

```
.TS H
Global Table Format (one line only)
Data Format Lines
Title Lines (Initial Part of Input Data)
.TH
Table Data
.TE
.TS H
Global Table Format (one line only)
Data Format Lines
Title Lines (Initial Part of Input Data)
.TH N
Table Data
.TE
```

Title lines at the beginning of the second table will be printed only if the two tables are printed on different pages. Subsequent title lines of the second table will be printed as usual.

---

20. To be precise, the multi-page table feature is supported by mm and is not really a part of `tbl`.

8.2 Automatically-Numbered Table Captions

Automatically-numbered table captions can be printed by using the `mm` instruction `.TB` which has the form

`.TB` [*caption-string* [*modifier* [*modifier-control*]]]

where

1. *caption-string* is the caption to be associated with the table and
2. arguments *modifier* and *modifier-control* are used to modify the default numbering style:
   a. if *modifier-control* is missing or has the value zero, then *modifier* is used as a prefix of the table number.
   b. if *modifier-control* is equal to one, then *modifier* is used as a suffix of the table number.
   c. if *modifier-control* is equal to two, then *modifier* replaces the table number.

For example, a `.TB` instruction of the form

`.TB` *caption-string*

generates a caption of the form

TABLE n. *caption-string*

where **n** is the table number.

Here are two examples of captioned tables:

TABLE 1. Exchange Rates: December 14, 1984

Foreign Currency	**Units per US Dollar**
German Mark	3.09
Swiss Franc	2.55
Japanese Yen...................	247.00
British Pound...................	0.85
Canadian Dollar..............	1.39
French Franc...................	9.46

TABLE 2. Exchange Rates: 1974 Average

Foreign Currency	Units per US Dollar
German Mark	2.59
Swiss Franc	2.98
Japanese Yen...................	292.00
British Pound...................	0.43
Canadian Dollar..............	0.98
French Franc...................	4.81

The table captions were generated by the instructions

```
.TB "Exchange Rates: December 14, 1984"
.TB "Exchange Rates: 1974 Average"
```

which were placed before the table specifications; the table specifications and the corresponding `.TB` instructions were placed inside `mm` displays. By convention, table headings are placed above tables. A list of tables whose captions were specified with the `.TB` instructions is printed by the table-of-contents instruction; printing of this list can be suppressed by setting register `Lt` to 0 (default value of `Lt` is 1).

8.3 Including Files Containing Tables

Keeping `tbl` specifications in separate files allows tables to be formatted, printed and checked without processing the whole document. Unfortunately, `tbl` does not provide a facility for reading in specifications kept in separate files. Fortunately, `tbl` specifications kept in separate files can be included in the document by using the `pic` instruction `.PS`. Using the `.PS` instruction requires preprocessing the document with the `pic` preprocessor.

The `.PS` instruction, which has the form

`.PS` <*file-name*

causes the contents of the specified file *file-name* to be included. For example, the effect of the instruction

```
.PS <table1
```

will be to include the contents of the file `table1`.

9. Checking for Errors: `tbl`

`tbl` can be used to check for table specification errors prior to typesetting the document. To check for `tbl` errors, use the UNIX commands[21]

```
tbl files >/dev/null
```

or

```
tbl files >temp
```

Error messages, if any, are printed on the standard error output. The first command discards the output of `tbl` while the second command stores the output in file `temp` for possible later examination by the user.

10. Restrictions on Table Specifications

Tables specified using `tbl` instructions are subject to the following restrictions and limitations:

1. The maximum number of columns allowed is 20.
2. A column cannot have items in both the `n` and `a` formats.
3. Column widths are computed using the first 200 lines of input data.
4. Table continuations `.T&` are not recognized after the first 200 lines of a table.
5. The maximum number of text blocks allowed in a table is about 30.
6. Use of arbitrary `troff` requests may confuse `tbl` in calculating column widths. For example, `troff` instructions to change the font or change the point size should be used with care because, in calculating the column widths, `tbl` uses the font and point size that were in effect when the table-start instruction `.TS` was encountered. There are two exceptions to this rule which are handled by `tbl` without any problem:
   i. Fonts and point sizes specified in the data format lines (by means of font qualifiers).
   ii. Fonts and point sizes specified in the data; even here the user must be careful to ensure that the font and point size on leaving a column entry are the same as those encountered on entering the column entry, for example,

---

21. If the `.PS` instruction has been used to include files containing `tbl` specifications, then the document must be preprocessed by the `pic` preprocessor before checking for `tbl` errors, for example,

    ```
    pic files | tbl >/dev/null
    ```

    Otherwise, `tbl` errors in the included files will not be detected.

```
\f(CWand then\fP☛\fIand\fP☛Boolean
```

7. Numeric or alphabetic columns cannot span; `tbl` changes a numeric-spanning column to a centered-spanning column and an alphabetic-spanning column to a left-adjusted-spanning column.

8. The global table attribute `allbox` does not work with staggered-column entries.

9. When a file contains both tables and equations, `tbl` should be used before `eqn`. If there are no equations within the tables, then `eqn` may be used before `tbl` or vice versa. However, it is better to run `tbl` before `eqn` for efficiency reasons—the transformations produced by `eqn` are larger than those produced by `tbl`.

10. `troff` number registers 31 through 99 should not be used because they are used by `tbl`.

11. `troff` string names of the form #*x*, ^*x*, *x*+, *x*¦, *x*-, ##, #- and #^, where *x* is a lower-case letter, should not be used.

11. Examples

In this section, I will give a variety of examples illustrating the versatility and flexibility of `tbl`. In each example, I will first show the table and then give its specification. The first example illustrates the use of `troff` escape sequences in table entries. The second example shows how tables can be used to align items vertically. The third example illustrates the use of text blocks and the specification of column separation and point size. The fourth example illustrates the use of `eqn` expressions and `troff` instructions within `tbl` specifications and use of the backslash character \ to continue a data line on to the next line. The final example, a picture of an array, illustrates the versatility of `tbl`.

11.1 Table Entries With `troff` Escape Sequences to Change Fonts

Consider the following table in which the headings are printed in bold font:

procedures	**functions**
CREATE	MODE
OPEN	NAME
CLOSE	FORM
DELETE	IS_OPEN
RESET	

This table was specified as

```
.TS
center;
l l.
\fBprocedures\fP☛\fBfunctions\fP

CREATE☛MODE
OPEN☛NAME
CLOSE☛FORM
DELETE☛IS_OPEN
RESET
.TE
```

A blank data input line causes an empty row. The bold fonts could also have been specified in the table data format lines by using the following two format lines

```
lb lb
l l.
```

instead of just one, that is,

```
l l.
```

After this, the data input line

```
\fBprocedures\fP☛\fBfunctions\fP
```

can be replaced by the line

```
procedures☛functions
```

11.2 Using Tables to Align Items Vertically

Tables are a convenient way of displaying vertically-aligned items. For example, consider the vertically-aligned items

device	**register**	**address**
Keyboard	status	8#177560#
	buffer	8#177562#
Display	status	8#177564#
	buffer	8#177566#

These items were vertically aligned by specifying them as elements of a table:

```
.TS
center;
ab ab ab
a a a.
device☛register☛address

Keyboard☛status☛8#177560#
☛buffer☛8#177562#

Display☛status☛8#177564#
☛buffer☛8#177566#
.TE
```

As another example of vertically-aligned items, consider the following list of words:

auto	break	case	char
continue	default	do	double
else	entry	enum	extern
float	for	goto	if
int	long	register	return
short	sizeof	static	struct
switch	typedef	union	unsigned
void	while		

As before, these items are vertically aligned by specifying them as elements of a table:

```
.TS
center;
lfCW lfCW lfCW lfCW.
auto☛break☛case☛char
continue☛default☛do☛double
else☛entry☛enum☛extern
float☛for☛goto☛if
int☛long☛register☛return
short☛sizeof☛static☛struct
switch☛typedef☛union☛unsigned
void☛while
.TE
```

11.3 Text Blocks, and Specification of Column Separation and Point Size

The following table illustrates the use of text blocks, explicit specification of the separation between columns, specification of the point size to be used for the entries and use of the `troff` instruction `.na` to turn off right adjustment:

operator	**name**	**operand types**	**result type**	**comments**
*	multiplication	arithmetic	`int, unsigned, long, double`	
/	division	arithmetic	`int, unsigned, long, double`	when positive integers are divided, truncation is towards 0; if either operand is negative, then the truncation is machine dependent
%	remainder	integral	`int, unsigned, long`	remainder has same sign as dividend

This table was specified as

```
.DS L F
.na
.TS
box, center;
cw(.6i)|cw(.7i) 1|cw(.7i) 1|cw(.75i) 1|cw(1.3i) 1
cw(.6i)|cw(.7i) 1|cw(.7i) 1|cw(.75i) 1|cw(1.3i) 1
cw(.6i)|lw(.7i) 1|lw(.7i) 1|lw(.75i) 1|lw(1.3i) 1.
\fBoperator\fP☛\fBname\fP☛\fBoperand\fP☛\fBresult\fP\
☛\fBcomments\fP
☛☛\fBtypes\fP☛\fBtype\fP
=
\f(CW*\fP☛multiplication☛arithmetic☛T{
\f(CWint,
unsigned,
long,
double\fP
T}
_
\f(CW/\fP☛division☛arithmetic☛T{
\f(CWint,
unsigned,
```

```
long,
double\fP
T}☛T{
when positive
integers are
divided, truncation
is towards 0; if
either operand is
negative, then the
truncation is machine
dependent
T}
_
\f(CW%\fP☛remainder☛integral☛T{
\f(CWint,
unsigned,
long\fP
T}☛T{
remainder has
same sign as
dividend
T}
.TE
.ad
.DE
```

The column separation in the above table was specified to be 1 en (overriding the default separation, 3 ens). Right adjustment for all the text blocks was turned off by using the `troff` instruction `.na` just before the table-start instruction `.TS`; right adjustment is restored at the end of the table by using the `troff` instruction `.ad`.

11.4 Tables With Equations

Consider the following table with equations as entries:

Euler's Identities

expression	**identity**
$\sin\theta$	$\frac{e^{i\theta} - e^{-i\theta}}{2i}$
$\cos\theta$	$\frac{e^{i\theta} + e^{-i\theta}}{2}$
$\tan\theta$	$\frac{e^{i\theta} - e^{-i\theta}}{i(e^{i\theta} + e^{-i\theta})}$

This table was specified as

```
.DS
.ce
\fBEuler’s Identities\fR
.sp 3p
.TS
center box;
c c
l l.
\fBexpression\fR☛\fBidentity\fR
.sp 0.05i
.vs +3p
$sin~theta$☛\
${e sup {i theta}~-~e sup {-i theta}} over 2i$
$cos~theta$☛\
${e sup {i theta}~+~e sup {-i theta}} over 2$
$tan~theta$☛\
${e sup {i theta}~-~e sup {-i theta}} over \
  {i(e sup {i theta}~+~e sup{-i theta})}$
.vs -3p
.sp 0.05i
.TE
.DE
```

where `$` is the `eqn` delimiter. Note the use of the

1. `troff` instruction `.vs` to increase the vertical spacing between the rows by three points and to restore the original vertical spacing.
2. backslash character \ at the end of a line to continue an input data line; the continuation occurs in the middle of an `eqn` expression.

11.5 Versatility of `tbl`

The versatility of `tbl` is illustrated by using it to draw the following pictorial representation of an array and its contents:

B	e	l	l		L	a	b	s	\0
0	1	2	3	4	5	6	7	8	9

The figure was specified as

```
.TS
center;
| c | c | c | c | c | c | c | c | c | c |
c c c c c c c c c c.
_
\f(CWB☞e☞l☞l☞ ☞L☞a☞b☞s☞\e0\fR
_
\f(CW0☞1☞2☞3☞4☞5☞6☞7☞8☞9\fR
.TE
```

Note the use of the `troff` escape sequence `\e` to specify the backslash character \; the escape sequence `\e` evaluates to the backslash character.

12. Exercises

1. Modify the `tbl` specification of the *tic-tac-toe* game figure so that the horizontal lines are drawn by placing the underscore character in the data lines instead of the data format lines. What are the advantages and disadvantages of these two approaches?

2. What are the pros and cons of specifying the font and point size in the data format instead of in the data itself?

3. Write a `tbl` specification for the figure that illustrates an object with three components:

VALUE	
LEFT	RIGHT

4. Write a `tbl` specification to print the following table that contains both horizontally and vertically spanning entries [Lesk 1976]:

Composition of Foods			
Food	Percent by Weight		
	Protein	Fat	Carbo-hydrate
Apples	.4	.5	13.0
Halibut	18.4	5.2	...
Lima Beans	7.5	0.8	22.0
Milk	3.3	4.0	5.0
Mushrooms	3.5	.4	6.0
Rye Bread	9.0	.6	52.7

5. Write a `tbl` specification for the table

Production Function Crude Oil Pipeline

Line diameter	Horsepower (thousands)				
	20	30	40	50	60
(inches)	Output rate (thousands of barrels per day)				
14	70	90	95	100	104
18	115	140	155	165	170
22	160	190	215	235	250
26	220	255	290	320	340

6. Write a `tbl` specification for the table (an example from business):

Balance Sheet, Buffalo Works, as of December 31, 1981

Assets (dollars)		Liabilities and net worth (dollars)	
Current assets:		Current liabilities:	
Cash	20,000	Accounts payable	20,000
Inventory	120,000	Notes payable	40,000
Fixed assets:		Long-term liabilities:	
Equipment	160,000	Bonds	160,000
Buildings	180,000		
		Net worth:	
		Preferred stock	100,000
		Common stock	100,000
		Retained earnings	60,000
Total	480,000	Total	48,000

7. Write a specification for the following table with several horizontal lines:

<table>
<tr><td>Vertical
Local Motion</td><td colspan="2">Effect in
troff nroff</td><td>Horizontal
Local Motion</td><td colspan="2">Effect in
troff nroff</td></tr>
<tr><td>\v'n'</td><td colspan="2">Move distance n</td><td>\h'n'
\(space)
\0</td><td colspan="2">Move distance n
Unpaddable space-size space
Digit-size space</td></tr>
<tr><td>\u
\d
\r</td><td>½ em up
½ em down
1 em up</td><td>½ line up
½ line down
1 line up</td><td>\|
\^</td><td>1/6 em space
1/12 em space</td><td>ignored
ignored</td></tr>
</table>

Note: Use the `troff` escape sequence `\e` to print a backslash character.

Chapter 4
Specifying Figures

pic is a troff preprocessor, designed by B. W. Kernighan, for specifying figures in documents [DWB 1984c; Kernighan 1981, 1982a, 1984]. Before the advent of pic, figures were drawn manually and then pasted on the document. This approach had many disadvantages:

1. Figures were usually drawn by a person other than the document preparer. Drawing figures and making changes, even small ones, often delayed completion of the document because the appropriate artist or draftsperson was not immediately available.
2. Figures had to be pasted on the document every time the document was reformatted.
3. The complete document could not be mailed electronically.

pic eliminates these problems by providing a mechanism for specifying figures in documents, just as equations and tables can be specified using eqn and tbl.

Drawing figures with pic is straightforward; the user can think of pic as a "pen" that can be guided along a two-dimensional surface. Figures are drawn by using lines and other primitive graphic objects such as boxes, circles, arrows, ellipses, arcs and spline curves.

Selected points of pic objects, called *corners*, can be referenced for positioning or connecting objects. pic also allows arbitrary text to be associated with the objects; this text is placed automatically by pic at appropriate places within the object or in close proximity to the object. Alternatively, the user can explicitly specify the text position.

An object position is specified in terms of absolute or relative coordinates. *Absolute coordinates* are coordinates whose values are given in terms of some fixed point, for example, the origin (0.0, 0.0). *Relative coordinates* are coordinates whose values are given in terms of positions of other objects. In general, relative coordinates are preferred to absolute coordinates, because of

1. *convenience*: when specifying a figure containing numerous objects that are to be positioned with respect to each other, it is easier to think in terms of distances separating the objects instead of distances from some

fixed point.

2. *robustness*: when changing the position of an object, the relative position of dependent objects will be automatically preserved.

1. An Example `pic` Specification

As an example of a figure specified using `pic`, consider the figure:

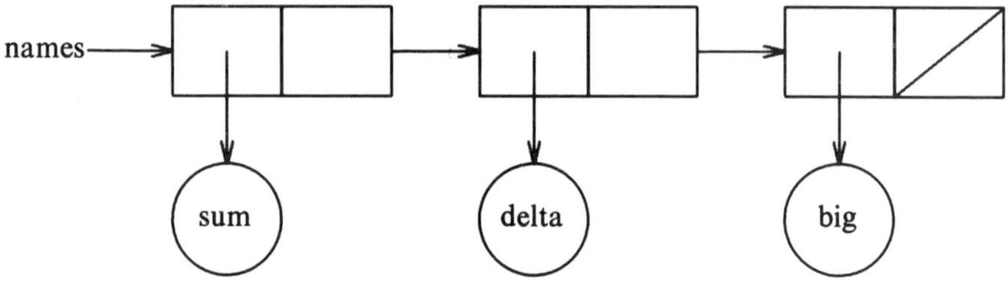

This figure was drawn (specified) by the following instructions:

```
.DS CB
.PS
#figure illustrating the internal representation
#of a list of names

boxwid = 0.5; boxht = 0.4
linewid = 0.4

arrow
B1: box; box

arrow
B2: box; box

arrow
B3: box; box
line from last box.sw to last box.ne

"names" at 1st arrow.start rjust

arrow down from B1.c; circle "sum"
arrow down from B2.c; circle "delta"
arrow down from B3.c; circle "big"
.PE
.DE
```

The first two lines of the specification signal the beginning of a centered mm display and a pic specification. The last two lines signal the end of the pic specification and of the mm display enclosing the pic specification. pic specifications should be enclosed in displays if the specified figure is to be centered and to prevent the figure from being split across pages. Lines 3 and 4 are comments. Comments begin with the character "#" and are terminated by the end of a line.

The default width and height of a box are specified by the values of the special variables boxwid and boxht, respectively. The default lengths of horizontal lines and arrows are specified by the value of the special variable linewid. The next two lines (ignoring the blank lines) assign values to these variables. All numbers representing dimensions are assumed to have inch units.[22] Note that line 5 contains two instructions; several instructions can be given on a line if they are separated by semicolons.

Lines 7 and 8 contain instructions specifying objects, that is, an arrow and two boxes:

```
arrow
B1: box; box
```

The first box is labeled B1 for future reference. By default, pic places objects next to each other in a left-to-right order. Like lines 7 and 8, each of the next two pairs of lines (lines 9 and 10, and 11 and 12) contain instructions specifying an arrow and two boxes. Line 13

```
line from last box.sw to last box.ne
```

instructs pic to draw a line from the south-west corner of the last box drawn to its north-east corner. Line 14

```
"names" at 1st arrow.start rjust
```

instructs pic to place the quoted text to the left (indicated by the keyword rjust) of the starting point of the first arrow.

Each of the next three lines (lines 15-18) contains two pic instructions: draw an arrow down from the center of the named box (B1, B2 and B3) and then draw a circle with the specified text inside it:

22. In older versions of pic [Kernighan 1981, 1982a] numbers with decimal points specified values in inches while numbers without decimal points specified values in the internal units used by pic. All numbers immediately followed by the letter i also specified values in inches.

```
arrow down from B1.c; circle "sum"
arrow down from B2.c; circle "delta"
arrow down from B3.c; circle "big"
```

Notice that this time, `pic` places the circles at the ends of the arrows instead of placing them adjacent to the arrows (on their right). This is because the initial drawing direction, which was "left-to-right", was implicitly changed to "top-to-bottom" by the arrows, which were drawn downwards.

2. Format of a Figure Specification

A `pic` figure specification has the form

`.PS`
macro definitions
variable assignments
other `pic` *instructions*
`.PE`

where `.PS` and `.PE` are the picture-start and picture-end instructions, respectively.

Suppose a figure is to be overprinted with another figure, a table, an equation or some text. Then the flyback picture-end instruction `.PF` can be used instead of the ordinary picture-end instruction `.PE`; the `.PF` instruction causes printing of the document portion following the `pic` specification to start at the beginning of the figure (printing is resumed as if no figure had been printed).

3. Primitive Objects—Basics

`pic` provides a variety of primitive objects: boxes, circles, lines, arrows, ellipses, arcs, spline curves and text. Technically speaking, moves (motion from one point to another without drawing anything) are also considered to be (invisible) objects. The following keywords are used to specify the primitive objects:

```
box        circle    line
ellipse    arrow     arc
spline     move
```

A text object is specified by enclosing it in double quotes.

In the rest of this section, I will discuss the general form of object specifications, object dimensions, object names, object interconnections, placement of objects, object positions, variables and expressions, and the overall figure size.

3.1 General Form of Object Specifications

The general form of an object specification is

[*label* :] *object list-of-attributes*

An object specification can span more than one line provided the lines being continued are terminated with the escape character \. Object labels are used for symbolically referring to objects. Object attributes describe the placement, the orientation and the size of an object, and the text, if any, associated with it. Default values are used for missing attributes. `pic` does not give rules for determining appropriate attribute combinations; instead it silently ignores inappropriate attributes.

3.2 Object Dimensions

The default dimensions of objects and related attributes are given by the values of the special variables associated with them:

object attribute	special variable	initial default value	description/comments
box	`boxwid`	0.75 inches	box width
	`boxht`	0.50 inches	box height
circle	`circlerad`	0.25 inches	circle radius
ellipse	`ellipsewid`	0.75 inches	ellipse width
	`ellipseht`	0.50 inches	ellipse height
arc	`arcrad`	0.25 inches	arc radius
line or arrow	`linewid`	0.50 inches	horizontal line or arrow width
	`lineht`	0.50 inches	vertical line or arrow height
move	`movewid`	0.50 inches	width of a horizontal move
	`moveht`	0.50 inches	height of a vertical move
arrowhead	`arrowht`	0.10 inches	arrowhead height
	`arrowwid`	0.05 inches	arrowhead width
	`arrowhead`	2	arrowhead style (i.e., fill)
dash	`dashwid`	0.10 inches	width of dashes in a dashed object and distance between dots in a dotted object
text	`textht`	0.00 inches	height of the invisible box containing the text object
	`textwid`	0.00 inches	width of the invisible box containing the text object

Default dimensions can be changed by simply assigning new values to the associated special variables. For example, the assignments

```
boxwid = 1.0; boxht = 1.0
circlerad = 0.2
```

change both the default width and height of a box to be 1.0 inches (makes a one-inch square), and the default circle radius to be 0.2 inches.

The special variable `arrowhead` is used to specify the arrowhead style, that is, the amount of filling used for the arrowhead; the default value of `arrowhead` is 2. Here are some examples of arrows with different types of arrowheads (`arrowhead` values used are indicated on top of the arrows):

3.2.1 Resetting the Special Variables to Their Original Values: The `reset` instruction can be used to reset some or all of the special variables to their original values.. Instruction

`reset` [i_1 i_2 ... i_n]

resets the variables i_1, i_2, ..., i_n. If no variables are specified, then all the variables are reset.

3.2.2 Specifying Alternative Object Dimensions: There are several ways of specifying alternative object dimensions:

1. Default object dimensions can be changed by changing the values of the associated special variables.
2. Object dimensions can be explicitly specified when specifying the object; these dimensions override the default object dimensions.
3. Specification of the maximum height and width of a figure causes objects in the figure to be scaled appropriately (see Section 17.1).

3.3 Object Names

Object names are used for referencing previously defined objects. There are two kinds of object names: labels, which must be specified explicitly, and ordinal names, which are constructed by using ordinal numbers.

3.3.1 Labels: Objects are labeled by using specifications of the form

label: *object specification*

where *label* is a string of letters and digits that begins with an upper-case letter.

3.3.2 Ordinal Names: There are two denotations for ordinal names:

ordinal name	meaning
n`th` *a*	n^{th} object of type *a*
n`th last` *a*	n^{th} last (previous) object of type *a*.

Each object type has its own set of ordinal numbers. Ordinal numbers such as `1st`, `2nd` and `last` are accepted as synonyms for `1th`, `2th` and `1th last`.

Ordinal names can be more convenient than labels for referencing objects; however, they are very sensitive to changes in a figure specification.

3.4 Object Coordinates

Object names denote Cartesian coordinate pairs of the geometric centers of boxes, circles, ellipses, arcs and text, the starting points of lines, arrows and splines and the end points of moves. The *x* and *y* components of the absolute coordinates of the position associated with an object name can be accessed as

object-name`.x` and *object-name*`.y`

Object names (and their *x* and *y* components) are used for positioning other objects relative to the objects associated with them.

3.5 Object Corners

An object *corner* is one of the eight compass points associated with an object, or it is the start, the center or the end point of the object:

corner	comments
`.n (.t)`	north (top)
`.e (.r)`	east (right)
`.w (.l)`	west (left)
`.s (.b)`	south (bottom)
`.ne`	northeast
`.se`	southeast
`.nw`	northwest
`.sw`	southwest
`.c`	center
`.start`	starting point
`.end`	end point

Compass points apply only to boxes, circles, arcs and ellipses; start and end points apply only to lines, arrows, splines and moves.

Object corners are referenced as

object-name . *corner*

Some examples of object corners are

```
last box.c
C.c
B.ne
L.start
```

Corners are used for positioning objects and for drawing lines, arrows, arcs or splines connecting two objects. Corners, like object names, are Cartesian coordinate pairs. The x and y components of object corners are accessed as

object-corner `.x` and *object-corner* `.y`

3.6 Connecting the Primitive Objects—Entry and Exit Points

Each primitive object drawn by `pic` has an entry point and an exit point. The *entry point* of an object is the point where the drawing of the object was started. The *exit point* of an object is the point where the drawing of the object was completed. The default entry point of the first object is the location with coordinates (0.0, 0.0); the entry point of the first object can be changed by explicitly specifying the position of the first object.

`pic` connects the primitive objects it draws by using the exit point of the last object as the entry point for the next object. Entry and exit points for boxes, circles and ellipses are on opposite sides; for example, if objects are being drawn in a left-to-right direction, then the entry point of a box is its west compass point, and the exit point is its east corner. Entry and exit points for arrows, lines, arcs, splines and moves are their start and end points, respectively.

3.7 Placement of Objects/Drawing Direction

By default, `pic` starts off by drawing objects in a left-to-right direction; that is, objects are placed in a left-to-right order. The drawing direction can be changed by using the following operators:

direction operator
`up`
`down`
`left`
`right`

The direction operators can be used by themselves[23] or in conjunction with instructions specifying objects such as lines and arrows. In either case, the drawing direction is changed.

3.8 Drawing Direction: Some Examples

Consider the following figure

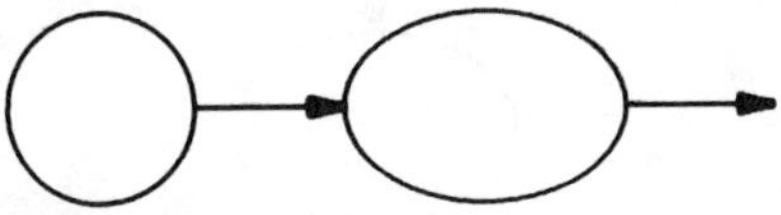

which was drawn with the instructions

```
circle; arrow; ellipse; arrow
```

and then centered because the `pic` specification was enclosed in a centering mm display.

There are four objects in this figure: a circle, an arrow, an ellipse and another arrow. By default, they were placed left-to-right. The entry point of the circle is its west corner because the initial drawing direction is left-to-right. The exit point of the circle, that is, its east corner, is used as the entry point of the first arrow, that is, as its start corner. Similarly, the exit point of the first arrow is used as the entry point of the ellipse. The exit point of the ellipse, that is, its east corner, is used as the entry point of the second arrow.

Now let us experiment with the drawing direction: the initial drawing direction is changed from "right" (left-to-right) to "down" (top-to-bottom) by adding the direction-changing instruction `down` at the beginning of the specification:

```
down; circle; arrow; ellipse; arrow
```

The figure is now printed as

23. I will refer to uses of the direction operators by themselves as direction-changing instructions.

As far as the individual objects are concerned, only the orientation of the arrows is different; they are now placed vertically instead of horizontally. However, the objects are connected differently because their entry and exit points have changed. The entry and exit points of the circle and ellipse have changed from the west and east corners to the north and south corners, respectively. The entry and exit points of the arrows are still their start and end corners, respectively; however, these points now correspond to the north and south compass points instead of the west and east compass points.

We continue our experiment with the drawing direction by using the `down` operator in conjunction with `arrow` instruction instead of using it, by itself, as the first instruction:

```
circle; arrow down; ellipse; arrow
```

The `down` operator, when used with the `arrow` instruction, specifies that the arrow and all subsequent objects should be drawn downwards:

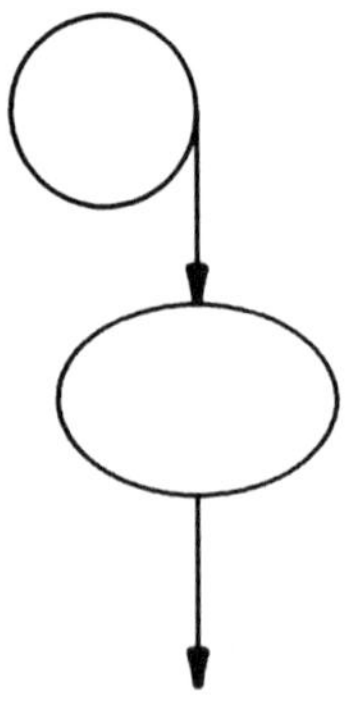

However, the exit point of the circle is still its east corner.

3.9 Positions and Places

3.9.1 Positions: A *position* denotes a point in the Cartesian plane: its value is a Cartesian coordinate pair. Positions are used for placing objects, specifying the start and end points of lines and arrows, guiding points for splines and so on. A position can be specified in several ways:

1. Directly as a Cartesian coordinate pair[24]

   $$(x,\ y)$$

   where x and y are floating-point expressions. Positions can be added or subtracted to give new positions, for example,

   ```
   (a, b) + (c, d)
   ```

   which is equivalent to

   ```
   (a+c, b+d)
   ```

2. As an offset from a place (defined later in this section):

   $$place \pm (x,\ y)$$

   where x and y are floating-point expressions.

3. As a point on the line between two points (positions) p_1 and p_2:

   $$e <p_1,\ p_2>$$

   This expression specifies a point between p_1 and p_2 that is located at p_1 plus e times the distance between p_1 and p_2. Note that e can be negative or greater than one in which case the point will not be between p_1 and p_2.

3.9.2 Places: A *place* is a point associated with an object or the current drawing position (places were used above in defining positions). Places are denoted by the following expressions:

placename [*corner*]
`Here`
nth [`last`] *primitive* [*corner*]

where

24. The parentheses used in denoting a coordinate pair are optional but are recommended for readability.

1. *placename* is

   - an object label or
   - a label recording a position:

     label : `Here`
     label : `(`*x*`,` *y*`)`

     In the first case, the current position (`Here`) is associated with *label*, while in the second case, the coordinate pair (*x*, *y*) is associated with *label*.

2. *corner* denotes an object corner.

3. *n*`th` **[**`last`**]** is an ordinal number used for referring to an object.

4. *primitive* is one of the primitive object types, for example, `box`.

3.9.3 Example: The example figure of a rake illustrates several things: the use of positions, places, labels, the direction operators and the *for* instruction:[25]

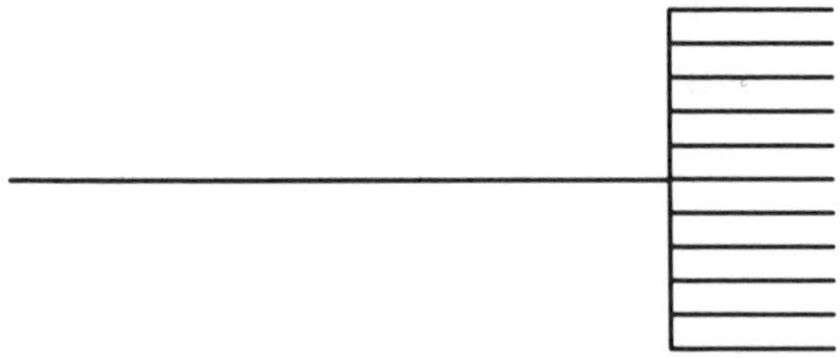

This figure was specified as

```
.PS
h = 2.0; y = 0.5; x = 0.5; n = 10
H: line right h
L1: line up y from H.end
L2: line down y from H.end
for i = 0 to n do
{
  line right x from i/n <L1.end, L2.end>
}
.PE
```

25. The *for* instruction is a recent addition to `pic` [Kernighan 1984].

Line 2 consists of assignments to variables that are used in subsequent instructions. Line 3 instructs `pic` to draw a horizontal line, labeled `H`, from left to right; the length of the line is specified to be 2.0 inches (the value of `h`). Line 4 instructs `pic` to draw a vertical line, of length `y`, going up from the end of the first line (i.e., `H.end`). Line 5 is similar to line 4, except that it specifies a line going down instead of up.

Line 6 is the header of the `for` loop instruction (see Section 13 for details) which specifies that its body

```
line right x from i/n <L1.end, L2.end>
```

is to be executed `n+1` times with the loop variable `i` being successively assigned the values from 0 to `n`. Lines 7 and 9 delimit the loop body. The loop body specifies that a horizontal line is to be drawn such that its starting point is

$$\frac{\mathtt{i}}{\mathtt{n}} \times \text{(the distance between } \mathtt{L1.end} \text{ and } \mathtt{L2.end})$$

below `L1.end`.

3.10 Variables, Expressions and Built-In Functions

`pic` allows the user to define floating-point variables and construct floating-point and position expressions using these variables and built-in functions.

3.10.1 Variables: Variables are not declared explicitly. The first variable assignment also serves as the declaration of the variable. Some example assignments are

```
x = 2.0; dx = 0.1
depth = 2.25
```

Within a document, variable definitions carry over from one figure specification to another. Variables should be used instead of literal values for the usual reasons:

1. Figures can be parameterized.

2. Symbolic names improve readability and simplify change.

There are no variables of type position; however, labels can be used as substitutes for variables of type position. Further, label values can be changed as follows:

label: *label* ± *position*

For example,

```
Cur: Cur + (1.0, 1.0)
```

3.10.2 Expressions: Expressions can be of two types: floating-point or position. *Floating point* expressions are constructed by using variables, floating-point and integer literals, the operators `+`, `-`, `*`, `/` and `%` (modulus), parentheses, built-in functions, and the following attributes associated with objects and positions:

attribute	description/comments
p`.x`	The x-coordinate of the object, object corner or a position denoted by *p*.
p`.y`	The y-coordinate of the object, object corner or a position denoted by *p*.
obj`.ht`	If *obj* is a box or an ellipse, then `ht` refers to the height of *obj*; if *obj* is a line, an arc, an arrow or a spline, then `ht` refers to the arrowhead height.
obj`.wid`	If *obj* is a box or an ellipse, then `wid` refers to the width of *obj*; if *obj* is a line, an arc, an arrow or a spline, then `wid` refers to the arrowhead width.
obj`.rad`	Radius of the circle or the arc specified by *obj*.

Some examples of floating-point expressions are

```
last box.c.x + 2.0
B1.nw.y         #B1 is a box label
last box.wid
```

A *position expression* is a position or a position plus or minus another position. Some examples of position expressions are

```
move to 1st circle.ne + (x, y)
"I/O Hardware" at C.s - (0.0, 0.2) below
arc with .c at C.e + (r/2, 0.0) from C.se to C.ne
```

Line 1 specifies a move to a point which is offset by (`x`, `y`) from the northeast corner of the first circle. Line 2 specifies that a text string is to be placed below a point that is 0.2 inches under the south corner of circle `C`. Line 3 specifies an arc whose center is located at a point that is `r`/2 inches to the right of `C.e`.

3.10.3 Built-In Functions: `pic` provides several built-in functions:

function	description/comments
`sin(`e`)`	sine of e (e must be in radians)
`cos(`e`)`	cosine of e (e must be in radians)
`atan2(`e_1`,`e_2`)`	the arctangent of e_1/e_2
`log(`e`)`	logarithm base 10 of e
`exp(`e`)`	10^e
`sqrt(`e`)`	square root of e
`max(`e_1`,`e_2`)`	maximum of e_1 and e_2
`min(`e_1`,`e_2`)`	minimum of e_1 and e_2
`int(`e`)`	integer part (by truncation) of e
`rand(`n`)`	random number between 1 and n

4. Moves

The current drawing position can be changed by using the `move` instruction which has the form

`move` *attributes*

Movement is specified by giving the new drawing position or distance to be moved from the current position and the direction of movement. If the direction is not specified explicitly, then the current drawing direction is used. If the distance to be moved is not specified explicitly, then for horizontal moves the distance moved is equal to the value of the special variable `movewid`; for vertical moves, the distance moved is equal to the value of the special variable `moveht`. The initial value of both of these variables is 0.5 inches.

4.1 Move Attributes

Attributes that can be associated with moves are summarized in the following table:

`move` **attributes**	**description/comments**
`up` [*e*]	Move up by *e*; if *e* is omitted, then move up by `moveht`.
`down` [*e*]	Move down by *e*; if *e* is omitted, then move down by `moveht`.
`left` [*e*]	Move left by *e*; if *e* is omitted, then move left by `movewid`.
`right` [*e*]	Move right by *e*; if *e* is omitted, then move right by `movewid`.
`to` *p*	Move to position *p*
`by (`*x*`,` *y*`)`	Move to current position + (*x*, *y*).
`"`*text*`"` [*positioning-attributes*]	The text item is placed at the end of the move; positioning attributes are `ljust`, `rjust`, `above` and `below`.

In the above table, *e*, *x* and *y* denote floating-point expressions and *p* denotes a position expression.

4.2 Move Examples

As an example of the `move` instruction, consider the figure:

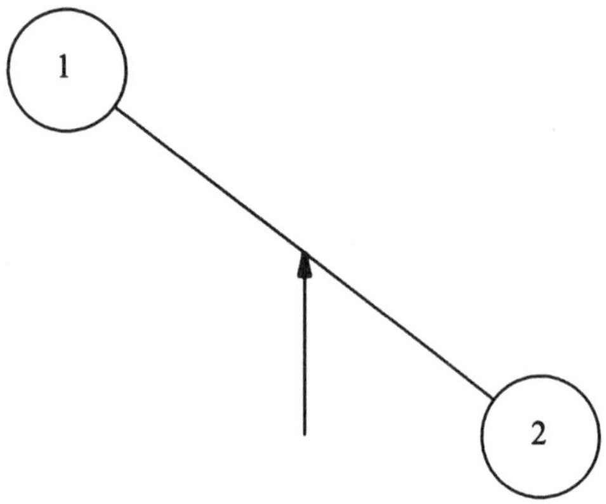

This figure was specified as

```
.PS
a = 1.5

C1: circle "1"
move down a right a
C2: circle "2"
L: line from C1 to C2 chop
move to 0.5 <L.start, L.end> + (0.0, -a/2)
arrow up a/2
.PE
```

After the first circle has been drawn (line 3), the `move` instruction (line 4) moves the current drawing position down by 1.5 inches and right by 1.5 inches. Notice the simultaneous use of the `down` and `right` attributes. The next two instructions draw the second circle and then a line connecting the two circles; portions of this line within the circles are chopped off (specified by attribute `chop`). The next instruction (line 7) moves the current drawing position to a point that is 0.75 inches below the middle point of the connecting line. Finally, the last instruction (line 8) draws an arrow.

5. Lines and Arrows

Lines and arrows are drawn using the `line` and `arrow` instructions, respectively; these instructions have the forms

`line` *attributes*
`arrow` *attributes*

Arrows can alternatively be specified as lines with the arrowhead attribute `->`.

The default length of horizontal lines and arrows is given by the value of the special variable `linewid`; special variable `lineht` denotes the default length of vertical lines and arrows. The initial value of both of these special variables is 0.5 inches. The default arrowhead length and width are given by the values of the special variables `arrowht` and `arrowwid`. The default values of these variables are 0.1 inches and 0.05 inches, respectively.

5.1 Line/Arrow Attributes

Attributes that can be associated with lines and arrows are summarized in the following table:

`line/arrow` **attributes**	**comments**
`up` [*e*]	Vertical line/arrow, *e* inches long, going up; if *e* is omitted, then the value of `lineht` is used as the default length.
`down` [*e*]	Vertical line/arrow, *e* inches long, going down; if *e* is omitted, then the value of `lineht` is used as the default length.
`left` [*e*]	Horizontal line/arrow, *e* inches long, going left; if *e* is omitted, then the value of `linewid` is used as the default length.
`right` [*e*]	Horizontal line/arrow, *e* inches long, going right; if *e* is omitted, then the value of `linewid` is used as the default length.
`from` *p*	The starting point of the line/arrow is *p*.
`to` *p*	The end point of the line/arrow is *p*.
`by (`*x*`,` *y*`)`	Draw a line/arrow from the current position to the current position + (*x*, *y*).
`then` *attributes*	Specifies the next segment of a path line/arrow (see Section 5.3).
`at` *p*	Start line/arrow from position *p*.
`dotted` [*e*]	Specifies a dotted line/arrow; *e* specifies the distance between the dots; if *e* is omitted, then the value of `dashwid` is used as the default distance between the dots.
`dashed` [*e*]	Specifies a dashed line/arrow with dashes of length *e*; if *e* is omitted, then the value of `dashwid` is used as the default dash length; spaces between the dashes will be of approximately the same size as the dashes.
`invisible`	Makes the line or arrow invisible (abbreviation `invis`).
`chop` [*r*]	Used in conjunction with lines connecting circles; specifies that segments of length *r* are to be chopped from both ends of the line; if *r* is omitted, then the distance chopped is equal to the radius of the corresponding circle.

`line/arrow` **attributes**	**comments**
`<-`	Arrowhead at the start of the line.
`->`	Arrowhead at the end of the line.
`<->`	Arrowheads at both ends of a line.
`height` *e*	Arrowhead height (abbreviation `ht`).
`width` *e*	Arrowhead width (abbreviation `wid`).
`"`*text*`"` [*positioning-attributes*]	Text item to be associated with the line/arrow; several text items can be specified and they will be placed on top of each other; positioning attributes are `ljust`, `rjust`, `above` and `below`.

5.2 Line/Arrow Examples

As examples of how lines are specified, consider the lines:

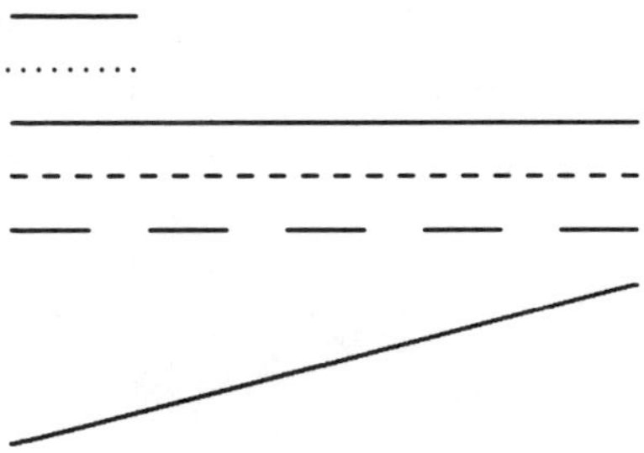

These six lines were specified independently; that is, each line was specified inside a separate "`.PS/.PE`" instruction pair containing one of the following input lines:

```
line
line dotted
line right 2.0
line right 2.0 dashed
line right 2.0 dashed 0.25
line from (0.0, 0.0) to (2.0, 0.5)
```

The first instruction draws a line in the current drawing direction (left-to-right); the line length is, by default, taken to be the value of `linewid` (0.5 inches). The second instruction is similar to the first one except that the line is specified to be dotted. The third instruction explicitly specifies the line length; it was necessary to give the direction attribute because a line length cannot be given by itself. The next two instructions specify dashed lines with dashes of length `dashwid` and 0.25 inches, respectively. The final instruction explicitly specifies the start and end points of the line.

Lines are easily connected and the direction attributes can be combined; for example, consider the lines

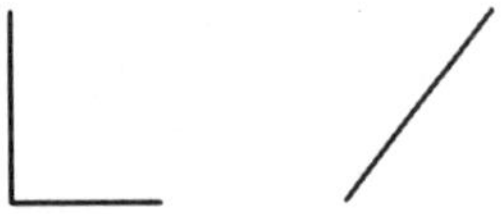

These lines were specified as

```
.PS
line down; line right
move;
line up right
.PE
```

The line bent at right angles actually consists of two lines. `pic` automatically connects the second line to the first one by drawing the second line from the end point of the first line. The end point of the sloping line is determined by moving distance `lineht` upwards and the distance `linewid` to the right.

As an example illustrating the use of lines to construct objects, consider the diamond:

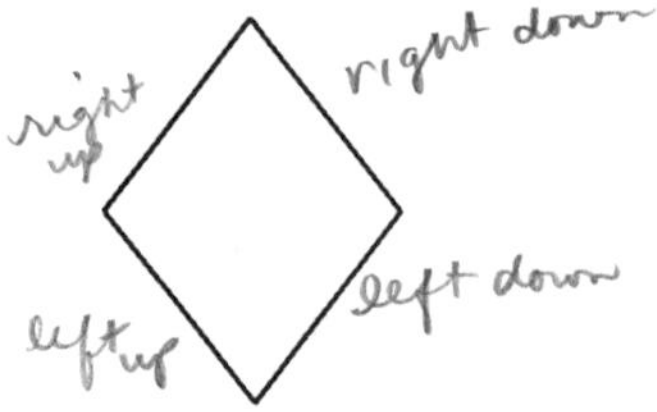

This diamond was specified as

```
.PS
line right down
line left down
line left up
line right up
.PE
```

Now it is time to look at some examples of arrows:

These arrows were specified as

```
.PS
arrow; move
line ->; move
line <-; move
line <->
.PE
```

Notice that except for the first arrow, all the other arrows were specified as lines with arrowheads.

Text can be easily associated with lines and arrows [Kernighan 1984]; for example, consider the arrows that have text items associated with them:

These arrows and the associated text were specified as

```
.PS
movewid = 0.3

arrow "on top of"; move
arrow "above" "below"; move
arrow "above" above; move
arrow "below" below; move
arrow "above" "on top of" "below"; move
.PE
```

If text positioning attributes such as `below` and `above` are not used, then `pic` will center the text items with respect to the associated object.

5.3 Lines Specified as Path Lines

A line can be specified as a *path* line, that is, as a series of connected segments (component lines) by using an instruction of the form[26]

`line` *segment*$_1$ `then` *segment*$_2$ `then ... then` *segment*$_n$

---

26. The use of the keyword `then` to separate segments is necessary only in ambiguous cases; however, its use is recommended for clarity.

Segments contain attributes normally associated with lines. However, some attributes given in a segment will apply to the whole line instead of just the segment containing the attribute. For example, the arrowhead and text attributes given in a path line segment apply to the whole line and not just to the segment containing them; if it is necessary to have segments with arrowheads or to associate text with them, then the path line should be specified as a set of independent but connected lines.

An example of a path line is the zig-zag line:

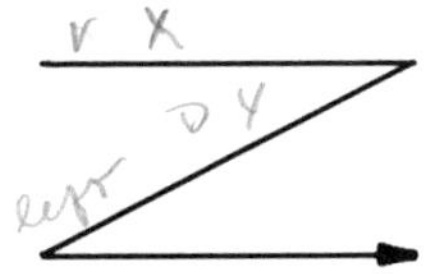

This zig-zag line was specified as

```
.PS
x = 1.0; y = 0.5

line -> right x then down y left x then right x
.PE
```

Finally, here is an example that illustrates and compares a path line and an equivalent line constructed by connecting simple lines. In this example, the box

will be specified in two different ways: the first specification uses four simple lines to construct the box and the second specification uses one path line. Using four lines, this box can be drawn as

```
line; line down; line left; line up
```

Alternatively, by using one path line, this box can be drawn as

```
line right then down then left then up
```

Drawing the box by using four separate lines creates four different objects while drawing it as a path line creates one object. In the first case, the box sides are full-fledged lines, but in the second case they are segments of one line. All line attributes can be associated with full-fledged lines but not with line segments; for example, arrowheads cannot be associated with line segments.

6. Boxes

Boxes are drawn using the `box` instruction[27] which has the form

`box` *attributes*

The default width and height of a box are given by the values of the special variables `boxwid` and `boxht`, respectively; the initial value of `boxwid` is 0.75 inches and that of `boxht` is 0.5 inches. The following figure shows the corners associated with each box:

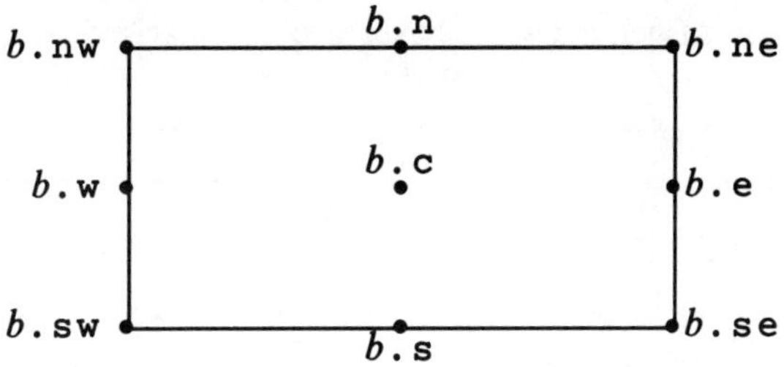

The box was specified as

```
.PS
B: box "\s-3\(bu\s0" wid 2.0 ht 1.0
"\s-3\(bu\s0" at B.n;   "\s-3\(bu\s0" at B.e
"\s-3\(bu\s0" at B.s;   "\s-3\(bu\s0" at B.w
"\s-3\(bu\s0" at B.ne;  "\s-3\(bu\s0" at B.se
"\s-3\(bu\s0" at B.sw;  "\s-3\(bu\s0" at B.nw
"\fIb\fP\f(CW.n\fP" above at B.n
" \fIb\fP\f(CW.e\fP" ljust at B.e
"\fIb\fP\f(CW.s\fP" below at B.s
"\fIb\fP\f(CW.w\fP  " rjust at B.w
" \fIb\fP\f(CW.ne\fP" ljust at B.ne
" \fIb\fP\f(CW.se\fP" ljust at B.se
"\fIb\fP\f(CW.sw\fP  " rjust at B.sw
"\fIb\fP\f(CW.nw\fP  " rjust at B.nw
"\fIb\fP\f(CW.c\fP" above at B.c
.PE
```

In the specification, the box dimensions (2.0 inches × 1.0 inch) and a text item are specified in the `box` instruction (line 2). The text item is automatically

---

27. A box can also be constructed by using lines. However, such a box is not a box object as far as `pic` is concerned; for example, `pic` will not automatically center text items in such a box.

centered within the box. The box is labeled `B` for easy reference in later instructions. Note the use of in-line point size changes and the escape sequence denoting the bullet symbol. Point size and font changes in a text item must be undone within the text item itself [Kernighan 1984]. The next 8 instructions (lines 3 to 6) place bullets at the box corners; the following 9 instructions (lines 7-15) place labels at the box corners. Note the use of blanks in the text objects to separate them from the sides of the box.

6.1 Box Attributes

Attributes that can be associated with boxes are summarized in the following table:

`box` **attributes**	**description/comments**
`height` *h*	Box height (abbreviation `ht`).
`width` *w*	Box width (abbreviation `wid`).
`at` *p*	Place box at position *p* (if the `with` attribute is not specified then the box will be centered at *p*).
`with` *c*	Used with the `at` attribute; the box is placed with its corner *c* at the position specified in the `at` attribute.
`dotted` [*e*]	Dotted box; *e* specifies the distance separating the dots; if *e* is omitted, then the value of `dashwid` is used as the default separation.
`dashed` [*e*]	Dashed box; the optional expression *e* specifies the dash length; if *e* is omitted, then the value of `dashwid` is used as the default dash length; spaces between the dashes will be of approximately the same size as the dashes.
`invisible`	Invisible box (abbreviation `invis`).
"*text*" [*positioning-attributes*]	Text items are centered in the box; several text items can be associated with a box; these items are placed on top of each other; positioning attributes are `ljust`, `rjust`, `above` and `below`.

6.2 Box Examples

The first example illustrates how to draw diagonals of a box:

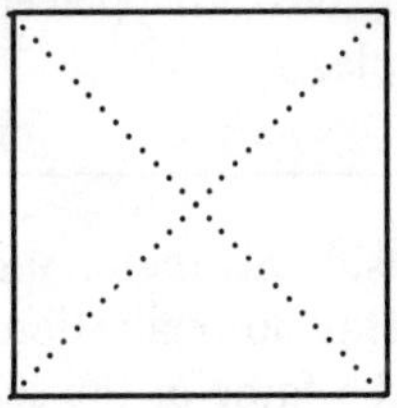

This box was specified as

```
.PS
a = 1.0

B: box wid a ht a
line dotted from B.sw to B.ne
line dotted from B.se to B.nw
.PE
```

Boxes of all shapes and sizes can be easily drawn by explicitly specifying their dimensions; for example, here are two boxes, one narrow and one wide:

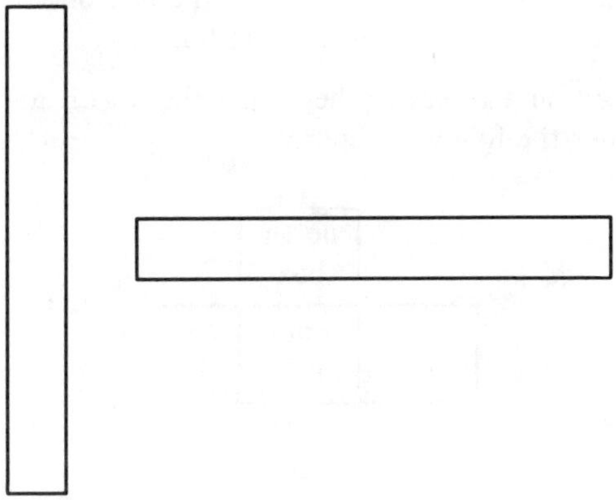

Theses boxes were specified as

```
.PS
a = 2.0; b = 0.25

box height a width b
move
box height b width a
.PE
```

Text items associated with a box are placed on top of each other and individually centered; for example,

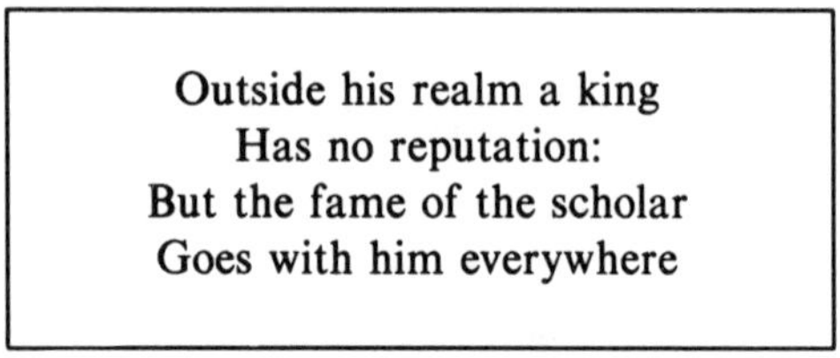
Outside his realm a king
Has no reputation:
But the fame of the scholar
Goes with him everywhere

The box was specified as

```
.PS
box width 2.5 height 1.0\
    "Outside his realm a king"\
    "Has no reputation:"\
    "But the fame of the scholar"\
    "Goes with him everywhere"
.PE
```

Note the use of the escape character "\" at the end of a line to indicate that the instruction is being continued on the next line.

Boxes can be placed next to each other using the `with` and `at` attributes; as an example, consider the following figure:

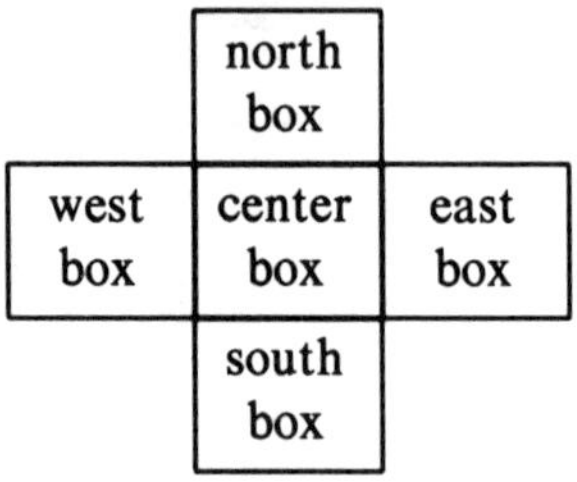
north
box
west
box
center
box
east
box
south
box

This figure was specified as

```
.PS
box "center" "box"
box "east" "box" with .w at 1st box .e
box "west" "box" with .e at 1st box .w
box "north" "box" with .s at 1st box .n
box "south" "box" with .n at 1st box .s
.PE
```

Note the use of the ordinal name "`1st box`" to refer to the box at the center of the figure.

Object dimensions can be parameterized by using variables. As an example, consider the following set of nested boxes:

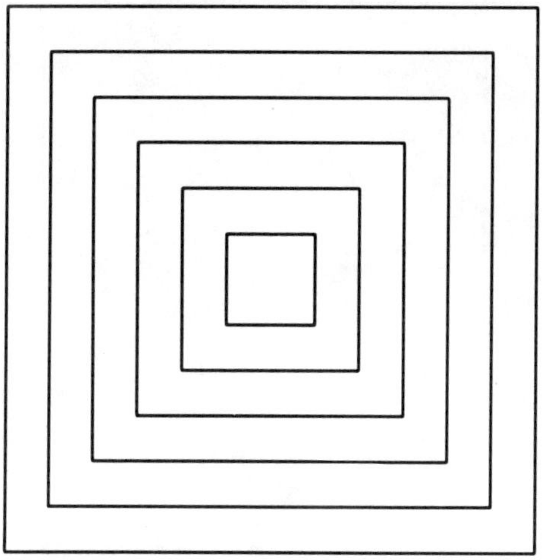

These boxes were specified as

```
.PS
a = 2.4; da = 0.4; n = 5

B: box wid a ht a
for i = 1 to n do
{
  box wid a-i*da ht a-i*da at B.c
}
.PE
```

There are several interesting things about this specification:

- the nested boxes are parameterized with respect to the two variables `a` and `da` which specify the dimensions of the outer box,
- expressions are used to specify the dimensions of the inner boxes and
- a `for` loop has been used to construct the five nested boxes. This loop executes the instructions in its body once for each value of the loop variable `i` which successively takes on the values 1 through `n` (`for` loops are discussed in Section 13.2).

The next example illustrates one use of an invisible box. Consider the following figure of a cube (the dashed lines represent the hidden edges):

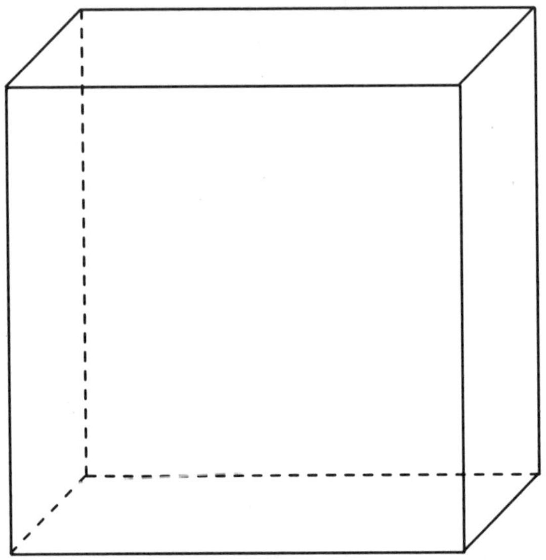

Front face edges of this cube were drawn by using a box and the remaining edges by using lines. For ease of specification, the corners of the back face of the cube are represented by the corners of an invisible box; these corners are connected by appropriate lines to the front face corners to draw the remaining edges. The cube was specified as

```
.PS
a = 2.4; x = 0.4; y = 0.4

B1: box wid a ht a
B2: box invis wid a ht a at B1.c + (x, y)
line dashed from B2.sw to B2.nw
line dashed from B2.sw to B2.se
line from B2.ne to B2.se
line from B2.ne to B2.nw
line from B1.nw to B2.nw
line from B1.se to B2.se
line from B1.ne to B2.ne
line dashed from B1.sw to B2.sw
.PE
```

Note the use of position arithmetic "`B1.c + (x, y)`" to position box `B2`.

7. Circles

Circles are specified by using the `circle` instruction which has the form

`circle` *attributes*

The default radius of a circle is given by the value of the special variable `circlerad`; its initial value is 0.25 inches. Like boxes, circles have corners:

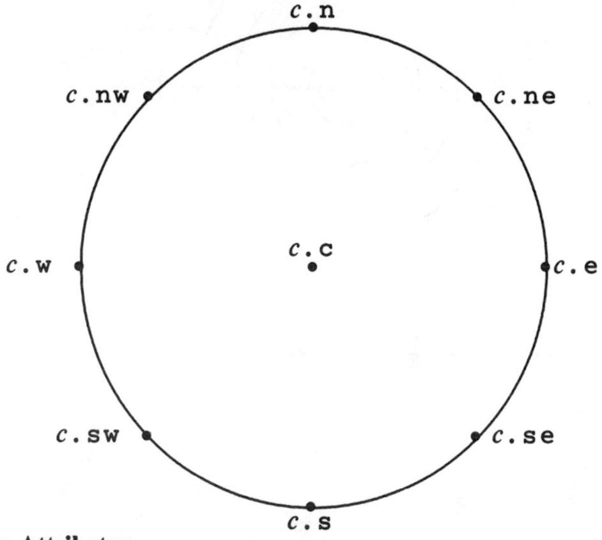

7.1 Circle Attributes

Attributes that can be associated with circles are summarized below:

`circle` attributes	description/comments
`radius` *r*	Circle radius (abbreviation `rad`).
`diameter` *d*	Circle diameter (abbreviation `diam`).
`at` *p*	Place circle at position *p* (if the `with` attribute is not specified then the circle will be centered at *p*).
`with` *c*	Used with the `at` attribute; the circle is placed with its corner *c* at the position specified in the `at` attribute.
`invisible`	Invisible circle (abbreviation `invis`).
"*text*" [*positioning-attributes*]	Text items are centered in the circle; several text items can be associated with a circle; these items are placed on top of each other; positioning attributes are `ljust`, `rjust`, `above` and `below`.

Circles cannot be dotted or dashed.

7.2 Circle Examples

Consider the concentric circles and arrows in the figure of an archer's target:

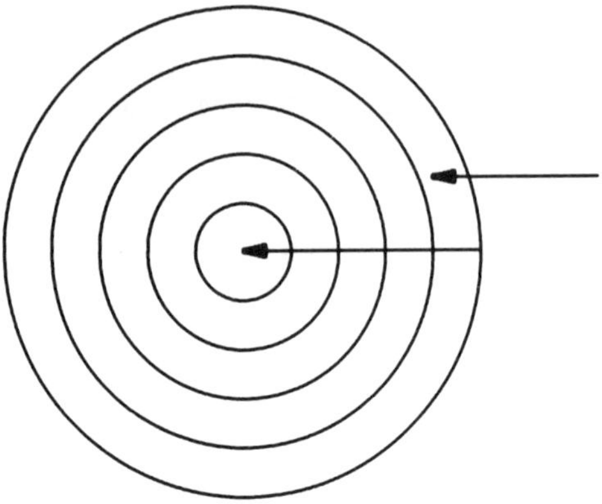

The target was specified as

```
.PS
r = 0.2; dr = 0.2; al = 1.0

C1: circle rad r
for i = 1 to 4 do
{
  circle rad r+i*dr with .c at C1.c
}
arrow left from C1.c + (al, 0.0) to C1.c
arrow left from C1.c + (al + 0.5, 0.3)\
           to C1.c + (al - 0.2 , 0.3)
.PE
```

As another example, consider the following figure of a clock:

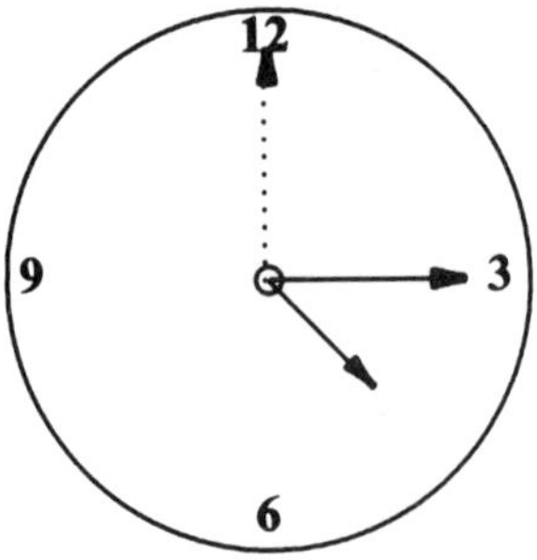

This clock was specified as

```
.PS
r = 0.75

C1: circle rad r
C2: circle rad 0.05*r at C1.c

"\fB12\fP" below at C1.n
"\fB6\fP" above at C1.s
" \fB9\fP" ljust at C1.w
"\fB3\fP " rjust at C1.e

#hour hand
  arrow from C2.c down 0.4*r right 0.4*r
#minute hand
  arrow from C1.c right 0.75*r
#second hand
  arrow dotted from C1.c up 0.85*r
.PE
```

7.3 Chopping Ends of Lines/Arrows Connecting Circles

Consider the following two circles:

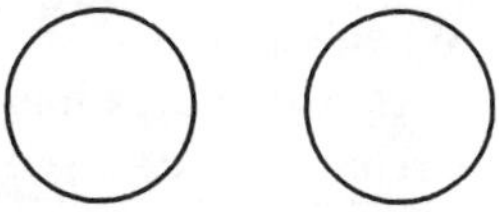

Specifying a connecting line from one circle to the other

```
.PS
C1: circle
move
C2: circle
line from C1 to C2
.PE
```

creates a line connecting the centers of the two circles:

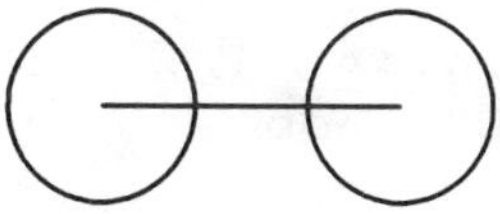

Now consider the following line connecting the two circles:

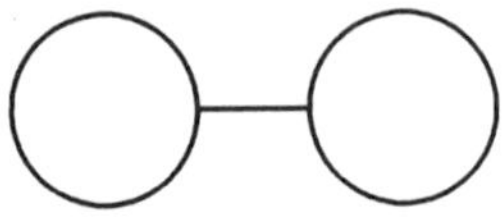

The connecting line stops at the circumferences of the two circles. Specifying such a connecting line is easy in this case because the connecting line intersects each circle at one of its corners. The difficulty arises when the intersection points are not circle corners and they have to be computed, for example,

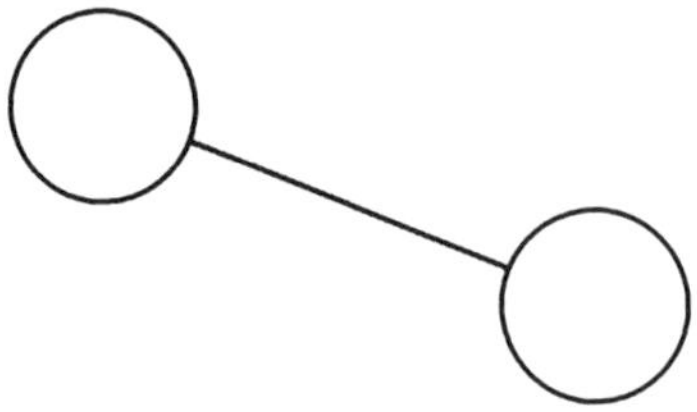

Fortunately, `pic` provides a special facility, the `chop` attribute, for drawing connecting lines that stop at the circle circumferences. Qualifying a line or an arrow connecting two circles with the `chop` attribute causes portions of the lines within the circles to be chopped off. The `chop` attribute has three forms:

form	description/comments
`chop`	When used with a line/arrow connecting two circles, it causes line/arrow segments within the circles to be chopped off.
`chop` *r*	Chop segments of length *r* from both ends of a line/arrow.
`chop` r_1 `chop` r_2	Chop a segment of length r_1 from the beginning of a line/arrow and a segment of length r_2 from its end.

Using the `chop` attribute, the above figure was specified as

```
.PS
x = 4.25 * circlerad

C1: circle
C2: circle with .c at C1.e + (x, -x/2)
line from C1 to C2 chop
.PE
```

8. Ellipses

An *ellipse* (oval) is a closed plane curve generated by moving a point in such a way that the sum of its distance from two fixed points, called *focuses* or *foci*, is constant. Ellipses are drawn by using the `ellipse` instruction which has the form

`ellipse` *attributes*

The default width and height of an ellipse are given by the values of the special variables `ellipsewid` and `ellipseht` whose initial values are 0.75 inches and 0.5 inches, respectively. Like boxes and circles, ellipses have corners:

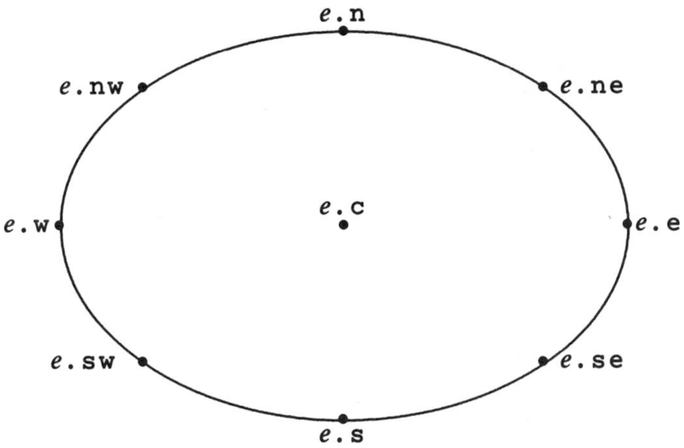

8.1 Ellipse Attributes

Attributes that can be associated with ellipses are summarized below:

`ellipse` **attributes**	**description/comments**
`height` *h*	Ellipse height (abbreviation `ht`).
`width` *w*	Ellipse width (abbreviation `wid`).
`at` *p*	Place ellipse at position *p* (if the `with` attribute is not specified then, by default, the ellipse is centered at *p*).
`with` *c*	Used with the `at` attribute; the ellipse is placed so that its corner *c* resides at the position specified by the `at` attribute.
`invisible`	Makes the ellipse invisible (abbreviation `invis`).
"*text*" [*positioning-attributes*]	Text items are centered in the ellipse; several text items can be associated with an ellipse; these items are placed on top of each other; positioning attributes are `ljust`, `rjust`, `above` and `below`.

Ellipses cannot be dotted or dashed.

8.2 Ellipse Examples

Consider the figure of a cone:

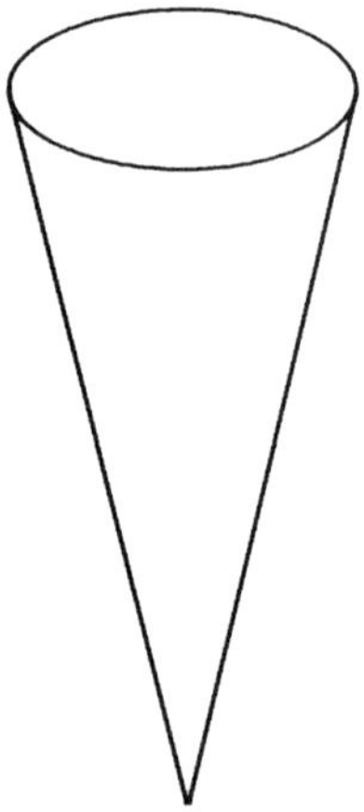

This cone was specified as

```
.PS
w = 1.0; h = 0.45; y = 2.0

E: ellipse wid w ht h
line from E.w to E.c + (0.0, -y)
line from E.e to E.c + (0.0, -y)
.PE
```

Another example illustrating the use of ellipses is the following flowchart:

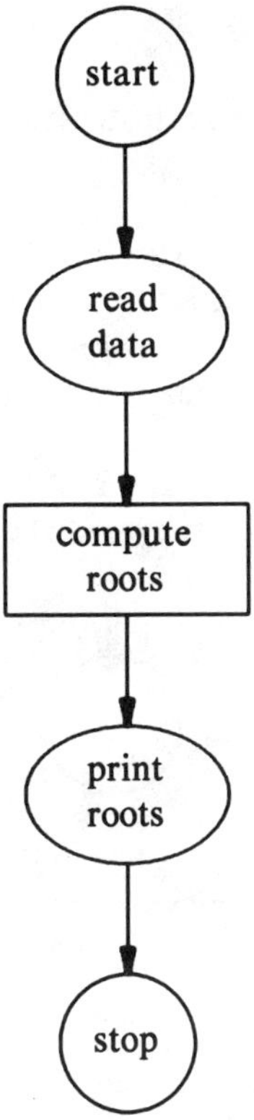

Different objects are used to specify different components of a flowchart; here boxes have been used to specify computations, ellipses have been used to specify input/output operations and circles have been used to specify program starting and stopping operations.

The flowchart was specified as

```
.PS
lineht = 0.4
down
circle "start"; arrow
ellipse "read" "data"; arrow
box wid 0.9 "compute" "roots"; arrow
ellipse "print" "roots"; arrow
circle "stop"
.PE
```

9. Arcs

Arcs are specified by using the `arc` instruction which has the form

`arc` *attributes*

By default, the radius of the arc is taken to be the value of the special variable `arcrad` whose initial value of is 0.25 inches. Again by default, arcs are drawn, starting from the current position, in a *counterclockwise* direction turning 90 degrees (¼ circle) from the current direction. Four arcs can be used to draw a circle. Associated with every arc is an invisible circle on which the arc lies. Arc corners are the corners of this invisible circle. The following figure illustrates an arc (within the arrowheads) and the normally invisible circle associated with it:

The figure was specified as

```
.PS
arc <->
circle with .c at last arc.c
.PE
```

Arcs are typically specified by giving their start and end points using the `from` and `to` attributes; `pic` automatically determines the radius of an appropriate circle for the arc.

9.1 Arc Attributes

Attributes that can be associated with arcs are summarized in the following table:

`arc` **attributes**	**description/comments**
`up`	Draw the arc after changing the current drawing direction to up.
`down`	Draw the arc after changing the current drawing direction to down.
`left`	Draw the arc after changing the current drawing direction to left.
`right`	Draw the arc after changing the current drawing direction to right.
`height` *e*	Arrowhead height (abbreviation `ht`).
`width` *e*	Arrowhead width (abbreviation `wid`).
`from` *p*	Start point of the arc.
`to` *p*	End point of the arc.
`at` *p*	Place arc at position *p* (if the `with` attribute is not specified then, by default, the arc is centered at *p*).
`with` *c*	Used with the `at` attribute; the arc is placed so that its corner *c* resides at the position specified in the `at` attribute.
`radius`	Radius of the arc (abbreviation is `rad`).
`invisible`	Makes arc invisible (abbreviation `invis`).
`cw`	Draw the arc clockwise.
`<-`	Arrowhead for a head at the beginning of an arc.
`->`	Arrowhead for a head at the end of an arc.
`<->`	Arrowhead for heads at both ends of an arc.
"*text*" [*positioning-attributes*]	Text items are centered in the invisible circle of which the arc is a part; several text items can be associated with an arc; these items are placed on top of each other; positioning attributes are `ljust`, `rjust`, `above` and `below`.

Arcs cannot be dotted or dashed.

9.2 Arc Examples

The first example illustrates the association of text with an arc:

The arc and the associated text items were specified as

```
.PS
arc -> cw "clock-" "wise"
.PE
```

The same text associated with the normally invisible circle corresponding to the arc looks like:

As another example, consider the arc drawn between the two points (0.0, 0.5) and (0.5, 0.0)

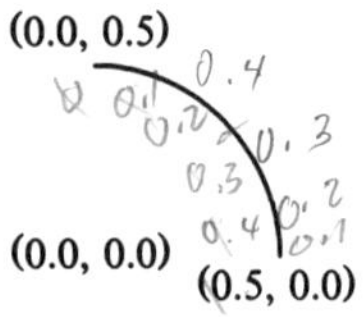

This arc was specified as

```
.PS
arc from (0.5, 0.0) to (0.0, 0.5)\
                  with .c at (0.0, 0.0)
"\s-2(0.5, 0.0)\s0" below at (0.5, 0.0)
"\s-2(0.0, 0.5)\s0" above at (0.0, 0.5)
"\s-2(0.0, 0.0)\s0" at (0.0, 0.0)
.PE
```

`pic` draws the shorter arc, instead of the longer arc, between the two points (0.0, 0.5) and (0.5, 0.0). By default, `pic` draws arcs in a counterclockwise direction. Remember that the default drawing direction is left-to-right and that the starting point of the above arc was specified to be (0.0, 0.5). The longer arc between these two points, shown below,

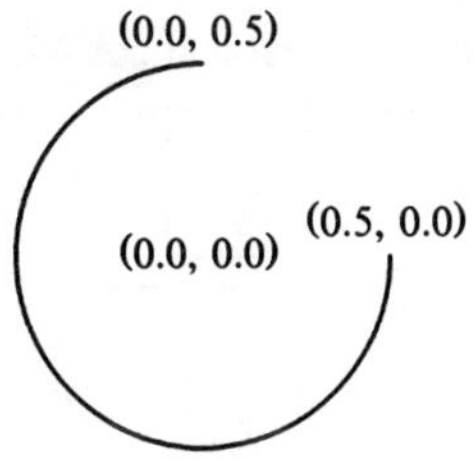

can be drawn by explicitly specifying its direction to be clockwise:

```
.PS
arc cw from (0.5, 0.0) to (0.0, 0.5)\
                  with .c at (0.0, 0.0)
"\s-2(0.5, 0.0)\s0" above at (0.5, 0.0)
"\s-2(0.0, 0.5)\s0" above at (0.0, 0.5)
"\s-2(0.0, 0.0)\s0" at (0.0, 0.0)
.PE
```

Alternatively, it can be drawn by interchanging the start and end points of the arc:

```
.PS
arc from (0.0, 0.5) to (0.5, 0.0)\
                  with .c at (0.0, 0.0)
"\s-2(0.5, 0.0)\s0" above at (0.5, 0.0)
"\s-2(0.0, 0.5)\s0" above at (0.0, 0.5)
"\s-2(0.0, 0.0)\s0" at (0.0, 0.0)
.PE
```

As another example, consider the figure of an arc connecting two circles:

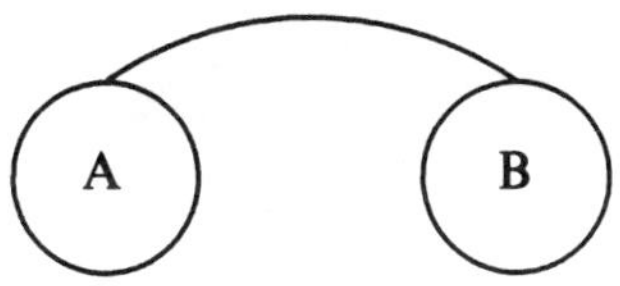

This figure was specified as

```
.PS
A: circle "A"
move; move
B: circle "B"
arc cw from A.n to B.n
.PE
```

The arc radius can also be explicitly specified; for example, here are several arcs of different radii connecting the same two points:

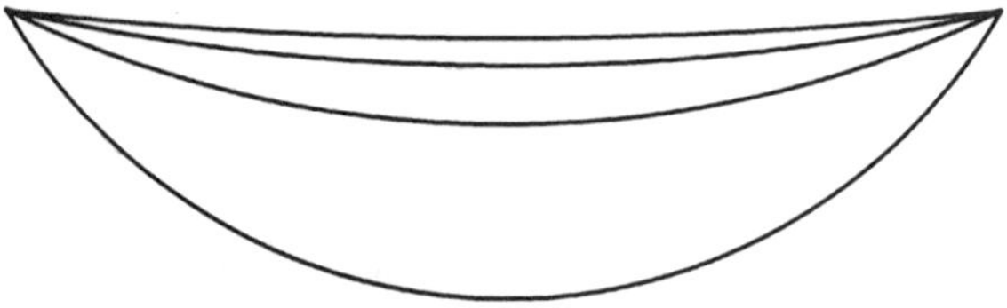

These arcs were specified as

```
.PS
r = 1.75

A: Here
B: A + (3.0, 0.0)

j = 1
for i = 1 to 4 do
{
  arc from A to B rad j*r; j = j * 2
}
.PE
```

The radius of each adjacent arc differs by a factor of 2. Notice the use of

1. the keyword `Here` to associate the current position (0.0, 0.0) with the label `A`.
2. the use of label `B` and position arithmetic to record a position relative to position `A`.

Finally, consider the following figure:

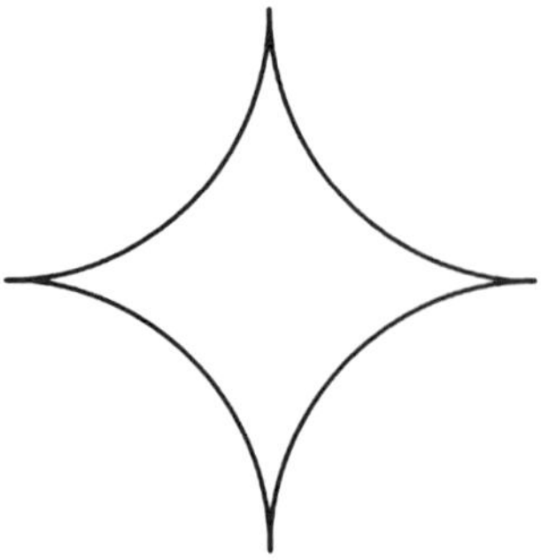

This figure was specified as

```
.PS
arcrad = 0.8
arc; arc down; arc left; arc up
.PE
```

10. Splines

A *spline* is a smooth curve guided by a set of points that are specified either explicitly or implicitly by using the direction operators `right`, `left`, `up` and `down`. The guiding points can also serve as the specification of a path line, called the *guiding-path line*. The spline starts and ends at the same points as the guiding-path line and is tangent to the mid-points of the guiding-path line segments. None of the guiding points, except the start and end points, lie on the spline. Unlike arcs, splines can be made to bend in any direction by specifying appropriate guiding points.

Splines are specified using the `spline` instruction which has the form

`spline` *segment*$_1$ `then` *segment*$_2$ `then ... then` *segment*$_n$

The syntax of a spline specification is identical to that of a path line specification except that the keyword `spline` is used instead of the keyword `line`.

As a comparison of splines and path lines consider the following figure of a spline and its guiding-path line (the path line is dashed) [Kernighan 1982a]:

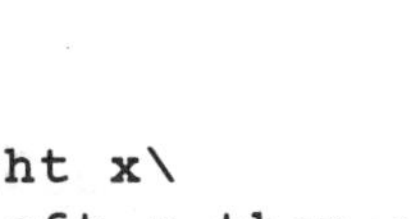

This figure was specified as

```
.PS
x = 1.0; y = 0.5

L: line dashed right x\
     then down y left x then right x
  spline from L.start right x\
     then down y left x then right x
.PE
```

10.1 Spline Attributes

Spline attributes are identical to path line attributes with the following exception: splines, like the other curved objects in `pic`, cannot be dotted or dashed.

10.2 Spline Examples

Splines are useful for drawing smooth curves. For example, consider the following figure illustrating the cross-section of a curved mirror being held in a frame:

This cross-section was specified as

```
.PS
x = 0.75; y = 0.75

.ps 18
L: line left x down y then down 2*y\
      then right x down y
spline from L.start left x down y then down 2*y\
      then right x down y
.ps
.PE
```

As another example, consider the figure of a hot-air balloon:

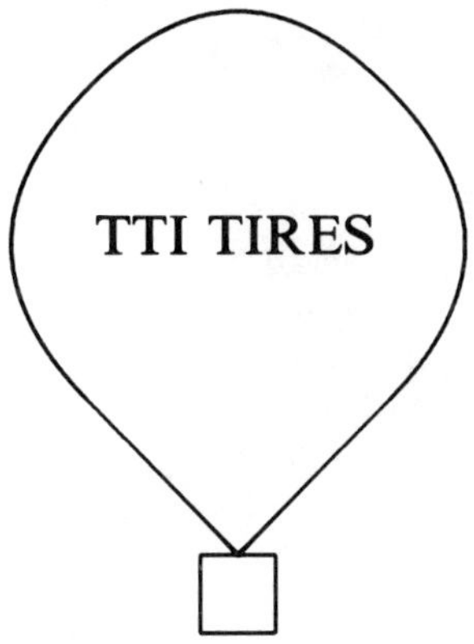

The hot-air balloon was specified as

```
.PS
a = 1.0

S: spline right a up a\
  then left a up a\
  then left a down a\
  then right a down a

box wid a/4 ht a/4 with .n at S.start

"\s+3TTI TIRES\s0" at S.start + (0.0, a)
.PE
```

As a final example, consider the following figure of a finite automaton:

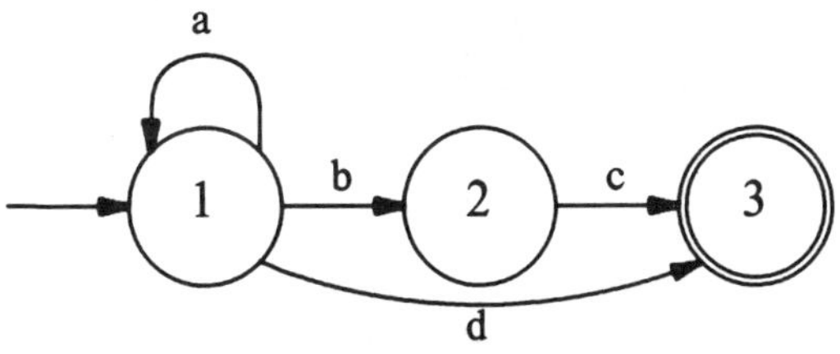

The finite automaton shown above was specified as

```
.PS
r1 = circlerad - 0.025
y = circlerad

arrow
C1: circle "\s+21\s0"
    arrow "b" above
C2: circle "\s+22\s0"
    arrow "c" above
C3: circle "\s+23\s0"
    circle rad r1 with .c at C3.c

spline -> from C1.ne to C1.ne + (0.0, y)\
  then to C1.n + (0.0, y)\
  then to C1.nw + (0.0, y)\
  then to C1.nw
"a" above at C1.n + (0.0, y)

A: arc -> from C1.se to C3.sw rad 2.0
"d" below at A.s
.PE
```

Of course, drawing complex figures such as this one is a trial-and-error process that may require several attempts for satisfactory completion.

11. Text

Although text strings are frequently specified as attributes of primitive objects,[28] they can also be full-fledged primitive objects that are specified independently of other objects. A text object specification has the form

"*text*" *attributes*

Text objects can contain `troff` escape sequences such as those specifying font and size changes, and local motion. These escape sequences can be used without any problems provided their effects are undone within the text item; for example, if a font is changed within a text object, then the original font must be restored within the text object itself.

28. Specification of an object with a text object as an attribute has the form

primitive-object attributes "*text*" [*positioning-attributes*] *attributes*

11.1 Text Attributes

Attributes that can be associated with text are summarized in the following table:

"*text*" attributes	description/comments
`at` *p*	Place the text item at position *p*.
positioning-attributes	Modify the placement of the text object with respect to the position specified in the `at` attribute; positioning attributes are `ljust`, `rjust`, `above` and `below` (see discussion below for details).
"*text*" [*positioning-attributes*]	Text objects can be given as attributes of a text object; all text objects are positioned by placing them in the center of an invisible box (subject to the positioning attributes) whose height and width are given by the values of `textwid` and `textht`. Default values of each of these variables is 0.0, but these values can be changed. The height and width of the invisible box associated with a text object can also be specified explicitly by using the `height` and `width` modifiers.

Text object attributes of a non-text object are, by default, centered vertically and horizontally with respect to the object. Stand-alone text objects and their text-object attributes are centered vertically and horizontally within the invisible box associated with the stand-alone text object. Placement of text objects can be modified using the following positioning attributes:

positioning attribute	description/comments
`ljust`	Text is placed on the right of the specified location.
`rjust`	Text is placed on the left of the specified location.
`above`	Text is placed ½ line above the specified location.
`below`	Text is placed ½ line below the specified location.

`pic` is not intelligent enough to fit text within an object by changing the font size of the text. Consequently, fitting and positioning of text is often a trial-and-error process.

The figure of a diamond illustrates the use of a text object with attributes that are text objects:

The figure was specified as

```
.PS
a = 1.0

line right a down a
line left a down a
line left a up a
line right a up a
move down a
"Diamonds" "are" "forever"
.PE
```

Note that the text object `"Diamonds"` has attributes that are themselves text objects, that is, `"are"` and `"forever"`.

11.1.1 Converting Numeric Expressions to Text Objects: Numeric expressions can be converted to text objects by using the `sprintf` function, which has the form

`sprintf("`*format-string*`",` e_1, e_2, ..., e_n`)`

One format item must be given for each numeric expression e_i in *format-string*. Only the `%f` and `%g` format conversions are appropriate. Format item `%f` converts the corresponding numeric expression to decimal notation, [-]*ddd*.*ddd*, where *d* is a digit. Format item `%g` converts the corresponding numeric expression to scientific notation, [-]*d*.*ddd*e±*dd*, or the decimal notation depending upon the value of the numeric expression. For more details, see the description of the C language `sprintf` function given in the *UNIX Reference Manual* [AT&T UNIX 1983b].

As an example, consider the circle with its radius specified within it:

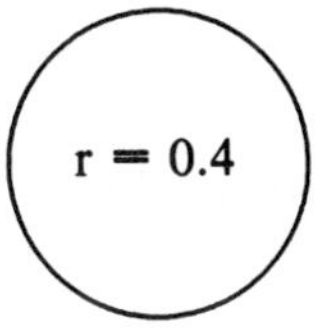

This circle was specified as

```
.PS
circlerad = 0.4
circle sprintf("r = %g", circlerad)
.PE
```

The function call

```
sprintf("r = %g", circlerad)
```

is used to specify the text attribute

`"r = ` *g*`"`

where *g* is the value of `circlerad` in the `%g` format.

12. Invisible Objects

Invisible objects are used mainly to control the placement and positioning of text and other objects. As an example, consider the following figure that illustrates document processing steps:

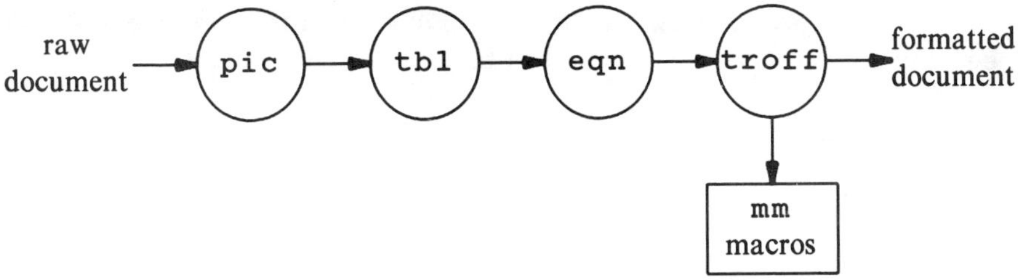

This figure was specified as

The text objects at the left and right ends of the figure were positioned with the help of invisible boxes.

13. Control Instructions

`pic` provides two control instructions: the `if` instruction for conditional execution and the `for` instruction for repeated execution.

13.1 `if` Instruction

The `if` statement has the form

`if` *e* `then { ` s_1 ` } [else { ` s_2 ` }]`

If expression *e* evaluates to true, then s_1 is executed; otherwise, s_2 is executed. Operators that can be used to construct the `if` expression are:

operator	meaning
==	equal (numeric and string)
!=	not equal (numeric and string)
>	greater than (numeric)
>=	greater than or equal to (numeric)
<	less than (numeric)
<=	less than or equal to (numeric)
&&	logical *and*
||	logical *or*

13.2 `for` Instruction

The `for` loop instruction has the form

`for` *i* `=` *a* `to` *b* `[by` *j*`] do {` *instructions* `}`

The body of the `for` loop (in curly braces) is executed once for each value of variable *i* which is initially assigned the value *a*. *i* is then increased in steps of *j* (1 if the `by` clause is absent) as long as it is less than or equal to *b*.

13.3 Examples of the `if` and `for` Instructions

`pic` does not provide facilities for shading objects; in this example, I will show how the `if` and `for` instructions can be used to shade an object:

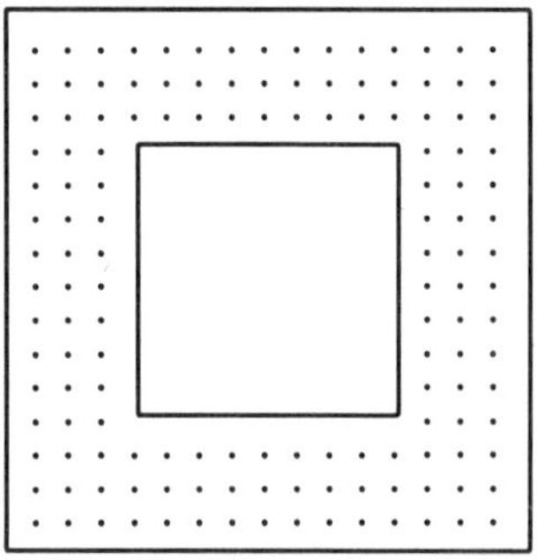

This figure was specified as

```
.PS
a = 1.6; h = 0.1; n = a/h

A: box wid a ht a
B: box wid a/2 ht a/2 with .c at last box.c

for i = 1 to n-1 do
{
  for j = 1 to n-1 do
  {
    if (i < n/4 || i > 3*n/4 ||\
                 j < n/4 || j > 3*n/4) then
    {"." at (A.nw.x + i*h, A.nw.y - j*h)}
  }
}
.PE
```

Variable a specifies the length of an outer square side, variable h specifies the distance between the dots. The `if` instruction ensures that dots are placed only in the region between the two squares.

14. Macros

`pic` macro definitions are of the form

`define` *macro-name* ***θ*** *macro-body* ***θ***

where *macro-name* is a character sequence not containing item separators such as blanks, tabs and quotes, and character ***θ*** is the delimiter enclosing the macro body; the delimiter must not appear in the macro body.

Items of the form $1, $2, ..., $*n*, have a special significance in a macro body; they represent the parameters.

Macro definitions can be removed by using the `undef` instruction:

`undef` *macro-name*

14.1 Macro Calls

Macros are invoked (called) as

macro-name(a_1 , a_2 , . . . , a_n)

where a_i is the ith argument corresponding to the parameter $*i*. A macro call is replaced by the corresponding macro body after the parameters have been replaced by the corresponding arguments. If a parameter is not supplied, then it is assumed to be the null string.

14.2 Examples of Macros

Consider the following figure in which each square and the text associated with it were drawn by using the macro `square`:

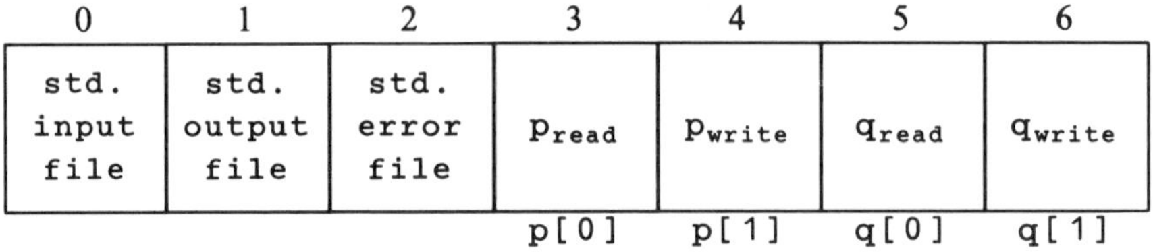

The figure was specified as

```
.PS
define square X
box $2 $3 $4 ht l wid l with .sw at last box.se
$1 at last box.n above
$5 at last box.s below
X

l = 0.65

box ht 0.0 wid 0.0 invisible
square("0", "\f(CW\s-1std.\s0\fP",\
                    "\f(CW\s-1input\s0\fP",\
                    "\f(CW\s-1file\s0\fP", "")
square("1", "\s-1\f(CWstd.\s0\fP",\
                    "\s-1\f(CWoutput\fP\s0",\
                    "\s-1\f(CWfile\fP\s0", "")
square("2", "\s-1\f(CWstd.\s0\fP",\
                    "\s-1\f(CWerror\fP\s0",\
                    "\s-1\f(CWfile\fP\s0", "")
square("3", "", "$font CW {p sub read}$", "",\
                    "\f(CWp[0]\fP")
square("4", "", "$font CW {p sub write}$", "",\
                    "\f(CWp[1]\fP")
square("5", "", "$font CW {q sub read}$", "",\
                    "\f(CWq[0]\fP")
square("6", "", "$font CW {q sub write}$", "",\
                    "\f(CWq[1]\fP")
.PE
```

Macro `square` references five parameters in its body: `$1`, `$2`, `$3`, `$4` and `$5`. Parameter `$1` represents the top label associated with the square, parameters `$2`, `$3` and `$4` represent the text to be placed within the square, and parameter `$5` represents the bottom label of the square.

Notice that each square is placed with its southwest corner (`.sw`) on top of the southeast corner (`.se`) of the last square. An invisible box was first drawn to provide an initial starting point for placing the squares. There are several ways to draw the figure without using this invisible box, for example,

- by supplying the positioning point for each square as an additional macro argument or
- by using an `if` instruction in macro `square` to avoid referring to the "last box" when drawing the first square.

As another example, consider the following binary tree figure:

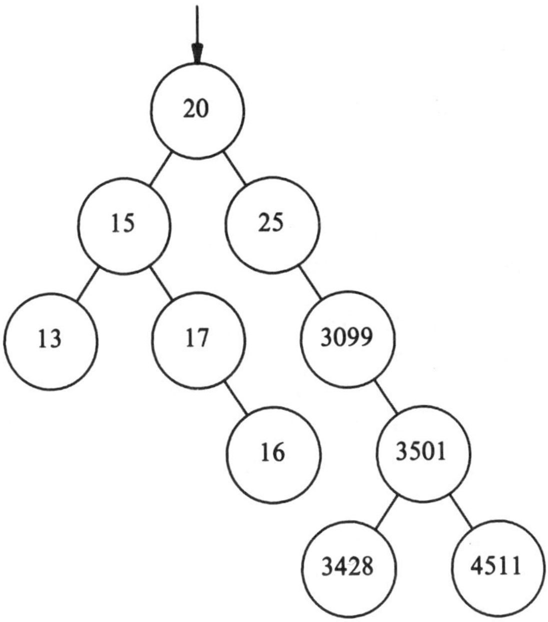

This figure was specified using two macros `leftson` and `rightson`:

```
.PS
define leftson X
$1: circle $3 at $2.c + (-x, -y)
line from $2 to last circle chop
X

define rightson X
$1: circle $3 at $2.c + (x, -y)
line from $2 to last circle chop
X

circlerad = 0.25
x = 0.4; y = 0.6

arrow down
ROOT: circle "20"

leftson(N15, ROOT, "15")
rightson(N25, ROOT, "25")

leftson(N13, N15, "13")
rightson(N17, N15, "17")
rightson(N16, N17, "16")

rightson(N30, N25, "3099")
rightson(N35, N30, "3501")
leftson(N34, N35, "3428")
rightson(N45, N35, "4511")
.PE
```

15. Blocks

`pic` provides two kinds of blocks: curly-brace blocks and square-bracket blocks. Curly-brace blocks are used to restore the original position and direction of motion after a set of `pic` instructions has been executed. Square-bracket blocks are used to combine several `pic` objects into one logical object.

15.1 Curly-Brace Blocks

Upon entry to a curly-braced block, the position and direction of motion are saved; this position and direction of motion are restored upon block exit. Curly-brace blocks have the form

{*set of* `pic` *instructions*}

As an example of the use of curly-brace blocks, consider the following figure:

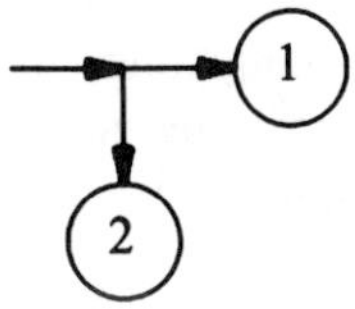

This figure was specified as

```
.DS CB
.PS
circlerad = 0.15

arrow
{arrow; circle "1"}
down
{arrow; circle "2"}
.PE
.DE
```

The curly-brace blocks simplify specification of the third arrow. Alternatively, this figure could have been specified without using blocks as follows:

```
.DS CB
.PS
circlerad = 0.15

arrow
arrow; circle "1"
arrow down from 1st arrow.end; circle "2"
.PE
.DE
```

15.2 Square-Bracket Blocks

Square-bracket blocks are used to combine several objects into one logical object. These blocks have the form

`[`*set of* `pic` *instructions*`]`

A block object may be thought of as the smallest box that encompasses the component objects. The corners of this box can be referenced like those of any other box. Like other objects, blocks can be placed at specific locations, for example,

```
[ ... ] with .c at C.c
[ ... A: ... ] with .A at B.s
```

As with blocks in programming languages, names of variables and labels are local to the block, and blocks can be nested. Blocks can be labeled and referred to either explicitly or implicitly by using ordinal names such as

```
last [].c
first [].A
```

As an example of a square-bracket block, consider the following figure showing the cross-section of some beams:

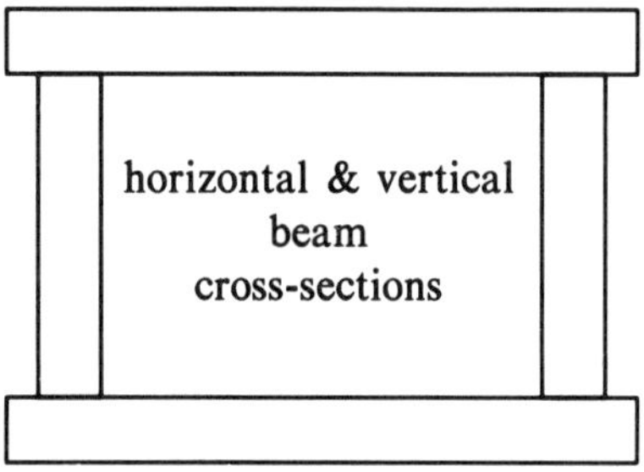

The figure was specified as a block consisting of four boxes:

```
.PS
a = 2.0; b = 1.0; c = 0.2
I: [
        T: box ht c wid a
        L: box ht b wid c with .n\
                          at T.sw + (c, 0.0)
        R: box ht b wid c with .n\
                          at T.se - (c, 0.0)
        B: box ht c wid a with .n\
                          at T.s - (0.0, b)
   ]
"horizontal & vertical" "beam"\
  "cross-sections" at I.c
.PE
```

Using the block facility, the four beams can be treated as one logical object; the text items are centered within the logical object, that is, at `I.c`.

16. Including Files Containing Pictures

`pic` provides two instructions for including files: the `copy` instruction [Kernighan 1984] and the `.PS` instruction[29]

16.1 `copy` Instruction

The `copy` instruction has the form

`copy "`*file-name*`"`

The `copy` instruction must be given inside a `pic` specification. All `.PS` instructions and `.PE` instructions within the included file are ignored. This allows files containing complete `pic` specifications to be included without modification.

16.2 `copy thru` Instruction

The `copy thru` instruction, a variant of the `copy` instruction, allows each line of an input file to be used as input for a macro. The specified macro is called, once for each input line. The fields in the input line (separated by blanks) are used as arguments of the macro call. The `copy thru` instruction is particularly useful when a figure is to be drawn based on data produced by another program or device. The `copy thru` instruction has the form

`copy "`*file-name*`" thru` *macro-name*

where *macro-name* is the name of the macro to be called once for each line of the file *file-name*. `pic` allows the body of the macro to be specified directly in `copy thru` instruction:

`copy "`*file-name*`" thru` ***θ*** *macro-body* ***θ***

where character ***θ*** is the delimiter enclosing the macro body.

As an example illustrating the use of the `copy thru` instruction, consider the following figure depicting a radar screen showing airplane positions at the time of a near collision:

---

29. The `copy` instruction is intended to replace the use of the `.PS` instruction to include files; consequently, if your version of `pic` supports the `copy` instruction, then you should use it instead of the `.PS` instruction to include files.

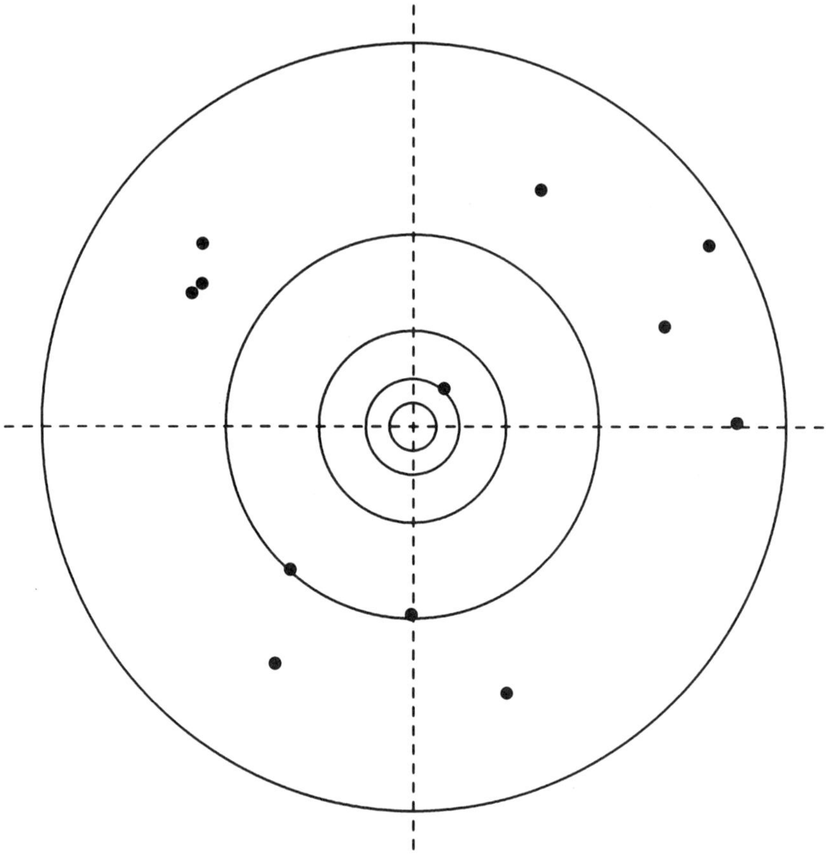

File `airplane-data` contains locations of the airplanes (in polar coordinates "r, θ") at the time of the near collision. Here are some sample lines from this file:

```
1.75 0
1.85 30
1.4 60
1.0 230
1.0 270
1.45 20
```

Using this information, the figure was specified as

```
.PS
pi = 3.1415926536; k = pi/180.0
r = 2.0; dr = r/10

define airplane X "\(bu" at\
            (1*cos(2*k), 1*sin(2*k)) X

C: circle rad r with .c at (0.0, 0.0)
line dashed from (C.n.x, C.n.y + dr)\
            to (C.s.x, C.s.y - dr)
line dashed from (C.w.x - dr, C.w.y)\
            to (C.e.x + dr, C.e.y)

r1 = r/2
for i = 1 to 4 do
{
  circle rad r1 with .c at C.c
  r1 = r1/2
}
copy "airplane-data" thru airplane
.PE
```

Notice the use of the trigonometric functions `sin` and `cos`.

16.3 `.PS` Instruction

The `.PS` instruction, in addition to specifying the start of a `pic` specification, can also be used to include files. The form of the `.PS` instruction used for including files is

`.PS` <*file-name*

Unlike in the case of the `copy` instruction, `.PS` and `.PE` instructions in the included file are not ignored.

17. Figure Size

The easiest way to draw figures [Kernighan 1982a] of the right size is to

1. first draw the figure, and

2. then, if necessary, scale the figure to an appropriate size; scaling the figure may require changing the point size used for the text objects.

Scaling can be done in two ways: by using the `.PS` instruction to specify the width and height of the figure (implicit scaling) or by using the explicit scaling facility.

17.1 `.PS` Instruction

The width and height of a figure can be explicitly specified as parameters in the picture-start instruction `.PS`:

`.PS` [*width-of-figure* [*height-of-figure*]]

These figure dimensions override the dimensions specified within the `pic` specification. The figure is expanded or contracted to match the width and height specified in the `.PS` instruction; if only the width is specified, then the height is adjusted automatically to match the width.

As an example, consider the figure that was given at the beginning of this chapter:

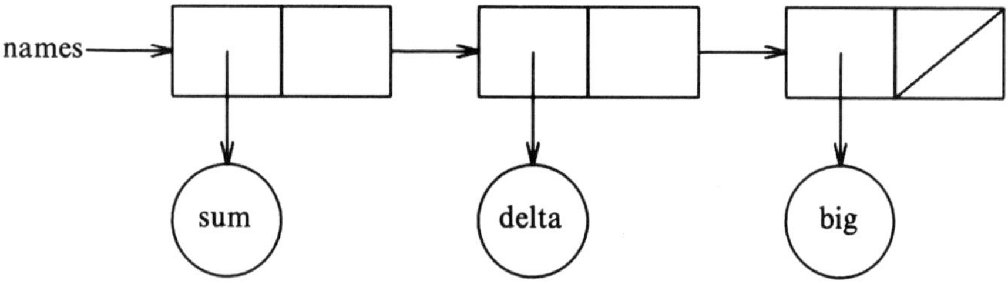

By using the instruction

```
.PS 3.0
```

the width of this figure is specified to be 3.0 inches:

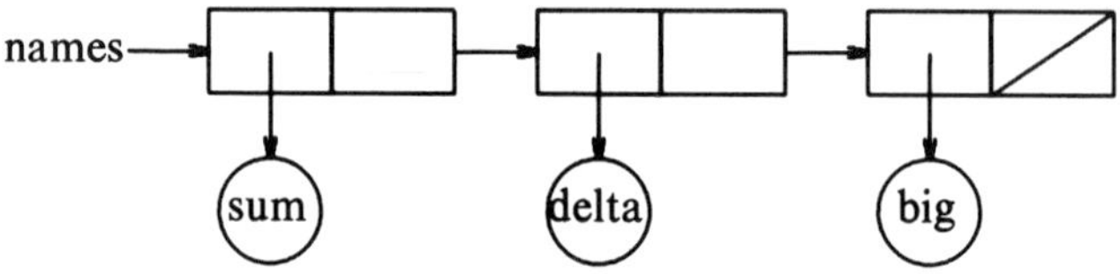

`pic` automatically adjusts the height of the figure to match the new width. Notice that the size of characters printed has not been reduced; appropriate `troff` font-control sequences to reduce and to restore the font size must be inserted explicitly in the text objects; for example, the text in the second circle was printed as

```
circle "delta"
```

The font size of "delta" could have been reduced by two points and then restored as follows:

```
circle "\s-2delta\s0"
```

17.2 Explicit Scaling

Assigning a value n to the special variable `scale` causes all dimensions to be scaled by $\frac{1}{n}$, that is, every dimension is divided by n. Explicit scaling affects the `pic` specification containing the assignment to variable `scale` and all subsequent `pic` specifications in the document. As an example of the use of scaling, suppose we want to interpret all dimensions in `pic` specifications to be in centimeters instead of in inches. This is accomplished by setting variable `scale` to 2.54:

```
scale = 2.54
```

Each dimension will now be divided by 2.54 causing them to be interpreted as centimeters.

18. Interface with mm and eqn

18.1 Interface with mm

`pic` specifications are normally enclosed in mm displays to center the figures and to ensure that figures are not split across pages, for example,

```
.DS parameters
.PS
figure specification
.PE
.DE
```

Text and other items associated with the figure, but which are not part of the figure, can also be placed in the display:

```
.DS parameters
text (or other items) to be placed above the figure
.PS
figure specification
.PE
text (or other items) to be placed below the figure
.DE
```

Several figures may be specified in one display:

```
.DS parameters
.PS
specification for figure_1
.PE
.PS
specification for figure_2
.PE
  :
.PS
specification for figure_n
.PE
.DE
```

18.1.1 Automatically-Numbered Figure Captions: The `mm` instruction `.FG`, which is used for printing automatically-numbered figure captions, has the form

`.FG` [*caption-string* [*modifier* [*modifier-control*]]]

The output of this instruction is

Figure [*modifier*] *n.* [*caption-string*]

where *n* is the number of times the `.FG` instruction has been executed.

Arguments *modifier* and *modifier-control* are used to modify the normal numbering:

1. If *modifier-control* is missing or is zero, then the *modifier* is used as a prefix of the figure number.
2. If *modifier-control* is equal to one, then the *modifier* is used as a suffix of the figure number.
3. If *modifier-control* is equal to two, then the *modifier* replaces the figure number.

Examples of captioned figures are the following two figures whose captions were generated by the instruction

```
.FG "Tic-Tac-Toe"
```

placed before each figure specification; both figure specifications and the `.FG` instructions were placed inside display blocks:

Figure 1. Tic-Tac-Toe

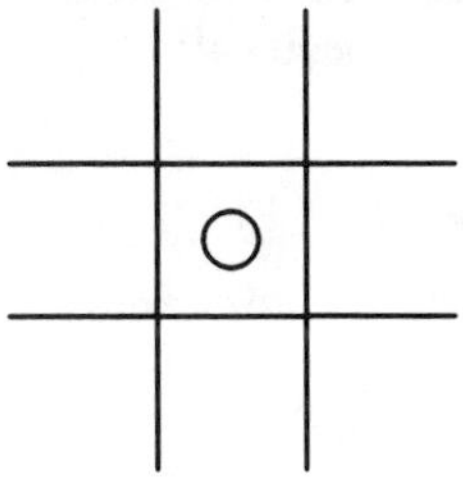

Figure 2. Tic-Tac-Toe

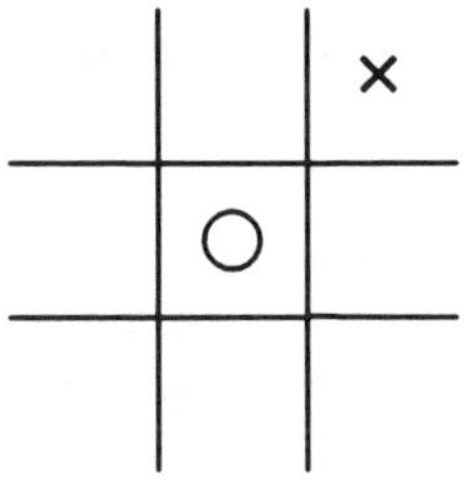

A list of figures (whose captions were specified by the `.FG` instruction) is printed along with the table of contents; this list will not be printed out if register `Lf` is set to 0 (default value of `Lf` is 1).

18.2 Interface with `eqn`

The interface between `eqn` and `pic` does not work correctly if `eqn` has to output some extra vertical space in the equation, for example, when an equation has fractions. As an example consider the figure [Kernighan 1981]

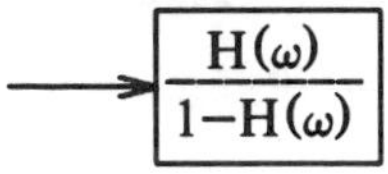

Specifying this as

```
arrow
box "${H( omega )} over {1 - H( omega )}$"
```

produces this figure

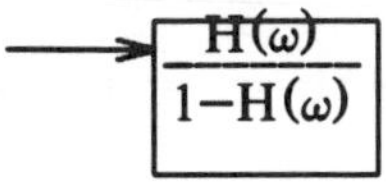

If an equation in a figure has things other than subscripts and superscripts, then the extra information "`space 0`" must be added to the beginning of each equation. For example, the specification

```
arrow
box "$space 0 {H( omega )} over {1 - H( omega )}$"
```

produces the first of the two figures shown above.

19. Checking for Errors: `pic`

`pic` can be used to check for figure specification errors prior to typesetting the document. To check for `pic` errors, use the UNIX commands

`pic` *files* `>/dev/null`

or

`pic` *files* `>temp`

Error messages, if any, are printed on the standard error output. The first command discards the output of `pic` while the second command stores the output in file `temp` for possible later examination by the user.

To help debug figure specifications, `pic` provides the `print` statement which has the form

`print` *expression-or-string*

Argument *expression-or-string* is printed on the standard error output.

20. Recent Changes to `pic`

As I have mentioned earlier, many changes have been made to `pic` recently [Kernighan 1984]; these changes are summarized in the following list for the benefit of the readers who have an older version of `pic`:

- `pic` now uses inches, instead of internal units, for internal computation.
- The output of `pic` is now produced in inches instead of typesetter units; consequently, it is not generally necessary to specify the typesetter for which the code is being produced (e.g., by using the `-T` option of the `pic` command).
- The following functions can now be used in `pic` expressions:
    1. trigonometric functions `log` (base 10), `exp` (base 10), `sqrt`, `sin`, `cos` and `atan2`.
    2. `max`, `min` (2 arguments only), `int` and `rand`.

- The special variable `arrowhead` can be used to control the arrowhead fill.
- Function `sprintf`, which allows numeric values to be converted to text objects, has been added.
- Instruction `reset`, which resets some or all of the special variables to their default values, has been added.
- The `same` attribute is not supported any more.
- A macro definition facility has been added.
- Instruction `copy` has been added with the purpose of replacing the use of the instruction `.PS` to include files. The `copy thru` variant of the `copy` instruction can be used to include a file after filtering it with the specified macro.
- An `if` instruction has been added providing a facility for conditional execution.
- A `for` instruction has been added providing a facility for specifying loops.
- Text objects are now full-fledged objects.
- Arc corners are now defined.
- Input numbers in scientific format are now allowed.
- `pic` now saves the fill/no-fill mode on entering a `pic` specification and restores it upon exit.
- The height of a figure can now be specified along with the width in the `.PS` instruction.
- The debugging statement `print` has been added.

21. Exercises

1. Write `pic` specifications of the following figures:

   a.

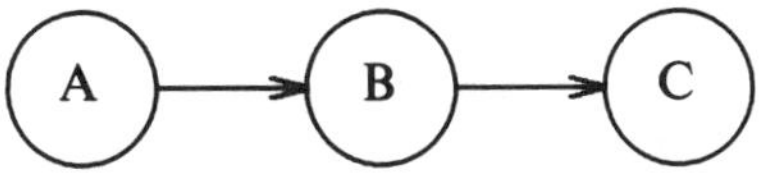

b.

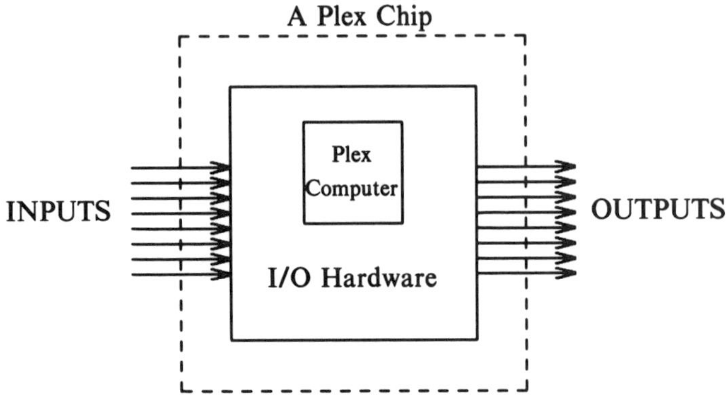

A Plex Computer System

c.

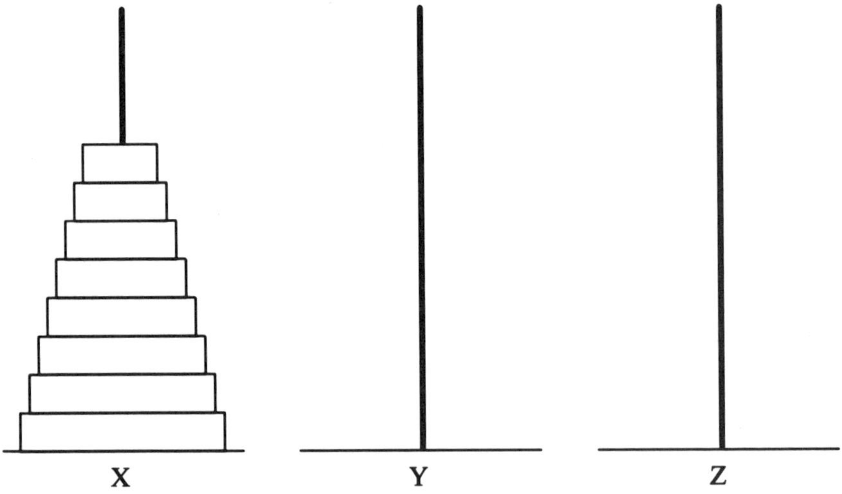

The Towers of Hanoi

d.

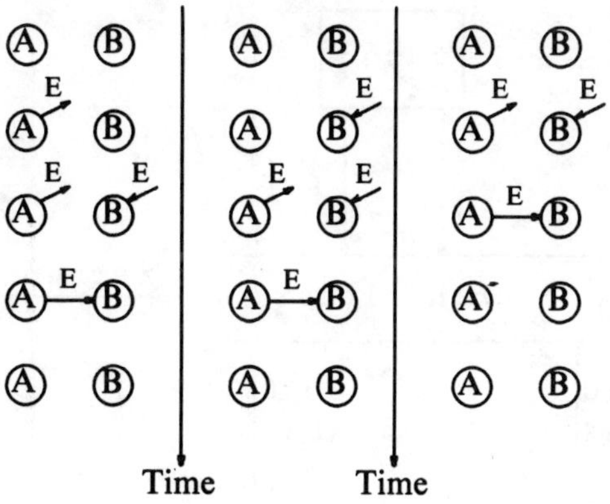

e.

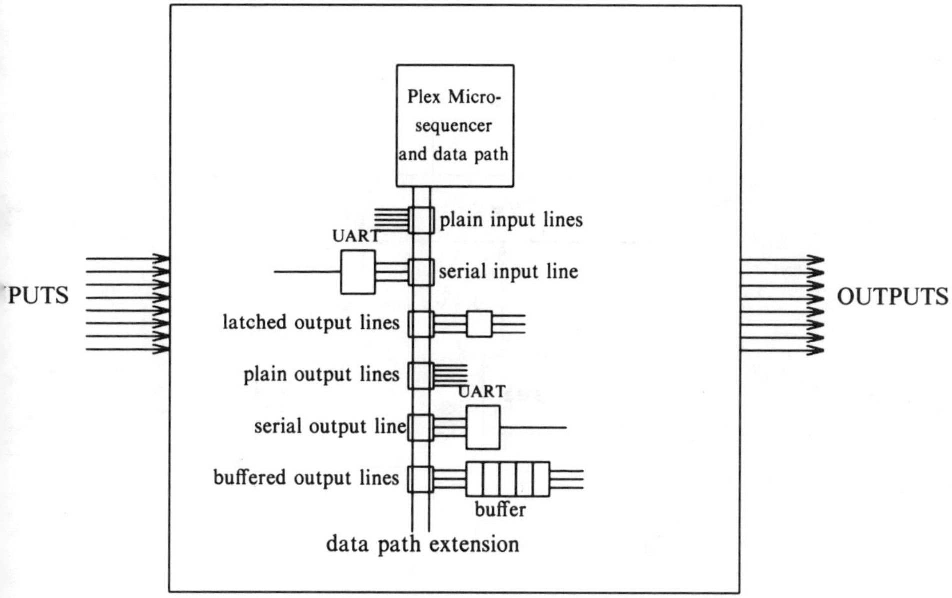

A Plex Computer System

f.

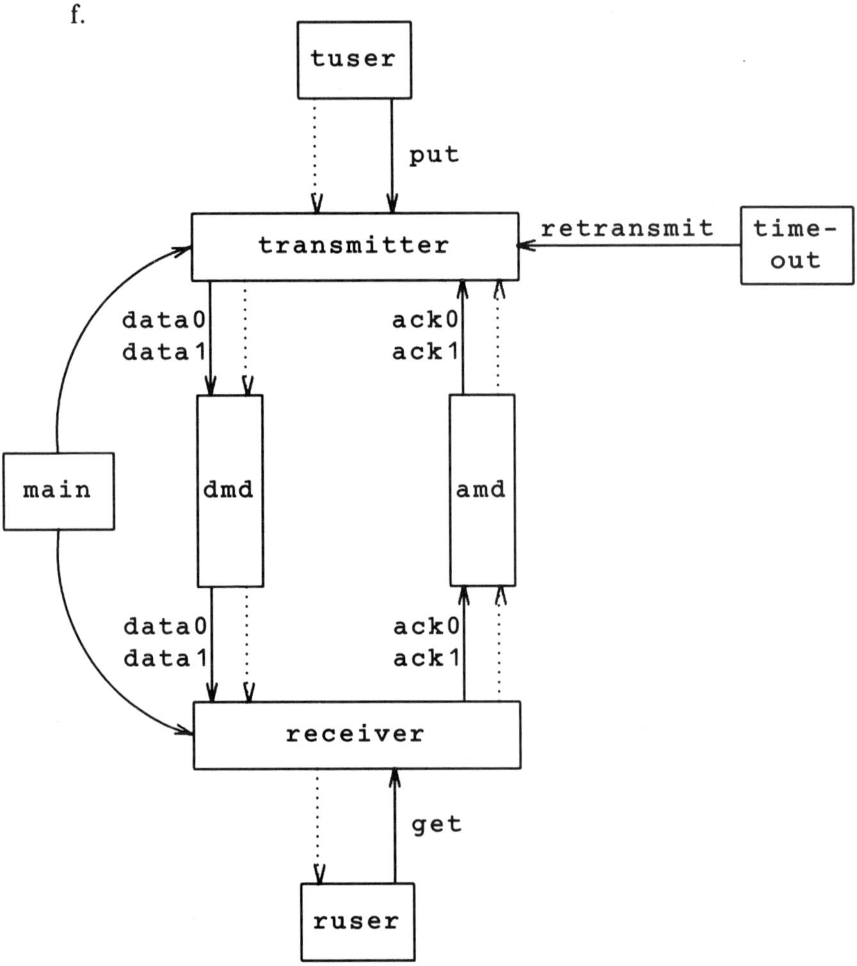

——> solid arrows indicate transaction calls

·······> dotted arrows indicate direction of information flow

Structure of the Concurrent C Program

g. Specify the following figure without using a special font such as the *chess* font:

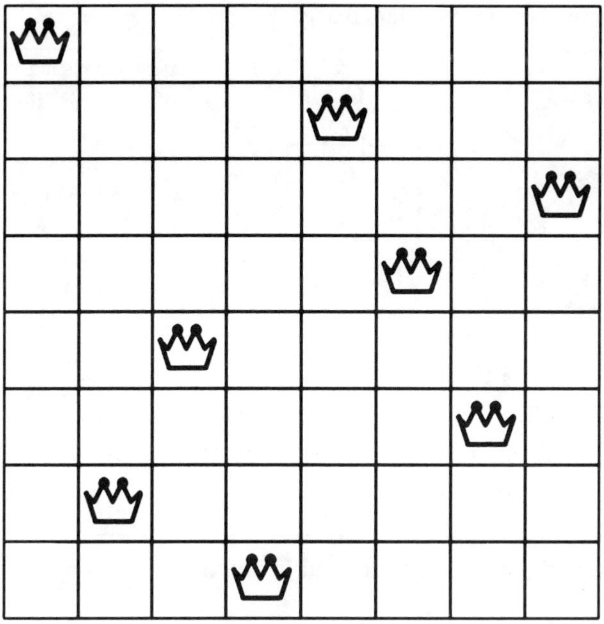

The Eight Queens
(safely placed)

h.

2. Use four arcs to draw a circle.
3. Rewrite the specification of the binary tree using a new macro called `son` which you are to define as a combination of the two macros `leftson` and `rightson`.
4. Rewrite the nested boxes example of Section 6 using macros.
5. Rewrite the box shading example of Section 13.3 using dotted lines instead of dots. What is the advantage of using dotted lines instead of

dots? (Problem suggested by John Linderman.)

6. Extend the specification of the beam cross-sections in Section 15.2 to shade the cross-sections with dots.

7. Write formatting instructions for the following figure and associated text (contributed by D. W. Hagelbarger):

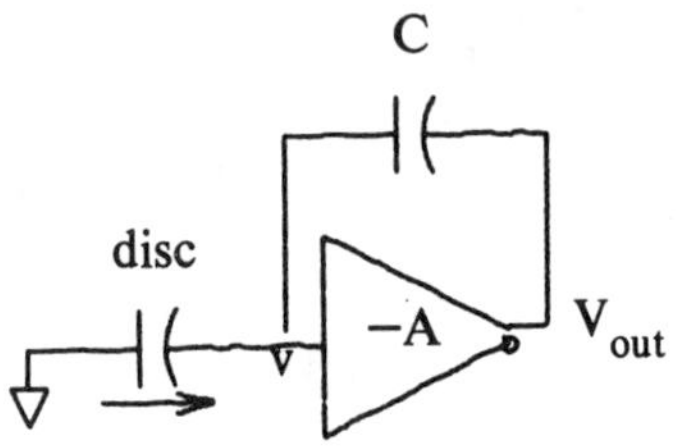

The figure on the left shows how we can use an operational amplifier (op amp) to convert the current flowing from our disc into a voltage. We find by measurement that the capacity of our disc to the box is 12 pf. The op amp has a large negative gain. This means the voltage v at the input is approximately zero. The op amp also has a very high input impedance.

Hint: Use the flyback picture-end instruction `.PF`.

Chapter 5
Specifying Formulas (Equations)

Mathematical formulas[30] can be specified by using the facilities provided by eqn, a troff preprocessor.[31] eqn, which was designed by B. W. Kernighan and L. Cherry [DWB 1984c; Kernighan and Cherry 1975], provides high-level facilities for specifying two-dimensional equations using a one-dimensional notation. For example, eqn provides names for the standard mathematical symbols, facilities for specifying subscripts, superscripts, fractions, matrices and vertical alignment of equations. eqn follows standard mathematical typesetting conventions, for example, it uses a smaller point size for subscripts and superscripts and uses italics for variable names. eqn specifications (expressions) can be intermixed with the document text, mm and troff instructions specifying the document format, and with tbl and pic specifications.

The designers of eqn believe that learning eqn is rather easy and straightforward [Kernighan and Cherry 1975]:

> [eqn] has been designed to be easy to learn and to be easy to use by people who know neither mathematics or typesetting. ... The learning time [of eqn] is short. A few minutes gives the general flavor and typing a page or two of a paper generally uncovers most of the misconceptions about how it works.

However [DWB 1984c],

> eqn is quite happy to set garbage (but it will look good).

---

30. An equation is a special case of formula. Kernighan and Cherry use "equation" as a synonym for "formula"; I shall also do the same in this book.

31. neqn is the corresponding preprocessor for nroff. The same formula specifications can be used with both eqn and neqn. neqn, because of nroff limitations, does not provide the variety of characters, fonts and point sizes that are provided by eqn. neqn is normally used for producing draft output for proofreading.

    Unless it is ambiguous or inappropriate, I will use "eqn" to refer to both eqn and neqn.

1. An Example eqn Specification

As an example of how equations are specified using eqn, consider the equation

$$r_1, r_2 = \frac{-b \pm \sqrt{b^2 - 4ac}}{2a}$$

for computing the two roots r_1 and r_2 of a quadratic equation. This equation was specified as follows:

```
.DS CB
.EQ
r sub 1 , ~ r sub 2 ~=~
  {-b~+-~sqrt {b sup 2 ~ - ~ 4 a c}} over {2 a}
.EN
.DE
```

The first and last lines are mm instructions specifying the beginning and end of a centered display; specifications of equations that are to be displayed separate from the document text[32] *must* be enclosed within mm displays.

The second and fifth lines are the equation-start and equation-end instructions .EQ and .EN, respectively. The equation itself is specified by the eqn expression given in lines 3 and 4. eqn expressions can span several lines; they are interpreted according to the precedence of the operators, such as sub, sup and over, much like the evaluation of mathematical expressions.

Space and newline characters in eqn expressions are just item separators; they do not cause any spaces to be printed in the formatted equation. These characters are also used to improve the readability of eqn specifications. Special characters must be used to print spaces in equations. For example, the tilde character ~ specifies that one space is to be printed; the circumflex ^ specifies a half space.

Let us now examine the eqn specification in detail. Subexpression "r sub 1" specifies the formula "r_1"; sub is a binary infix operator for specifying subscripts. Following this subexpression is the character sequence ", ~ ". The comma character has no special meaning in eqn; therefore, it is output without any interpretation.

Next there is the subexpression "r sub 2" which produces "r_2". Then comes the character sequence "~=~". Character "=" by itself has no special

32. eqn provides a special notation for embedding equations in the document text, in mm instructions, and in tbl and pic specifications.

meaning in `eqn` and it is therefore passed directly to the output. Finally, we have the subexpression

```
{-b~+-~sqrt {b sup 2 ~ - ~ 4 a c}} over {2 a}
```

This subexpression has the form

numerator `over` *denominator*

and denotes a fraction which is printed as

$$\frac{numerator}{denominator}$$

The subexpression shown produces the fraction

$$\frac{-b \pm \sqrt{b^2 - 4ac}}{2a}$$

Let us now examine the final subexpression in more detail. It contains three pairs of curly braces ({ and }); braces are used to combine several items to produce one logical item. This allows several items to be supplied as a single argument to an operator. In this example, braces have been used to construct arguments for the binary operator `over` and the unary operator `sqrt`.

The final subexpression contains a nested subexpression of the form

`sqrt` *argument*

which prints an equation of the form

$$\sqrt{argument}$$

Note that the sequence of characters `+-` in the final subexpression has a special meaning in `eqn`; it denotes the symbol $\pm$.

2. Specifying Equations

Equations can be printed in two ways:

1. Equations can be displayed in blocks that are separate from the document text, for example,

   $$y^{\frac{1}{3}} + \sqrt{x}$$

   Such equations are called *displayed* equations.

2. Equations can be embedded in the document text, tables and figures, for example, $y^3 + \sqrt{x}$. Such equations are called *in-line* equations.

2.1 Displayed Equations

Displayed equation specifications have the form

```
.DS parameters
.EQ
expression specifying an equation
.EN
.DE
```

The `mm-eqn` interface requires that equations specified using the equation-start and equation-end instructions `.EQ` and `.EN`, respectively, be enclosed within a "`.DS/.DE`" display. Parameters of the `.DS` instruction are used to control the placement of the displayed equations, for example, parameter `CB` is used to print centered equations. I will normally omit the instructions specifying the display.

2.2 In-Line Equations

In-line equations are specified by enclosing `eqn` expressions in user-specified `eqn` delimiters. Equation delimiters are specified by the using the `delim` instruction which has the form

`delim` $\alpha\beta$

Characters α and β are designated as the new left and right delimiters for in-line `eqn` expressions. The `.EQ/.EN` instructions should not be enclosed in an `mm` display when specifying delimiters, deactivating delimiters and defining symbols but *not* specifying any equations; otherwise, extra blank lines will be printed.[33]

By convention, the same character is used for the left and right delimiters; for example, the instructions

```
.EQ
delim $$
.EN
```

specify that the dollar character will be used as both the left and right delimiter.

33. I encountered a bug in the `mm-eqn` interface when using `.EQ/.EN` instructions that were not enclosed within a display. Some document text prior to the `.EQ` instruction was lost. Apparently, some buffer was not being flushed properly. I was able to bypass this problem by putting the `troff` break instruction `.br` before the `.EQ` instruction. The `.br` instruction forces output of the current line.

I normally use the dollar character "$" as the delimiter. I can then use the special symbol `dollar` to denote the dollar character in `eqn` expressions without conflicting with the use of `$` as an `eqn` delimiter. However, if the equation contains many occurrences of the dollar character, then I use another character such as the percent character "%" to delimit in-line equations (unlike for the `$` character, there is no special symbol for the `%` character).

Here is an example illustrating the use of in-line `eqn` expressions:

```
Bold and bigger characters will be used for the
BNF meta symbols $lb rb ~ and ~ lc rc$
to distinguish them from
Flex language characters.
.P
... elements of the array $y$ are
output serially in the order
$y sub 0 , ~ y sub 1 , ~ ..., ~ y sub 7$.
```

where `lb`, `rb`, `lc` and `rc` are user-defined `eqn` abbreviations (discussed in Section 9) for large brackets and curly braces.

The above text is printed as

> Bold and bigger characters will be used for the BNF meta symbols **[ ]** and **{ }** to distinguish them from Flex language characters.
>
> ... elements of the array y are output serially in the order y_0, y_1, ..., y_7.

In-line equation specifications, like displayed equation specifications, can span several lines.

Delimiters can be "turned off" (deactivated) as follows:

```
.EQ
delim off
.EN
```

3. Basics

Components of `eqn` expressions are called *items*; items are separated from each other by *item separators*. Items that are not properly separated from other items are not recognized as distinct items. In this section, I will discuss items, item separators and how to specify output spaces in equations.

3.1 Items

There are three kinds of `eqn` items:

- Operators, which control the 2-dimensional display of an equation, for example, `over` (fractions), `sub` (subscripts) and `sup` (superscripts).
- Predefined or user-defined `eqn` items denoting characters, symbols, other items or item sequences. Two examples of predefined items are `theta`, which denotes the symbol θ, and `times`, which denotes the multiplication symbol $\times$.
- Items that have no special meaning in `eqn`. Such items are passed directly to the output, for example, `n` and `Russian`. Quoted items or item sequences are also passed directly to the output without any interpretation by `eqn`, for example, `"over"` and `"\f(CW"`. Quoted items can contain `troff` escape sequences specifying font and point size changes, but the original font and point size must be restored before the second double quote.

3.2 Item Separators

In addition to the separator characters (blanks, tabs and newlines), the following characters are also recognized as item separators:

- tilde "`~`" and circumflex "`^`" characters,
- the left curly brace "`{`" and the right curly brace "`}`", and
- the double-quote character "`"`".

If items are not separated properly, then the resulting output may not be correct. As an example, consider the subexpression

```
(x sub 1 , ~ y sub 2 )
```

which is printed as

$$(x_1, y_2)$$

Omitting the spaces before the comma and the right parentheses, that is,

```
(x sub 1, ~ y sub 2)
```

will create the output

$$(x_{1,}\ y_{2)}$$

in which the comma and right parenthesis have erroneously become components of the two subscripts. This has happened because now the two `sub` operators consider "`1,`" and "`2)`" to be their right arguments. Note that the left argument of the first `sub` operator is "`(x`" and not just "`x`"; making "`(`" and "`x`" distinct items in this case is not important. Omitting the space before or after the `sub` operators will result in their not being recognized by `eqn` as special operators. For example, the output of

```
(xsub 1 , ~ y sub2 )
```

will be

$$(xsub 1,\ ysub 2)$$

because `eqn` considers each of `xsub` and `sub2` to be single items; these items have no special meaning in `eqn`.

3.3 Null Items

The *null* item `""` is an item that is not printed. Null items are used in places where `eqn` requires an item to be present even though the item is not going to be printed in the equation. As an example of the use of a null item, consider the specification of the equation

$$^{2}\mathrm{He}$$

this symbol can be specified as [Kernighan and Cherry 1975]

```
"" sup 2 roman He
```

where `sup` is the superscript operator and `roman` is an operator that prints its argument in Roman font.

3.4 Quoting Items to Suppress Interpretation

Enclosing a sequence of characters in double quotes suppresses any special meaning that might otherwise be associated with items in the sequence; quoted character sequences are passed directly to the output without any interpretation by `eqn`. For example, suppose we want to print the equation

$$e^{sqrt(a_1 * a_2)}$$

Specifying this equation as

```
e sup {sqrt (a sub 1 * a sub 2 )}
```

will produce

$$e^{\sqrt{(a_1} * a_2)}$$

which is not what we want. "`sqrt`" is an `eqn` operator that is used to draw the square root symbol $\sqrt{\ }$ over an expression. Interpretation of "`sqrt`" as an operator can be suppressed by quoting it, for example,

```
e sup {"sqrt" (a sub 1 * a sub 2 )}
```

3.5 Combining Several Items into One Logical Item

Curly braces ("`{`" and "`}`") are used to combine several items into one logical item. Curly braces can be nested. As an example, consider the equation

$$a_{i+j}$$

Specifying this equation as

```
a sub i + j
```

is not correct because it will print the equation

$$a_i + j$$

This happens because `sub` takes only one item (`i` in this example) as its second argument instead of all the three items `i`, `+` and `j`. To produce the equation a_{i+j}, these three items must be combined into one logical item using braces:

```
a sub {i + j}
```

Alternatively, because in this equation there is no need to treat `i`, `+` and `j` as distinct items, we can treat them as a single item by removing the spaces separating them:

```
a sub i+j
```

This strategy of combining several items into one item by not separating them (to avoid the use of braces) does not always work. As an example, consider the equation

$$a_{\frac{i}{2}}$$

which was specified as

```
a sub { i over 2 }
```

and not as

```
a sub iover2
```

which would produce the equation

$$a_{iover2}$$

Eliminating the spaces between `i`, `over` and `2` prevents `over` from being recognized as a distinct item.

If you want to print braces, then they must be enclosed within double quotes, for example, the equation

$$\{a_2+b\}$$

is specified as

```
"{" a sub 2 + b "}"
```

3.6 Specification of Spaces in Equations

Spaces and newlines are used as item separators and for enhancing the readability of `eqn` specifications. They are normally gobbled up by `eqn` and not reproduced in the output; for example, writing

```
y  =  alpha x + beta
```

is the same as writing

```
y     =
alpha   x    +    beta
```

Both of these specifications will produce the same equation:

$$y{=}\alpha x{+}\beta$$

Spaces may be printed in equations by using the following characters in `eqn` specifications:

character	output effect
~	One blank space.
^	Half a blank space.
☛ (the tab character)	Move to the next tab stop (tab settings can be changed with the `troff` instruction `.ta`).

For example, spaces can be specified in the equation $y{=}\alpha x{+}\beta$ as follows:

```
y  ~  =
~  alpha  x
~ + ~  beta
```

This equation will now be printed as

$$y\ =\ \alpha x\ +\ \beta$$

4. Subscripts/Superscripts

Operators `sub` and `sup` are used for specifying subscripts and superscripts, respectively. Each of these operators takes two arguments

item `sub` *subscript*
item `sup` *superscript*

and prints equations of the form

$$item_{subscript}$$

$$item^{superscript}$$

Notice that the *subscript* and *superscript* are automatically printed in a smaller point size. Both `sub` and `sup` must be surrounded by spaces. Some examples of subscripts and superscripts are

$$a_i \qquad x_{ij} \qquad x_{x+\sqrt{\pi}\theta} \qquad b^e \qquad b^{i*j}$$

These equations were specified as

```
.EQ
a sub i ~~~~~
x sub ij ~~~~~
x sub { x + sqrt pi theta} ~~~~~
b sup e ~~~~~
b sup { i star j }
.EN
```

Several subscripts or superscripts, or a combination of subscripts and superscripts may be associated with an item. Here are some examples illustrating the interplay between subscript and superscript operators:

`eqn` expression	equation
`a sub i sub j`	a_{i_j}
`a sub i sub j sub k`	$a_{i_{j_k}}$
`a sup i sup j`	a^{i^j}
`a sup i sup j sup k`	$a^{i^{j^k}}$
`a sup i sub j`	a^{i_j}
`a sub i sup j`	a_i^j
`a sub {i sup j}`	a_{i^j}

Operator `sub` has a higher precedence than operator `sup`. Notice that in the case of the second last `eqn` expression, the superscript is placed on top of the subscript; a subscript followed by a superscript is treated as a special case because it is a common mathematical occurrence.

5. Fractions

Fractions are specified with the operator `over`:

numerator `over` *denominator*

For example, the fractions

$$\frac{du}{dx} = \frac{du/dy}{dx/dy} \qquad \frac{du}{dx} = \frac{\frac{du}{dy}}{\frac{dx}{dy}}$$

were specified as

```
.EQ
du over dx ~=~ du/dy over dx/dy
~~~~~~~~~~
du over dx ~=~ {du over dy} over {dx over dy}
.EN
```

6. Square Roots

The square root symbol $\sqrt{\ }$ is specified with the `sqrt` operator; the square root of an expression *exp* is specified as

`sqrt` *exp*

which produces the equation

$$\sqrt{exp}$$

The square root operator ensures that the size of the square root symbol $\sqrt{\ }$ matches the size of its argument.

Some example equations containing the square root symbol are

$$i = \sqrt{-1} \qquad \frac{\sqrt{a+b}}{c-d} \qquad \sqrt{\sqrt{x} + \frac{1}{\sqrt{x}}}$$

These equations were specified as

```
.EQ
i ~= sqrt { - ~ 1 } ~~~~~~
sqrt a+b over c-d ~~~~~~
sqrt { sqrt x ~+~ 1 over sqrt x }
.EN
```

7. Associating Limits With Items

`eqn` provides facilities for specifying equations of the form

$$\mathop{\theta}\limits_{lower\text{-}limit}^{upper\text{-}limit}$$

where *lower-limit* and *upper-limit* are limits associated with the item θ. Such equations are specified using expressions of the form

θ `from` *lower-limit* `to` *upper-limit*

where θ can be any item. Specification of either the lower limit, "`from` *lower-limit*", or the upper limit, "`to` *upper-limit*", may be omitted. If a limit consists of several items, then curly braces should be used to combine them into one logical item.

Some items with which limits are often associated are

item denotation	item
`sum`	Σ
`int`	$\int$
`prod`	Π
`union`	$\cup$
`inter`	$\cap$
`oppE`	$\exists$
`oppA`	$\forall$
`lim`	lim
`max`	max
`min`	min

Here are some examples illustrating the use of limits:

1. Equation

$$\int_{x=a}^{x=b} f(x)\, dx$$

was specified as

```
int from {x = a} to {x = b} f(x) ~ dx
```

The use of curly braces could have been avoided by deleting the spaces in the limits to make them single items:

```
int from x=a to x=b f(x) ~ dx
```

2. Equation

$$\forall_{a \in S} a > 0$$

which has no upper limit, was specified as

```
oppA from {a member S} a~>~0
```

Deleting blanks in the limits to avoid the use of curly braces will not work here because `member` will then not be recognized as a distinct item.

3. The equation

$$\int_{\mathbf{R}} f(x, y)\, d\mathbf{A} = \lim_{n \to \infty} \sum_{p=1}^{n} f(x_p, y_p) \Delta_p$$

which has several items with limits was specified as

```
.EQ
int from {fat R} f(x, ^ y) ^ d {fat A} ~ = ~
    lim from {n -> inf}
    sum from p=1 to n f(x sub p , ^ y sub p )
         DELTA sub p
.EN
```

The `fat` operator makes its argument look bold by "fattening" it.

4. Finally, the equation [Knuth 1984] with several lower limits

$$\sum_{\substack{1 \leqslant i \leqslant p \\ 1 \leqslant j \leqslant q \\ 1 \leqslant k \leqslant r}} a_{ij}\, b_{jk}\, c_{ki}$$

was specified as

```
.EQ
{{sum from {1 <= i <= p}} from {1 <= j <= q}}
    from {1 <= k <= r} a sub ij ^ b sub jk
                                ^ c sub ki
.EN
```

Notice the use of curly braces to specify the multiple limits and the order in which the lower limits are specified.

8. Large Brackets for Grouping

Components of an equation are often grouped together by using the following pairs of symbols:

$$() \quad [] \quad \{\} \quad \| \quad \lfloor\rfloor \quad \lceil\rceil$$

If these grouping symbols are used in conjunction with the `left` and `right` operators, then their height is adjusted automatically to match the items enclosed by them.

Big grouping symbols are specified by using an expression of the form

`left` θ_1 *items-to-be-grouped* `right` θ_2

where θ_1 and θ_2 are the left and right grouping symbols. Big parentheses, curly braces, square brackets and bars are produced by using these characters with the `left` and `right` operators. Big versions of $\lfloor$ and $\rfloor$ are produced by using the name `floor` with the operators `left` and `right`, respectively. Similarly, big versions of the symbols $\lceil$ and $\rceil$ are produced by using the name `ceiling`.[34]

In the following example, the height of the grouping symbols $\lfloor$ and $\rfloor$ was automatically increased by the `left` and `right` operators to match the enclosed items:

$$\left\lfloor \theta \right\rfloor \quad \left\lfloor {\large\theta} \right\rfloor \quad \left\lfloor {\Large\theta} \right\rfloor$$

These equations were specified as

```
.EQ
left floor theta right floor ~~~~
left floor {size +2 theta } right floor ~~~~
left floor {size +5 theta } right floor
.EN
```

The expression "`size +`*n* *x*" specifies that *x* is to be printed after increasing the point size by *n* points.

Another example of an equation with grouping symbols is

$$\left(\frac{a^2 + \frac{b^2}{4} + \frac{ab}{2}}{a^2 + \frac{b^2}{4} - \frac{ab}{2}} \right) = \frac{\left(a + \frac{b}{2} \right)}{\left(a - \frac{b}{2} \right)}$$

34. Names `floor` and `ceiling` work only with the `left` and `right` grouping operators. In other contexts, the symbols $\lfloor$, $\rfloor$, $\lceil$ and $\rceil$ can be produced by using their `troff` names, which are `\(lf`, `\(rf`, `\(lc` and `\(rc`, respectively.

This equation was specified as

```
.EQ
left ( { a sup 2 ^+^ {b sup 2} over
    4 ^+^ ab over 2} over
  { a sup 2 ^+^ {b sup 2} over
    4 ^-^ ab over 2 } right ) ~=~
  { left ( a ^+^ b over 2 right ) } over
    { left ( a ^-^ b over 2 right ) }
.EN
```

It is not necessary to use matching left and right grouping symbols:

$$\left[\frac{a}{2} \cdots 0 \right)$$

This equation was specified as

```
left [ a over 2 ~...~ 0 right )
```

Every `right` operator must have a corresponding `left` operator. However, the reverse is not true; that is, a `left` operator does not have to have a matching `right` operator. To print an equation with a right grouping symbol that does not have a corresponding left grouping symbol, the `left` operator is used with a null item; this satisfies the requirement that every `right` operator must have a matching `left` operator.

As an example, consider the equation, in which there is no matching left grouping symbol:

$$\left. \frac{x+\sqrt{x}}{x^2-1} \right|_0^3$$

This equation was specified as

```
left "" { x + sqrt x } over
    { x sup 2  - 1 } right ¦ sub 0 sup 3
```

Arbitrary characters can be used with the grouping operators `left` and `right`; however, the results may not be very appealing. As an example, consider the use of "/" with the `left` operator in the `eqn` expression

```
{ a over b } left / { c over d }
```

which is printed as

$$\frac{a}{b} \Big/ \frac{c}{d}$$

9. `eqn` Definitions

`eqn` definitions are used for giving symbolic and/or shorthand names to a sequence of characters, called the *replacement text*. All future occurrences of the symbolic-name in `eqn` expressions are automatically replaced by the associated replacement text.

9.1 Strings (Parameterless Definitions)

Strings, which are parameterless definitions, have the form

`define` *symbolic-name* ***θ*** *replacement text* ***θ***

where *symbolic-name* is an arbitrary character sequence that does not contain item separators; this is the name associated with the replacement text enclosed within the delimiter ***θ***. Delimiter ***θ*** can be any character; however, it must not occur within the replacement text.

Here are some example `eqn` definitions, all of which use `%` as the separator:

```
.EQ
define lb %size +1 bold [ \|%
define rb %\| size +1 bold ]%
define lc %size +1 bold "{" \|%
define rc %\| size +1 bold "}"%
define alt %size +1 bold |%
define ra %size +2 bold ->%
define tab %\(rh%
define xy %lb x alt y rb%
define x1sq %sqrt {x sub 1}%
.EN
```

These definitions create the following correspondences:

name	symbol
`lb`	[
`rb`	]
`lc`	{
`rc`	}
`alt`	|
`ra`	→
`tab`	☛
`xy`	$[x \mid y]$
`x1sq`	$\sqrt{x_1}$

New definitions can use existing definitions. For example, `xy` is defined in terms of `lb`, `alt` and `rb`.

The `eqn` definition mechanism is convenient for specifying abbreviations and it facilitates document modifications. Changing a definition for some replacement text *rt*, is straightforward; in the absence of a definition for *rt*, it will be necessary to change all occurrences of *rt* in the document.

The `eqn` definition mechanism can be used to give new names to `eqn` operators; for example, the subscript and superscript operators `sub` and `sup` can be given the aliases `¦` and `**`, respectively, by using the definitions

```
.EQ
define ¦ %sub%
define ** %sup%
.EN
```

Example expressions using the subscript and superscript operator aliases are

```
e ** e ** e
a ¦ i ¦ j ¦ k
x ¦ i ** j
```

These expressions print the equations

$$e^{e^{e}} \qquad a_{i_{jk}} \qquad x_i^j$$

Recursive definitions are not allowed. As an example, suppose we want to define `R` as the character sequence that constructs the symbol **R**.[35] The definition of `R`

```
define R % bold size +1 {I back 25 R}%
```

is erroneous because it is recursive; note the presence of the letter `R` within the definition. The correct definition of `R`, which suppresses the recursive invocation by enclosing `R` in double quotes, is

```
define R % bold size +1 {I back 25 "R"}%
```

9.2 Macros (Parameterized Definitions)

`eqn` has been recently enchanced to provide a macro-definition facility. Macros, which are really parameterized definitions, have the form

`define` *macro-name* ***θ*** *macro-body (replacement text)* ***θ***

Items of the form `$1`, `$2` ... `$`*n* within the macro body denote the parameters.

Macros are invoked (called) with expressions of the form

macro-name(a_1, a_2, . . . , a_n)

where a_i is the ith argument. A macro call is replaced by the corresponding macro body in which the parameters have been replaced by the corresponding arguments. Missing arguments are replaced by the null string.

As an example, consider the macro definition:

```
define sumi %sum from {i = $1} to {i = $2} $3%
```

Invoking the macro `sumi` (twice) as

```
sumi(1, n, i) ~~~~~ sumi(1, n+1, (x sub i ))
```

produces

$$\sum_{i=1}^{i=n} i \qquad \sum_{i=1}^{i=n+1} (x_i)$$

35. The symbol **R** is printed by partially overstriking the letter I with the letter R. The character sequence "`bold size +1 { I back 25 R}`" constructs symbol **R** by instructing `eqn` to first print the letter I, then to back up 25 hundredths of an em, and then to print the letter R. Both I and R are printed in bold font using a point size equal to the current point size plus one. Explicit specification of the font, point size and motion in `eqn` expressions are discussed in later sections.

9.3 Specifying Different Definitions for `eqn` and `neqn`

If a document contains `eqn` definitions that are appropriate for `eqn` but not for `neqn`, then alternative definitions are provided for use with `neqn`. Suppose, for example, that we have defined `mult` as the multiplication symbol × and a proof-reading version of the document is to be produced with `neqn` (and `nroff`). `nroff` does not support the symbol ×. An acceptable replacement of × is *. Unfortunately, × is printed as "x" by `nroff`. Printing * in the proofreading version requires changing the document.

Manually changing a document to ensure appropriate definitions are used with `eqn` and `neqn` will be a tedious and error-prone process, especially if the number of definitions is large. Fortunately, this problem is solved elegantly by using two other forms of the `define` instruction: `tdefine`, which is interpreted by `eqn` but ignored by `neqn`, and `ndefine`, which is interpreted by `neqn` but ignored by `eqn`. These two forms of the `define` instruction allow two different definitions of the same symbol, one each for `eqn` and `neqn`, to be included in the same file.

As an example of the use of different definitions for `eqn` and `neqn`, consider the following two definitions of `mult`:

```
tdefine mult % "\(mu" %
ndefine mult % * %
```

With `eqn`, `mult` will be printed as ×; with `neqn`, it will be printed as *.

10. Aligning Equations

`eqn` provides a facility for lining up (aligning) equations at points specified by the user. Vertically aligned equations are specified as

.EQ
specification of equation$_1$ must contain the keyword `mark`
.EN
.EQ
specification of equation$_2$ must contain the keyword `lineup`
.EN
⋮
.EQ
specification of equation$_n$ must contain the keyword `lineup`
.EN

The keyword `mark` in the first equation specifies the *alignment point* for all the equations. The keyword `lineup` in subsequent equations indicates the vertical-alignment point. As an example, consider the equations

$$y + z = 4$$
$$10x + 15y = 40$$
$$x + 10y + z = 24$$

Each of these equations is aligned with respect to its first character (they are left justified). They would look more pleasing if they aligned with respect to the character "=":

$$\begin{aligned} y + z &= 4 \\ 10x + 15y &= 40 \\ x + 10y + z &= 24 \end{aligned}$$

These vertically-aligned equations were specified as

```
.EQ
y ^+^ z mark ~=~ 4
.EN
.EQ
10x ^+^ 15y lineup ~=~ 40
.EN
.EQ
x ^+^ 10y ^+^ z lineup ~=~ 24
.EN
```

11. Piles

`eqn` provides the `pile` operator for piling up components of an equation on top of one another. A pile is specified by using an expression of the form

`pile` [s] {i_1 `above` i_2 `above` ... `above` i_n}

where i_j ($1 \leqslant j \leqslant n$) are the components of the pile and s is a signed integer specifying (in hundredths of an em) how much the default separation between the pile items is to be increased or decreased.

The pile specification (without changing the default separation) produces the pile

$$\begin{matrix} i_1 \\ i_2 \\ \cdots \\ i_n \end{matrix}$$

As another example of a pile, consider the equation

$$max\,(x, y) = \begin{cases} x & \text{if } x \geqslant y \\ y & \text{if } y \geqslant x \end{cases}$$

which was specified as

```
.EQ
max(x, ^y) ~=~ left {
  pile {{x ~~ if ~ x >= y}
    above {y ~~ if ~ y >= x}}
.EN
```

Notice the use of the operator `left` to specify a grouping symbol—there is no matching `right` operator.

Piles can be placed adjacent to one another; for example, the three adjacent piles

$$\begin{matrix}1\\2\\3\\4\\5\end{matrix}\;\begin{matrix}a\\b\\c\end{matrix}\;\begin{matrix}x_1\\x_2\\x_3\\x_4\\x_5\end{matrix}$$

were specified as

```
.EQ
pile { 1 above 2 above 3 above 4 above 5} ~~
pile { a above b above c} ~~
pile { x sub 1 above x sub 2 above x sub 3
  above x sub 4 above x sub 5}
.EN
```

Notice that adjacent piles may have a different number of items or items of different sizes.

Piles can also be nested as illustrated by the following equation which contains a pile whose components are piles:

$$\begin{matrix}a\\b\\ \left[\begin{matrix}1\\2\\3\end{matrix}\right]\end{matrix}$$

These nested piles were specified as

```
.EQ
pile {
  pile { a above b }
  above
  left [ pile { 1 above 2 above 3 } right ]
}
.EN
```

The `pile` operator is a synonym for the `cpile` operator which produces a centered pile, that is, a pile whose elements are centered with respect to each other. Left- and right-adjusted piles can be specified by using the `lpile` and `rpile` operators, respectively.

Matrices can be constructed by using adjacent piles. However, there can be alignment problems if the piles are of different heights. Consequently, `eqn` provides a separate facility for specifying matrices.

12. Matrices

Matrices are specified using expressions of the form

```
matrix {
     ccol{a11 above a21 above ... above am1}
     ccol{a12 above a22 above ... above am2}
     ...
     ccol{a1n above a2n above ... above amn}
}
```

where a_{ij} $(1 \leqslant i \leqslant m, 1 \leqslant j \leqslant n)$ is the element in the ith row and j^{th} column of the matrix being specified.

As an example, consider the matrix

$$\begin{bmatrix} 1 & 3 & -2 \\ 1 & 4 & 1 \\ 1 & 4 & 2 \\ 2 & 7 & -3 \end{bmatrix}$$

which was specified as

```
.EQ
left [
matrix {
     ccol { 1 above 1 above 1 above 2 }
     ccol { 3 above 4 above 4 above 7 }
     ccol { -2 above 1 above 2 above -3 }
}
right ]
.EN
```

Each column of a matrix must have the same number of elements. If some elements of a matrix are not to be printed, then the null item can be used in their place, for example,

$$\left(\begin{matrix} 0 & -1 & & \\ 1 & 0 & & \\ & & \sqrt{3} & \\ & & & -\sqrt{3} \end{matrix} \right)$$

This matrix was specified as

```
.EQ
left (
matrix {
    ccol { 0 above 1 above "" above "" }
    ccol { - 1 above 0 above "" above "" }
    ccol { "" above "" above sqrt 3 above ""}
    ccol { "" above "" above "" above - sqrt 3}
}
right )
.EN
```

Keyword `ccol` specifies a centered column. Left- and right- adjusted columns can also be specified by using the keywords `lcol` and `rcol`, respectively.

13. Diacritics

A *diacritic* is a modifying mark placed near a character:

diacritic	**associating diacritic with item** x	**effect**
·	`x dot`	$\dot{x}$
··	`x dotdot`	$\ddot{x}$
^	`x hat`	$\hat{x}$
~	`x tilde`	$\tilde{x}$
→	`x vec`	$\vec{x}$
↔	`x dyad`	$\overleftrightarrow{x}$
‾ (above)	`x bar`	$\bar{x}$
_ (under)	`x under`	$\underline{x}$

The lines produced by `bar` and `under` are extended to an appropriate length; other marks are centered.

Some examples of diacritics are

$$\overline{x+y+z} \quad \underline{x+y+z} \quad \underline{\overline{x+y+z}} \quad \underline{\ddot{x}}$$

These equations were specified as

```
{x + y + z} bar ~~~
{x + y + z} under ~~~
{{x + y + z} bar} under ~~~
{x dotdot} under
```

14. Local Motions

The position where `eqn` prints its next item can be changed by using the *motion* operators `up`, `down`, `fwd` and `back`:

operation	effect
`up` *x item*	move *item* up by *x*
`down` *x item*	move *item* down by *x*
`fwd` *x item*	move *item* right by *x*
`back` *x item*	move *item* left by *x*

where *x* is the distance to be moved in hundredths of an *em*. These operators can be used to construct new symbols and fine tune an equation.

An example illustrating the use of motion operators is the definition of the new symbol **ℝ** that was given earlier:

```
define R % bold size +1 { I back 25 "R"}%
```

(The amount of backward motion used in constructing **ℝ** was determined by trial-and-error.)

Another example is the *n*th-root symbol in the equation

$$G = \sqrt[n]{a_1 a_2 a_3 \cdots a_n}$$

`eqn` does not provide a mechanism for specifying how *n* is to be placed next to the square root symbol; consequently, an *n*th-root symbol, if needed, must be explicitly constructed. The equation was specified as

```
G ~=~~ up 40 {"" sup n} back 78
  sqrt {a sub 1 a sub 2 a sub 3 ... a sub n}
```

15. Labeling Equations

`eqn` provides a simple mechanism for labeling equations: the equation label is supplied as a parameter to the `.EQ` instruction. As an example, consider the labeled equation

$$r_1, r_2 = \frac{-b \pm \sqrt{b^2 - 4ac}}{2a} \qquad 5.4a$$

This equation was specified as

```
.DS CB
.EQ 5.4a
r sub 1 , ~ r sub 2 ~=~
    {-b ~ +- ~ sqrt {b sup 2 ~ - ~ 4 a c }}
    over { 2 a }
.EN
.DE
```

By default equation labels are printed on the right side; labels can be printed on the left side by setting register `Eq` to 1. Equations specified within centered displays are centered; equations specified within uncentered displays are adjusted at the margin opposite the label.

16. `eqn` Environment

`eqn` interprets equation specifications in its "environment". This environment can be modified on a *local* or a *global* basis. Local environment modifications are temporary, affecting only one item. On the other hand, global environment modifications have a longer lasting effect; they persist from the point of modification to the end of the document or up to the next related modification.

16.1 Default Environment

1. Equations are printed using the point size that was in effect just before the `eqn` specification was encountered.

2. Digits, parentheses, brackets, mathematical operators, punctuation characters and the following mathematical words are printed in Roman font:

```
Im Re
and arc cos cosh det exp for if
lim ln log max min sin sinh tan tanh
```

   Algebraic variable names are printed in italics.

16.2 Local `eqn` Environment Changes

Local environment changes, that is, point size and font changes, affect only one item.

16.2.1 Point Size: The point size used for printing an item can be changed with the `size` operator. This operator has two forms:

`size` *n item*
`size` ±*n item*

The first form of the `size` operator prints the specified item using point size *n*. The second form prints the specified item using a point size equal to the current point size ± *n*.

As examples illustrating the use of the `size` operator, consider the equations

$$\scriptstyle\int\ \textstyle\int\ \int\ \large\int\ \Large\int$$

$$r = \sqrt{(x^2+y^2)}$$

These equations were specified as

```
.EQ
size -2 int  ~ size -1 int ~ int ~
size +1 int ~ size +2 int
.EN
.SP 2
.EQ
size 14 { r ~=~
  sqrt { ( x sup 2 + y sup 2 ) } }
.EN
```

Notice that the third $\int$ symbol is printed in the default font size (10 point type); the effect of the `size` operator lasts for only one item.

Here is another example of equations produced using the `size` operator:

$$1\frac{15}{16}\quad 1\tfrac{15}{16}\quad 1\tfrac{\scriptscriptstyle 15}{\scriptscriptstyle 16}$$

These fractions were specified as

```
.EQ
1 15 over 16 ~~~
1 size -2 {15 over 16} ~~~
1 size -4 {15 over 16}
.EN
```

16.2.2 Fonts: The default font used to print items can be changed by using the `font` operator which has the form

`font` *c item*

where *c* is a one- or two-character font name.

As an example of the `font` operator, consider the equation

$$r = \sqrt{(\mathbf{x}^2+\mathbf{y}^2)}$$

in which **x** and **y** are printed in bold. This equation was specified as

```
r ~=~ sqrt { ( font B x sup 2 + font B y sup 2 ) }
```

Operators `roman`, `italic` and `bold` can be used to specify the three common fonts:

keyword	equivalent to
`roman`	`font R`
`italic`	`font I`
`bold`	`font B`

Using the `bold` operator, the expression could have been specified as

```
r ~=~ sqrt { ( bold x sup 2 +  bold y sup 2 ) }
```

An alternative way of printing bold characters is to use the operator `fat`, which "fattens" or "widens" its argument by overstriking. Operator `fat` can be used to produce bold (fat) versions of characters that are not available in the bold font. The `fat` operator can be used to approximate bold versions of any font.

Here are some examples of fattened items along with the normal (unfattened) versions:

$\boldsymbol{y+x}$ $y+x$ $\boldsymbol{\cup}$ $\cup$ ***typesetting*** *typesetting* **`x+y`** `x+y`

These items were specified as

```
fat {y+x} ~~ y+x ~~~~
fat  union  ~~ union ~~~~
fat typesetting ~~ typesetting ~~~~
fat { font CW {x+y} } ~~ { font CW {x+y }}
```

16.3 Global `eqn` Environment Changes

Operators `gfont` and `gsize` specify a default global font and global point size, respectively, that are to be used throughout the document. The global font and point specification must be enclosed within an `.EQ/.EN` instruction pair:

```
.EQ
  ⋮
```
global font specification
global point size specification
```
  ⋮
.EN
```

16.3.1 Fonts: As mentioned earlier, digits, parentheses, brackets, punctuation characters and some mathematical words are printed in Roman. All other words are, by default, printed in italics or in the font specified with the global font operator `gfont` which has the form

`gfont` *c*

where *c* is a one- or two-character font name.

16.3.2 Point Sizes: The global font size is changed by using the `gsize` operator, which, like the local font size operator `size`, has two forms:

`gsize` *n*
`gsize` ±*n*

The first form changes the default font size to *n*; the second form increases or decreases the default font size by *n*.

17. Operator Precedence and Association

Associated with each `eqn` operator is a precedence. In an expression with two or more operators, the actions indicated by operators with higher precedence are performed first. `eqn` operators are listed below in order of increasing precedence (operators on the same line have the same precedence).

```
from to
over sqrt
sup sub
size font roman italic bold fat
up down back fwd
left right
dot dotdot hat tilde bar under vec dyad
```

Now suppose that an expression contains two adjacent (ignoring the intervening operands) operators with the same precedence. Which operator should to be acted upon first? To break such ties, the order in which the operators associate is defined. If the two adjacent operators associate to the left, then the left operator is given precedence; otherwise, the right operator is given precedence. (Operators of equal precedence associate in the same direction.) Most `eqn` operators associate to the right; operators that associate to the left are

```
over sqrt left right
```

Curly braces can be used to change the order in which `eqn` expressions are interpreted. For example, the expression

```
a over b over c
```

is equivalent to

```
{a over b} over c
```

because operator `over` associates to the right; this expression specifies the equation

$$\frac{\frac{a}{b}}{c}$$

To print the equation

$$\frac{a}{\frac{b}{c}}$$

you must use curly braces to change the order in which the two `over` operators are acted upon:

```
a over {b over c}
```

As another example, consider the expression

```
a over b sub c
```

This expression is equivalent to

```
a over {b sub c}
```

because operator `sub` has higher precedence than operator `over`.

18. Special Characters and Symbols

`eqn` provides denotation for the Greek characters and most of the commonly used mathematical symbols. Definitions of the other symbols are kept in the file `/usr/pub/eqnchar`.

18.1 Mathematical Symbols

character sequence	symbol	character sequence	symbol
`>=`	$\geqslant$	`approx`	$\approx$
`<=`	$\leqslant$	`nothing`	
`==`	$\equiv$	`cdot`	$\cdot$
`!=`	$\neq$	`times`	$\times$
`+-`	$\pm$	`del`	∇
`->`	$\rightarrow$	`grad`	∇
`<-`	$\leftarrow$	`...`	$\cdots$
`<<`	$\ll$	`,...,`	$,\ldots,$
`>>`	$\gg$	`sum`	$\sum$
`inf`	∞	`int`	$\int$
`partial`	∂	`prod`	$\prod$
`half`	½	`union`	$\cup$
`prime`	$'$	`inter`	$\cap$
`dollar`	$\$$		

The character sequence `nothing` is an alternative denotation for the null item `""`.

18.2 Greek Characters

character sequence (lower case)	symbol	character sequence (upper case)	symbol
alpha	α		
beta	β		
chi	χ		
delta	δ	DELTA	Δ
epsilon	ϵ		
eta	η		
gamma	γ	GAMMA	Γ
lambda	λ	LAMBDA	Λ
mu	μ		
nu	ν		
omega	ω	OMEGA	Ω
omicron	o		
phi	ϕ	PHI	Φ
pi	π	PI	Π
psi	ψ	PSI	Ψ
rho	ρ		
sigma	σ	SIGMA	Σ
tau	τ		
theta	θ	THETA	Θ
upsilon	υ	UPSILON	Υ
xi	ξ	XI	Ξ
zeta	ζ		

18.3 Special eqn Character Definitions

character sequence	symbol	character sequence	symbol
`ciplus`	⊕	`¦>`	≯
`citimes`	⊗	`ang`	∠
`wig`	~	`rang`	∟
`-wig`	≃	`3dot`	⋮
`>wig`	≳	`thf`	∴
`<wig`	≲	`quarter`	¼
`=wig`	≅	`3quarter`	¾
`star`	*	`degree`	°
`bigstar`	✱	`angstrom`	Å
`=dot`	≐	`square`	□
`orsign`	∨	`circle`	○
`andsign`	∧	`blot`	■
`=del`	≜	`bullet`	•
`oppA`	∀	`prop`	∝
`oppE`	∃	`empty`	∅
`==>`	≧	`member`	∈
`==<`	≦	`nomem`	∉
`¦¦`	‖	`cup`	∪
`langle`	⟨	`cap`	∩
`rangle`	⟩	`incl`	⊑
`hbar`	ℏ	`subset`	⊂
`ppd`	⊥	`supset`	⊃
`<->`	↔	`!subset`	⊆
`<=>`	⇔	`!supset`	⊇
`¦<`	≮		

Definitions of these characters are stored in the file `/usr/pub/eqnchar`. Prior to using these characters, their definitions must be included the document (see section 19.3).

19. `eqn` Interface With `tbl`, `pic` and `mm`

In this section, I will briefly discuss how `eqn` expressions are included in `tbl` and `pic` specifications. I will also discuss the interface of `eqn` with `mm` and how to generate captions for equations.

19.1 `eqn` Expressions in `tbl` and `pic`

In-line equations (but not displayed equations) can be specified as `tbl` entries and in `pic` figures.

19.2 Interface with `mm`

Equations specified using the `.EQ/.EN` instructions must be enclosed within an `mm` `.DS/.DE` display. However, when the `.EQ/.EN` instruction pair is used only for specifying definitions and environmental changes, then the pair should not be enclosed in an `mm` display; otherwise, the output will contain extra blank lines.

Text and other items associated with the equation can also be placed in the display to ensure that they are printed on the same page as the equation:

```
.DS parameters
Text (and other items) to be placed above the equation
.EQ
expression specifying an equation
.EN
Text (or other items) to be placed below the equation
.DE
```

Several equations can also be specified in one display:

```
.DS parameters
.EQ
expression specifying equation_1
.EN
.EQ
expression specifying equation_2
.EN
⋮
.EQ
expression specifying equation_n
.EN
.DE
```

19.2.1 Equation Captions with Automatic Numbering: mm also provides a facility for specifying automatically-numbered equation captions; these captions will be printed by the table-of-contents instruction `.TC` if register `Le` is set to 1 (default value of `Le` is 0). Automatically-numbered captions are printed with the equation-caption instruction `.EC` which has the form

`.EC` [*caption-string* [*modifier* [*modifier-control*]]]

where argument *caption-string* specifies the equation caption, and arguments *modifier* and *modifier-control* are used to modify the normal automatic numbering style:

a. if *modifier-control* is missing or has the value zero, then the *modifier* is used as a prefix for the equation number.

b. if *modifier-control* is equal to one, then the *modifier* is used as a suffix for the equation number.

c. if *modifier-control* is equal to two, then the *modifier* replaces the equation number.

For example, a `.EC` instruction of the form

`.EC` *caption-string*

will generate a caption of the form

Equation *n*. *caption-string*

where ***n*** is number of times the `.EC` instruction has been invoked.

Here are two examples of captioned equations:

$$C_{i,j} = \sum_{k=L}^{k=U} A_{i,k} * B_{k,j}$$

Equation 1. Generalized Matrix Product

$$I = \int_{i=a}^{i=b} f(x)\, dx$$

Equation 2. Integrating Between Limits *a* and *b*

The captions were specified using `.EC` instructions placed after the specifications of the two equations. Both specifications and the associated `.EC` instructions were placed inside display blocks.

19.3 Including Files Containing Equations

`eqn` specifications can be kept in separate files and included in the document by using the recently added `include` (synonym `copy`) instruction or the `.PS` instruction, which is a `pic` preprocessor instruction. Keeping `eqn` specifications in separate files allows equations to be formatted, printed and checked without processing the whole document.

The `include` instruction has the form

`include` "*file-name*"

and its effect is to include the contents of file *file-name*. Of course, the `include` statement must be enclosed within a `.EQ/.EN` instruction pair. For example, the instructions

```
.EQ
include "/usr/pub/eqnchar"
.EN
```

will include the contents of the definitions file `/usr/pub/eqnchar`. Any `.EQ/.EN` instructions present within the included file are ignored.

Alternatively, if your `eqn` preprocessor does not support the `include` instruction, then you can use the `pic` instruction `.PS` to include files. The document must be preprocessed by `pic` for the files to be included.

The `.PS` instruction has the form

`.PS` <*file-name*

and its effect, like that of the `eqn` *include* instruction, is to include the contents of file *file-name*. For example, the instruction

```
.PS </usr/pub/eqnchar
```

will include the contents of the definitions file `/usr/pub/eqnchar`.

20. eqn Restrictions

1. Braces “{” and “}”, tildes “~”, circumflexes “^” and double quotes “"” should not be used as `eqn` delimiters.

2. In older versions of `eqn`, operators `gfont` and `font` take only one-character font names as arguments.

3. `eqn` is tuned for Roman, italic and bold fonts; other fonts may not look as good.

21. Checking for Errors: `eqn` and `checkmm`

`eqn` can be used to check for equation specification errors prior to typesetting the document. To check for `eqn` errors, use the UNIX commands[36]

`eqn` *files* `>/dev/null`

or

`eqn` *files* `>temp`

Error messages, if any, are printed on the standard error output by both these commands. The first command discards the output of `eqn` and prints just the error messages. The second command does not discard the output of `eqn`; instead it stores the output in file `temp` for possible later examination by the user. The `checkmm` UNIX command also checks for `eqn` errors.

22. Recent Enhancements to `eqn`

The following list summarizes recent changes to `eqn`:

- A more general macro facility, which allows definition of macros with arguments, has been added.
- `eqn` now has a file inclusion capability, the `include` instruction.
- Multi-character font names are accepted now, for example,

  `gfont CW`

  If you have an old version of `eqn`, then you can use appropriate quoted `troff` escape sequences to change to fonts with multi-character names. For example, the equation

  $\sqrt{\texttt{total}}$ *(operand name in constant-width font)*

  can be specified as

  ```
  sqrt {"\f(CWtotal\fP"} ~
  (operand ~ name ~ in ~
  constant "-" width ~ "font")
  ```

  The word "`font`" in the `eqn` specification was quoted to prevent it from being interpreted as the `font` operator. Because `eqn` does not know

36. If the `.PS` instruction has been used for including files containing `eqn` expressions, then the document must be first processed by the `pic` preprocessor; otherwise, `eqn` errors in the included files will not be detected.

about font changes made with `troff` escape sequences, it is the user's responsibility to switch back to the previous font when appropriate.

- `eqn` now prints equations using the appropriate point size in footnotes. Previously, it printed equations using a default point size of 10 (unless a different point size had been explicitly specified with `size` or `gsize`) regardless of the point size in effect when the `eqn` expression was encountered.
- Explicitly specified font changes in a document are now preserved across in-line equations. Previously, `eqn`, at the end of an in-line equation. would incorrectly switch to the Roman font, instead of to the font in use before the in-line equation,
- `eqn` now examines the UNIX system environment variable `TYPESETTER` to determine the typesetter in use so that it can produce appropriate code.
- The vertical distance separating the elements of a pile or a matrix can be increased or decreased by the user; the amount of change, in hundredths of an em, is specified after the keywords `pile`, `cpile`, `lpile`, `rpile`, `ccol`, `lcol` and `rcol`.
- A conditional compilation statement has been added; this statement has the form

  `ifdef` *name X one or more lines of text to be included X*

  where *name* is a typesetter name such as `aps` or `202`, and *X* is any character. If *name* matches the name of the current typesetter (from the environmental variable `TYPESETTER`), then the text specified will be considered as input; otherwise it will be ignored.

23. Examples

In this section, I will give examples to illustrate the versatility and power of `eqn`. The first example shows that in-line `eqn` expressions can be embedded in an mm instruction argument. The second example illustrates piles and big grouping symbols. The next example illustrates the use of a definition, specification of big left grouping symbols without matching right grouping symbols, and use of the square root symbols and piles. The fourth example illustrates vertically-aligned equations and the use of the special `eqn` characters. The final example illustrates the specification of nested matrices.

23.1 `eqn` and `mm`

Equation specifications can be freely intermixed with text and `mm` instructions. In particular, in-line `eqn` expressions can be given as arguments (or part of arguments) of `mm` instructions. For example, the unnumbered heading

Circle Area: $\pi \; r^2$

was specified as

```
.HU "Circle Area: $pi~r sup 2$"
```

23.2 Example Illustrating Piles and Big Grouping Symbols

The following equation contains two piles that are surrounded by big parentheses:

$$\begin{pmatrix} n \\ k \end{pmatrix} = \frac{n!}{k!\,(n-k)!} = \begin{pmatrix} n \\ n-k \end{pmatrix}$$

This equation was specified as

```
.DS CB
.EQ
left ( pile { n above k} right )
     ~=~ n! over {k! ^ (n - k)!}
     ~=~ left ( pile { n above {n - k }} right )
.EN
.DE
```

23.3 Example Illustrating Definitions, Unmatched Left Grouping Symbols, Math Symbols and Piles

This equation contains large left braces that are not matched by corresponding right braces.

$$\int \frac{dx}{x^2\sqrt{ax+b}} = \left\{ \begin{array}{l} \frac{1}{\sqrt{b}} \ln \left(\frac{\sqrt{ax+b}-\sqrt{b}}{\sqrt{ax+b}+\sqrt{b}} \right. \\ \frac{2}{\sqrt{-b}} \tan^{-1} \sqrt{\frac{ax+b}{-b}} \end{array} \right.$$

The equation was specified as

```
.DS CB
.EQ
define sr %sqrt ax+b%
int dx over { x sup 2 sr } ~ =~
    left {
        pile {
            { 1 over sqrt b ^ ln ^
                left (
                    { { sr - sqrt b} over
                        { sr + sqrt b }}}
        above
            2 over sqrt -b tan sup -1
                sqrt { ax+b over -b }
        }
.EN
.DE
```

Note that the integration symbol is an `eqn` character, but the square root symbol is not an `eqn` character; it is built by the `sqrt` operator.

23.4 Example Illustrating Vertically-Aligned Equations and Special `eqn` Characters

Consider the following equation which contains `eqn` special characters:

$$\nabla^2\Phi = \frac{1}{h_1h_2h_3}\left[\frac{\partial}{\partial u_1}\left(\frac{h_2h_3}{h_1}\frac{\partial\Phi}{\partial u_1}\right)+\frac{\partial}{\partial u_2}\left(\frac{h_3h_1}{h_2}\frac{\partial\Phi}{\partial u_2}\right)\right.$$

$$\left.+\frac{\partial}{\partial u_3}\left(\frac{h_1h_2}{h_3}\frac{\partial\Phi}{\partial u_3}\right)\right]$$

This equation was specified as

```
.DS CB
.EQ
grad sup 2  PHI ~ = ~
  1 over { h sub 1 h sub 2 h sub 3}
  left [
  mark
  partial over {partial u sub 1}
    left ( {h sub 2 h sub 3} over {h sub 1}
    {partial PHI} over {partial u sub 1} right )
  + partial over {partial u sub 2}
    left ( {h sub 3 h sub 1} over {h sub 2}
    {partial PHI} over {partial u sub 2} right )
.EN
.SP 2
.EQ
  lineup
  left ""
  + partial over {partial u sub 3}
    left ( {h sub 1 h sub 2} over {h sub 3}
    {partial PHI} over {partial u sub 3} right )
  right ]
.EN
.DE
```

Notice that the matching right bracket for the first large left bracket of the first equation is in the second equation. `eqn` requires every large right bracket to have a matching large left one; that is, for every `right` operator there must be matching `left` operator. To satisfy this rule, I was forced to use the `left` operator with the null item at the beginning of the second equation.

23.5 Example Illustrating Nested Matrices

The following equation consists of a 2×2 matrix whose elements are matrices themselves; note that the nested matrices are of different dimensions:

$$\begin{pmatrix} \begin{bmatrix} 0 & 2 \\ 3 & 4 \end{bmatrix} & \begin{bmatrix} \alpha & \sqrt{-1} \\ \beta & 4 \end{bmatrix} \\ \begin{bmatrix} 7 \\ 8 \end{bmatrix} & (1 \quad 4) \end{pmatrix}$$

These nested matrices were specified as

```
.DS CB
.EQ
left (
matrix {
    ccol {
        left (
        matrix {
            ccol {0 above 3}
            ccol {2 above 4}
        }
        right )
    above
        left (
        matrix {
            ccol {7 above 8}
        }
        right )
    }
    ccol {
        left (
        matrix {
            ccol {alpha above beta}
            ccol {sqrt -1 above 4}
        }
        right )
    above
        {( 1 ~~ 4 )}
    }
}
right )
.EN
.DE
```

Note the use of indentation to clarify the presentation.

24. Exercises

1. Write `eqn` expressions to print the equations [Knuth 1984]

   i.
$$\sqrt{1+\sqrt{1+\sqrt{1+\sqrt{1+\sqrt{1+\sqrt{1+x}}}}}}$$

ii.

$$a_0 + \cfrac{a}{a_1 + \cfrac{1}{a_2 + \cfrac{1}{a_3 + \cfrac{1}{a_4}}}}$$

iii.

$$\left(\frac{\partial^2}{\partial x^2} + \frac{\partial^2}{\partial y^2} \right) | \psi(x+iy) |^2 = 0$$

iv.

$$\{b\ c\}^{\frac{n}{2}}$$

Hint: Remember that curly braces have a special meaning in `eqn`.

2. Could the equation

$$\left. \frac{x}{x^2-1} \right|_0^3$$

have been specified as

```
x over {x sup 2  - 1} right ¦ sub 0 sup 3
```

Justify your answer.

3. Write `eqn` expressions to produce the matrices

i.

$$\begin{pmatrix} i & & & \\ & -i & & \\ & & \sqrt{3} & \\ & & & -\sqrt{3} \end{pmatrix}$$

ii.

$$\begin{pmatrix} a_{11} & a_{12} & \cdots & a_{1n} \\ a_{21} & a_{22} & \cdots & a_{2n} \\ \vdots & \vdots & \vdots & \vdots \\ a_{m1} & a_{m2} & \cdots & a_{mn} \end{pmatrix} \begin{pmatrix} x_1 \\ x_2 \\ \vdots \\ x_n \end{pmatrix} = \begin{pmatrix} b_1 \\ b_2 \\ \vdots \\ b_n \end{pmatrix}$$

4. Write `eqn` expressions to print the equations

$$[a] \oplus [b] = [a+b]$$

$$[a] \circledcirc [b] = [a \bullet b]$$

$$\alpha \circ \alpha^{-1} = \alpha^{-1} \circ \alpha$$

Hint Construct the symbol ◉ by overstriking two characters.

Chapter 6

troff/nroff—The Formatters

The UNIX system provides two formatting tools that are very similar: troff and nroff [DWB 1984a; Ossanna 1977; Kernighan 1978, 1982b; Kernighan, Lesk and Ossanna 1978]. nroff is used for typewriter-quality output on terminals such as the DASI-450. In contrast, troff is used for print-quality output that may be produced on matrix printers, laser printers, phototypesetters and bitmap displays. The same input can be used for both nroff and troff; nroff just ignores the things it cannot do such as changing font size or printing in fonts other than the standard fonts available on the terminal.[37] Otherwise, its behavior is the same as that of troff. As mentioned earlier, I will primarily discuss troff.

troff is a low-level but very powerful formatting language; it provides facilities for defining macros, defining text and arithmetic variables, numerical computation and testing, and conditional branching [Kernighan 1978]. troff can be used to specify document characteristics such as font, point size, page size, vertical spacing and whether or not the text should be right adjusted. However, troff is quite hard to use, especially when specifying things such as page layout, equations, tables and figures:

> The great strength of troff is the flexibility of the basic language and its programmability—it can be made to do almost any formatting task. But the flexibility comes at a high price—troff is often astonishingly hard to use. It is fair to say that almost all of the UNIX document formatting software is designed to cover up some part of naked troff [Kernighan and Pike 1984].

Because it is hard to use troff directly, I will not discuss its facilities in detail. I will only summarize troff facilities that can be useful with the other document formatting tools. For complete details of troff, please see

37. If bold and italic fonts are not available, then nroff can sometimes simulate a bold font by overstriking and indicate a italic font by underlining.

the nroff/troff *User's Manual* [DWB 1984a; Ossanna 1977].

There are two kinds of troff formatting instructions: stand-alone and embedded. Stand-alone formatting instructions occupy one complete line in the raw document; they begin with a . (period) or an ' (acute accent). troff formatting instructions that can be embedded in text are called troff *escape* sequences; they begin with a \ (backslash).

1. Stand-Alone troff Instructions

troff instructions are of the form

.*xx arguments*

where *xx* is a two-character instruction name that normally consists of lower-case letters. Breaks caused by some of the troff instructions can be suppressed by using the character ' instead of the period. Here are the troff instructions that can be used to advantage with mm and other formatting tools.

1.1 Controlling Font and Character Size

instruction name	instruction format	initial value	argument absent	explanation and comments
point size	.ps *n* .ps ±*n*	10 points	use previous value	Set the character point size[38] to *n* or, if the second form is used, to the current point size ± *n*. If the requested point size is not available, then use the closest available point size. (.ps is ignored by nroff.)
space size	.ss *n*	12/36 ems	ignored	Set the size of the space character to *n*/36 ems. (.ss is ignored by nroff.)
switch font	.ft *f*	Roman	switch to previous font	Switch to font with a one- or two-character name *f*; the font name P specifies the previous font.
mount font	.fp *n f*			Mount font *f* at position *n* ($n \geqslant 0$).

38. The set of available point sizes is implementation dependent.

1.2 Page Control

instruction name	instruction format	initial value	argument absent	explanation and comments
page length	`.pl` *n* `.pl` ±*n*	11 inches	11 inches	Set the current page length to *n* or to the current length ± *n*. Note that the top and bottom margins are not provided automatically; they must be accounted for in the page length.
begin page	`.bp`			Skip to a new page.
page number	`.pn` *n* `.pn` ±*n*	1	ignored	Set the next page number to *n* or to the current page number ± *n*. This instruction must occur before skipping to the next page (pseudo-skipping for the first page). Register `%` contains the current page number.
page offset	`.po` *n* `.po` ±*n*	26/27 inches for `troff` (0 for `nroff`)	previous	Set the next page offset to *n* or to the current page offset ± *n*. Register `.o` contains the current page offset.
need vertical space	`.ne` *n*		1v	If the distance to the bottom of the page is less than *n*, then this instruction causes a skip to the next page.
mark current vertical position	`.mk` [*r*]	none	internal register used	Mark the current vertical position in the internal register, or in register *r*, if given.
return to marked vertical position	`.rt` `.rt` ±*n*	none	internal register used	Return (*upward* only) to the marked vertical position stored in the internal register or to top of the page ± *n*. If the vertical place was stored in register *r* (instead of the internal register), then the `.sp` instruction must be used, e.g., `.sp |\n`*r*`u`

1.3 Text Filling, Adjusting and Centering

instruction name	instruction format	initial value	argument absent	explanation and comments
break	`.br`			Skip to the next output line without adjusting the current output line. Text input lines that begin with a blank produce an effect similar to this instruction.
fill	`.fi`	fill mode		Fill output lines.
no fill	`.nf`	fill mode		Switch to no-fill mode; subsequent input lines are output without filling or adjusting.
adjust	`.ad` *c*	adjust both margins	ignore	Line adjustment is started provided the formatter is in fill mode; otherwise, line adjustment is deferred until the formatter is switched to fill mode. The nature of the adjustment depends upon the value of the parameter *c*: `l` Adjust left margin only. `r` Adjust right margin only. `c` Fill and center each output line (no margin adjustment). `b` or `n` Adjust both margins (default).
no adjust	`.na`	adjust		Turn off the line adjustment.
center	`.ce` *n*		$n = 1$	Center the next *n* input lines. A break occurs after each of the *n* input lines. If an input line is too long, then it will be left adjusted. Line length minus line indent is used as the basis for centering lines.

1.4 Vertical Spacing

instruction name	instruction format	initial value	argument absent	explanation and comments
vertical spacing	`.vs` *n*	12 points	go back to previous vertical spacing	Set the spacing between the base lines of successive output lines to *n*. This space must be large enough to accommodate the characters. Vertical spacing is usually set to two points plus the current point size.
line spacing	`.ls` *n*	1	go back to previous line spacing	Append *n*−1 (0 by default) blank lines to each output line (text line). For example, instruction `.ls 2` specifies double spacing.
space vertically	`.sp` *n*		one vertical space (one blank line)	Space vertically by *n*. A positive *n* implies downward spacing while a negative *n* implies upward spacing. The spacing distance is truncated appropriately if it exceeds the distance to the top or bottom end of the page. A blank text input line is equivalent to `.sp 1`. No spacing occurs if the no-space mode is on.
turn on no-space mode	`.ns`	spacing mode		In this mode, `.sp` and `.bp` instructions are ignored. The no-space mode is in effect when crossing a page boundary. It is turned off implicitly after a line has been output or explicitly by using the `.rs` instruction.
restore spacing	`.rs`	spacing		Restore spacing (turn off no-space mode)

1.5 Line Length and Indenting

instruction name	instruction format	initial value	argument absent	explanation and comments
line length	`.ll n` `.ll ±n`	6.5 inches	use previous line length	Line length is set to *n* or to the current length ± *n*. The line length includes the line indent but not the page offset. The physical width of a page is the upper limit for the sum of the line length and page offset values.
line indent	`.in n` `.in ±n`	0 inches	use previous line indent	Indent all subsequent output lines by *n* or the current line indent ± *n*.
temporary indent	`.ti n` `.ti ±n`		ignored	Indent only the next output line by *n* or by the current line indent ± *n*.

1.6 Macros

instruction name	instruction format	argument absent	explanation and comments
define or redefine a macro	`.de m`		Define or redefine a macro with the one- or two-character name *m*. The contents of the macro body begin on the next line and are terminated by a line beginning with "`..`". Macro bodies can contain calls to other macros. Macros can be parameterized with up to 9 parameters; macro parameters are referred to in the macro body as `\\$`*i* ($1 \leqslant i \leqslant 9$).
append to a macro	`.am m`		Append lines to the body of macro *m*; the lines to be appended start on the following line and are terminated by a line beginning with "`..`".
remove macro	`.rm m`	ignored	Remove macro named *m*.

Macro calls have the format

.m arguments

where *m* is the name of the macro; arguments are separated by spaces and they must be enclosed within double quotes if they contain embedded blanks. If the arguments do not fit on one line, then they can be continued on the next line by terminating the current line with a backslash.

1.7 Strings

instruction name	instruction format	argument absent	explanation and comments
define a string	`.ds` *s str*	ignored	Define a string with one- or two-character name *s* and associate the value *str* with it. If *str* has leading blanks, then it must begin with " which is discarded (a matching " at the end of the string *should not* be used).
append to a string	`.as` *s str*	ignored	Append *str* to the definition of the string named *s*.
remove string	`.rm` *s*	ignored	Remove the string named *s*.

A one-character string with the name *x* is referenced as `\*`*x* and a two-character string with the name *xx* is referenced as `\*(`*xx*.

1.8 Number Registers

instruction name	instruction format	initial value	explanation and comments
define and set number register	`.nr` *r n* [*m*] `.nr` *r* ±*n* [*m*]		The first instruction defines a register *r* (one- or two-character name) and sets its to *n*; the second instruction changes, by *n*, the value of an existing register; both instructions associate the auto-increment *m* (default value is 1) with the register.
assign format to register	`.af` *r f*	arabic	Assign format *f* to register *r*; available formats are **format** **numbering sequence** `1` 0, 1, 2, 3, 4, 5, ... `i` 0, i, ii, iii, iv, v, ... `I` 0, I, II, III, IV, V, ... `a` 0, a, b, ..., z, aa, ..., az, aaa, ... `A` 0, A, B, ..., Z, AA, ..., AZ, AAA, ...
remove register	`.rr` *r*		remove register *r*

Number registers can be accessed and updated in a variety of ways:

register name	escape sequence	initial contents of register	auto-increment size	final contents of register	value yielded
x *xx*	`\n`*x* `\n(`*xx*	*i*			*i*
x *xx*	`\n+`*x* `\n+(`*xx*	*i*	*j*	*i*+*j*	*i*+*j*
x *xx*	`\n-`*x* `\n-(`*xx*	*i*	*j*	*i*−*j*	*i*−*j*

1.9 Tabs

instruction name	instruction format	initial value	argument absent	explanation and comments
set tabs	`.ta` x_1 x_2 ... x_n	0.5 inches (8 characters for `nroff`)	remove tab settings	Set tabs at positions x_1 x_2 ... x_n; if an x_i is preceded by a +, then it specifies tab stop at the last tab stop position + x_i.

1.10 Translating Input Characters

instruction name	instruction format	explanation and comments
translate characters	`.tr` *abcd...*	Translate *a* to *b*, *c* to *d* and so on; if an odd number of characters is given, then the last character is translated to a blank.

1.11 Title

instruction name	instruction format	initial value	argument absent	explanation and comments
title	`.tl` *'l'c'r'*			Arguments *l*, *c* and *r* are left adjusted, centered and right adjusted; this instruction is also used to print a right-adjusted string or a line with left-adjusted and right-adjusted components.
title length	`.lt` *n* `.lt` ±*n*	6.5 inches	use previous title length	Sets title length to *n* or to the current title length ±*n*

1.12 Hyphenation

instruction name	instruction format	initial value	argument absent	explanation and comments
turn off hyphenation	.nh			Turn off hyphenation
turn on hyphenation	.hy *n*		on (*n* assumed to be 1)	$n = 0$ Turn off hyphenation. $n = 1$ Turn on automatic hyphenation. $n = 2$ Turn on automatic hyphenation but do not hyphenate the last line on a page. $n = 4$ Turn on automatic hyphenation but do not split the last two characters of a word. $n = 8$ Turn on automatic hyphenation but do not split the first two characters of a word. $n = 14$ Combination of $n = 2$, 4 and 8.
hyphenation character specification	.hc *c*	\%	\%	Set the hyphenation-indicator character to *c*; this character, which does not appear in the final output, is used for specifying hyphenation points explicitly.

1.13 Conditional Input

In the following table, *anything* denotes a single input line or multiple input lines (where an input line is a line of text, a macro call or a `troff` instruction). Multiple input lines must be enclosed within the character pairs `\{` and `\}`, that is, use `\{`*anything*`\}`.

instruction name	instruction format	explanation and comments
if-condition	`.if` *c anything* `.if !`*c anything*	*c* is one of the four built-in conditions described below. The first form is used to accept input *anything* if condition *c* is true while the second form is used to accept the input if *c* is false. The four built-in conditions are **condition** — **meaning** `o` — current page number is odd. `e` — current page number is even. `t` — formatter is `troff`. `n` — formatter is `nroff`.
if-numeric-comparison	`.if` *n anything* `.if !`*n anything*	The first form is used to accept input *anything* if expression *n* is greater than 0; the second form is used to accept input if *n* is less than or equal to 0.
if-string-comparison	`.if` *'$string_1$'$string_2$' anything* `.if !`*'$string_1$'$string_2$' anything*	The first form is used to accept *anything* if $string_1$ and $string_2$ are identical; the second form is used to accept *anything* if the two strings are not identical.
if-else-branch	`.ie` *e* $anything_1$ `.el` $anything_2$	*e* is a built-in condition, numeric expression or string comparison as described above. Input $anything_1$ is accepted if *e* is true; otherwise $anything_2$ is accepted. (A `.el` instruction must follow a `.ie` instruction.)

1.14 Reading Standard Input, File Inclusion and Input Termination

instruction name	instruction format	argument absent	explanation and comments
read from standard input	`.rd` *prompt*	*bel* character is used as the default prompt	Read input until two blank lines are found; if the standard input is a keyboard then the *prompt* is written to the user's terminal.
write to standard error output	`.tm` *string*	blank line	Write *string* on the standard error output.
terminate input	`.ex`		Text processing is terminated as if all the input had finished.
include a file	`.so` *f*		Include file *f*; the `.so` instruction can be nested.
next input file	`.nx` *f*		Consider the current input file to have ended and use *f* as the next input file.
execute a UNIX system command	`.sy` *cmd args*		The command "*cmd args*" is executed.

Instructions `.rd` and `.nx` can be used to prepare multiple copies of a form letter. The text (data) read in using the `.rd` instruction is stored in a file (data file) which is used as standard input. The file containing the form letter reinvokes itself, for the next copy of the letter, by using the `.nx` instruction. The re-invocation process is eventually terminated by means of `.ex` instruction in the data file.

2. Escape Sequences for Characters, Indicators and Functions

escape sequence	meaning/explanation
`\\`	Backslash character \; the first \ suppresses or delays interpretation of the second backslash; generally used to suppress or delay the interpretation of escape sequences in macro definitions and invocations.
`\e`	Printable version of the current escape character (backslash by default).
`\'`	Acute accent ´; equivalent to `\(aa`.
`` \` ``	Grave accent `; equivalent to `\(ga`.
`\-`	Minus sign in the current font.
`\.`	Period (dot).
\ƀ	An unpaddable space (symbol ƀ indicates a space).
`\0`	Space whose width is equal to the width of a digit (all digits are of the same width).
|	Narrow space whose width is 1/6 em (zero width in `nroff`).
`\^`	Half narrow space whose width is 1/12 em (zero width in `nroff`).
`\&`	Non-printing zero-width character; the special interpretation of the control characters . and ' at the beginning of a line can be suppressed by prefixing them with `\&`.
`\"`	Beginning of comment (up to the end of the line).
`\$`*n*	Value of the nth ($1 \leqslant n \leqslant 9$) argument to a macro; the argument must be specified as `\\$`*n* in the macro definition to ensure that it is interpreted as `\$`*n*.
`\%`	Hyphenation-indication character used in words to specify hyphenation points explicitly; it does not appear in the output.
`\(`*xx*	Predefined character named *xx*.
`\*`*x* `\*(`*xx*	Value of a string with the one-character name *x* or two-character name *xx*.

escape sequence	meaning/explanation
\d	½ em downward vertical motion (½ line in nroff).
\f*x* \f(*xx*	Switch to font with the one-character name *x* or the two-character name *xx*.
\h'*n*'	Move horizontally to the right by *n*; the motion is to the left if *n* is negative.
\k*x*	Mark horizontal input place in register *x*
\l'*nc*'	Draw a horizontal line of length *n* using character *c*; if *n* is negative, then a backward horizontal motion of length *n* is made before drawing the line. If *c* is not specified then the underscore character is used to draw the line. In case of ambiguity, *c* may be separated from *n* by interposing the non-printing character \& between them; e.g., the sequence \l'15\&0' will print a 15n line of 0s.
\L'*nc*'	Draw a vertical line of length *n* using character *c*; if *n* is positive, then the line is drawn downwards; otherwise, it is drawn upwards. If *c* is not specified then the box rule character | (denoted as \(br) is used to draw the line. In case of ambiguity, *c* may be separated from *n* by interposing the non-printing character \& between them.
\D'l *x* *y*'	Draw a line from the current position to a point offset by (*x*, *y*).
\D'c *d*'	Draw a circle with diameter *d* with its left side at current position.
\D'e *d1* *d2*'	Draw an ellipse with diameters *d1* and *d2* with its left side at current position.
\D'a *x1* *y1* *x2* *y2*'	Draw an arc from current position to (*x1*+*x2*, *y1*+*y2*) with its center at (*x1*, *y1*) from current position.
\D'~ *x1* *y1* *x2* *y2* ...'	Draw a B-spline from current position by (*x1*, *y1*), then by (*x2*, *y2*), and so on.

escape sequence	meaning/explanation
\H'*n*'	Character height is set to *n* points independent of width (the .ps instruction and \s escape sequence set both height and width). If the height specification is of the form ±*n*, then the character height is set to current character height ± *n*.
\S'*n*'	Output is slanted by *n* degrees (*n* can be positive or negative).
\n*x* \n(*xx*	Value of a number register with the one-character name *x* or the two-character name *xx*.
\o'*string*'	Characters of *string* are overprinted with their centers aligned; the maximum length of *string* is 9 printable characters.
\r	1 em upward vertical motion (1 line in nroff).
\s0	Switch back to the previous point size.
\s*d* \s±*d* \s(*dd* \s(±*dd*	Switch to point size *d* or *dd*, or change current point size by ±*d* or ±*dd* (*d* must be a single digit). If the specified point size is not available, then switch to the closest available point size.
\u	½ em upward vertical motion (½ line in nroff).
\v'*n*'	Move down vertically by *n*; the motion is upward if *n* is negative.
\w'*string*'	Width of *string*.
\n̸	The new-line (carriage return) is to be ignored (symbol n̸ indicates a carriage return). This escape sequence allows the continuation of a logical line across input lines.
\{	Begin conditional input.
\}	End conditional input.

3. Naming Conventions for Non-ASCII Characters

Mathematical and Other Characters

char.	denotation	name	char.	denotation	name
+	`\(pl`	math plus	⊆	`\(ib`	improper subset
−	`\(mi`	math minus	⊇	`\(ip`	improper superset
=	`\(eq`	math equals	∞	`\(if`	infinity
∗	`\(**`	math star	∂	`\(pd`	partial derivative
§	`\(sc`	section	∇	`\(gr`	gradient
´	`\'` or `\(aa`	acute accent	¬	`\(no`	not
`	`` \` `` or `\(ga`	grave accent	∫	`\(is`	integral sign
_	_ or `\(ul`	underrule	∝	`\(pt`	proportional to
/	`\(sl` or `/`	slash	∅	`\(es`	empty set
√	`\(sr`	square root	∈	`\(mo`	member of
‾	`\(rn`	root extender	$\vert$	`\(br` or ¦	box vertical rule
⩾	`\(>=`	⩾	‡	`\(dd`	double dagger
⩽	`\(<=`	⩽	☛	`\(rh`	right hand
≡	`\(==`	equivalence	☚	`\(lh`	left hand
≃	`\(~=`	approx =	$\vert$	`\(or`	or
~	`\(ap`	approximates	○	`\(ci`	circle
≠	`\(!=`	not equal	⎧	`\(lt`	left top of big { and (
→	`\(->`	right arrow	⎩	`\(lb`	left bottom of big { and (
←	`\(<-`	left arrow	⎫	`\(rt`	right top of big } and)
↑	`\(ua`	up arrow	⎭	`\(rb`	right bottom of big } and)
↓	`\(da`	down arrow	⎨	`\(lk`	left center of big {
×	`\(mu`	multiply	⎬	`\(rk`	right center of big }
÷	`\(di`	divide	⎪	`\(bv`	bold vertical for center of big [,], (and)
±	`\(+-`	plus-minus	⌊	`\(lf`	left floor—bottom of [
∪	`\(cu`	cup (union)	⌋	`\(rf`	right floor—bottom of]
∩	`\(ca`	intersection	⌈	`\(lc`	left ceiling—top of [
⊂	`\(sb`	subset of	⌉	`\(rc`	right ceiling—top of]
⊃	`\(sp`	superset of			

Greek Characters

lower case			upper case		
character	denotation	name	character	denotation	name
α	\(*a	alpha	Α	\(*A	Alpha
β	\(*b	beta	Β	\(*B	Beta
γ	\(*g	gamma	Γ	\(*G	Gamma
δ	\(*d	delta	Δ	\(*D	Delta
ϵ	\(*e	epsilon	Ε	\(*E	Epsilon
ζ	\(*z	zeta	Ζ	\(*Z	Zeta
η	\(*y	eta	Η	\(*Y	Eta
θ	\(*h	theta	Θ	\(*H	Theta
ι	\(*i	iota	Ι	\(*I	Iota
κ	\(*k	kappa	Κ	\(*K	Kappa
λ	\(*l	lambda	Λ	\(*L	Lambda
μ	\(*m	mu	Μ	\(*M	Mu
ν	\(*n	nu	Ν	\(*N	Nu
ξ	\(*c	xi	Ξ	\(*C	Xi
ο	\(*o	omicron	Ο	\(*O	Omicron
π	\(*p	pi	Π	\(*P	Pi
ρ	\(*r	rho	Ρ	\(*R	Rho
σ	\(*s	sigma	Σ	\(*S	Sigma
ς	\(ts	terminal sigma			
τ	\(*t	tau	Τ	\(*T	Tau
υ	\(*u	upsilon	Υ	\(*U	Upsilon
ϕ	\(*f	phi	Φ	\(*F	Phi
χ	\(*x	chi	Χ	\(*X	Chi
ψ	\(*q	psi	Ψ	\(*Q	Psi
ω	\(*w	omega	Ω	\(*W	Omega

Non-ASCII Characters and *minus* on the Standard Fonts

character	denotation	name	character	denotation	name
‘	\`	open quote	¾	\(34	¾
’	´	close quote	fi	\(fi	fi
“	\`\`	open double quotes	fl	\(fl	fl
”	´´	close double quotes	ff	\(ff	ff
—	\(em	3/4 em dash	ffi	\(Fi	ffi
-	- or \(hy	hyphen	ffl	\(Fl	ffl
−	\-	minus	°	\(de	degree
●	\(bu	bullet	†	\(dg	dagger
□	\(sq	square	′	\(fm	footmark
_	\(ru	rule	¢	\(ct	cent sign
¼	\(14	1/4	®	\(rg	registered
½	\(12	1/2	©	\(co	copyright

4. Recent Changes to troff

troff has been recently extended to provide additional facilities, some of which are summarized in the following list:

1.
   - The new escape sequence \s(*dd*, where *d* is a single digit, can be used to change to point size *dd*; with the existing escape sequence \s*n*, the specified point size *n* cannot be greater than 36.
   - The new escape sequence \s(±*dd* can be used to change the point size by ±*dd*; with the escape sequence \s±*n*, *n* has to be a single digit.
2. troff examines the UNIX environment variable TYPESETTER to determine the type of typesetter to be used.

Chapter 7

WRITER'S WORKBENCH Software

The WRITER'S WORKBENCH software [Cherry 1981; WRITER'S WORKBENCH 1982; Macdonald 1982] is a set of tools (programs) that eliminates some of the tedious aspects of writing. These tools automate the mechanical parts of copy editing and proofreading; they provide the user with information about potential spelling mistakes, punctuation mistakes, poor word usage and writing quality.

In this chapter, I will give an overview of the WRITER'S WORKBENCH software[39] After the overview of the WRITER'S WORKBENCH software and a discussion of its components, I will show some sample document analysis that was produced by the WRITER'S WORKBENCH software.

1. Overview of the WRITER'S WORKBENCH Software

The UNIX System command `wwb` invokes all of the WRITER'S WORKBENCH tools, that is,

- `spellwwb` (checks for spelling errors),
- `punct` (checks for punctuation mistakes),
- `splitinf` (checks for split infinitives),
- `double` (checks for double words),
- `diction` (checks for poorly written phrases) and
- `style` (provides information about the writing style).

In addition to WRITER'S WORKBENCH tools, the UNIX system has other tools that can be invaluable to the writer; for example, `grope` is an online-interactive alternative to a dictionary for looking up the spelling of a misspelled word.

39. The reader interested in details of the WRITER'S WORKBENCH software should read [Cherry 1981; Frase 1983; Gingrich 1983; Macdonald 1982, 1983; WRITER'S WORKBENCH 1982].

The WRITER'S WORKBENCH software is organized as follows:

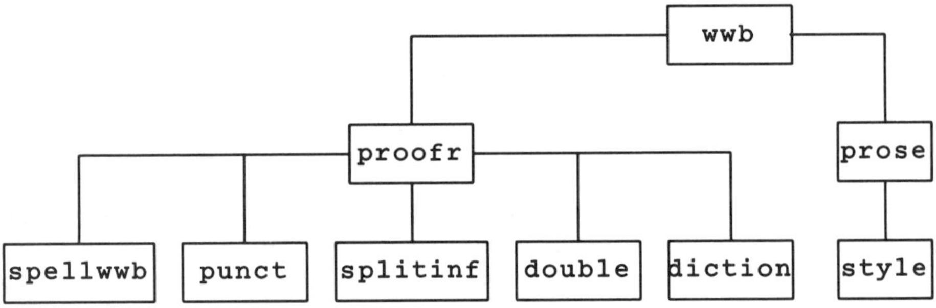

Organization of Writer's Workbench Tools

The UNIX command `wwb` is used to analyze a document with the WRITER'S WORKBENCH tools; this command has the form

`wwb` *document-files*

where *document-files* are files containing the documents to be analyzed. `wwb` writes the document analysis on the standard output.

The `wwb` command runs tools `proofr` and `prose`. `proofr` proofreads the document checking for spelling and punctuation errors, consecutive occurrences of words, wordy or misused phrases, and split infinitives. `prose` describes the writing style of a document, namely, readability and sentence characteristics, and suggests improvements.

The `wwb` command automatically invokes all of the WRITER'S WORKBENCH tools. If users do not want a complete analysis of a document, then they have the option of invoking individual components that make up the WRITER'S WORKBENCH software: `proofr`, `spellwwb`, `punct`, `splitinf`, `double`, `diction`, `style` and `prose`.

The analysis produced by `wwb` consists of suggestions to the writer. The writer, who is the final judge, is free to use some or all of the suggestions or to discard them.

In the following sections, I will describe the WRITER'S WORKBENCH components individually.

2. `proofr`

Program `proofr` runs the `wwb` component programs `spellwwb`, `punct`, `splitinf`, `double` and `diction` on the specified document.

2.1 `spell`, `spellwwb` and `grope`

The `spell` program is a standard UNIX system program that looks up each word of a document in a dictionary; words not found in the dictionary are listed as potential spelling mistakes. Names of persons, esoteric technical words and acronyms are flagged as errors because `spell` has no way of knowing that these words are spelled correctly. As far as `spell` is concerned, all words not in the dictionary are spelling mistakes.

The WRITER'S WORKBENCH program `spellwwb` remedies the above problem by examining, in addition to the dictionary, a user-supplied list of words.[40] This list can be built by the user with the help of the program `spelladd`.

`grope` is an online and interactive alternative to a dictionary for looking up the spelling of a misspelled word. It is used to find words that are close to the misspelled word. `grope` is not one of the `wwb` tools but it is available on many UNIX systems.

2.2 `punct`

Program `punct` identifies straightforward punctuation mistakes such as unbalanced parentheses and quotes. It prints the line with the error along with a corrected version of the line. If `punct` is used by itself, then it also stores the corrected version of the original document in file `pu.`*docname* where *docname* is the name of the file containing the document. .

2.3 `splitinf`

Split infinitives in a document can be located by means of `splitinf`.

An *infinitive* is a verb form that contains the word "to",[41] for example,

I told him to go.

A *split infinitive* is an infinitive with a word or phrase modifying the "to" that is placed between the "to" part of an infinitive and the rest of the infinitive, for example,

I told him to quickly go.

---

40. Newer versions of `spell` provide a similar capability.

41. To be more precise. an infinitive is a word form normally identical in English with the first person singular that performs some functions of a noun while at the same time it displays some characteristics of a verb; the infinitive is usually used with the word "to" [Webster's Dictionary 1977].

Although split infinitives are not grammatically incorrect, it is often better to not split [sic] the infinitive. For example, the above sentence can be improved by not splitting the infinitive:

I told him to go quickly.

2.4 `double`

A common mistake when editing text on a computer is to enter two identical words in succession. Such pairs of words can be located using the program `double`. For example, `double` will locate the two pairs of double words in the following two lines:

```
a sprinkle of of rain or
or a flurry of snow
```

2.5 `diction`

The `diction` program matches phrases in a document with those in its list of poorly written phrases. It prints the sentences containing poorly written phrases with the phrases in question identified clearly. Program `wwb` also uses another tool (`worduse`) to suggest alternative phrases to the user.

Some examples of the phrases that `diction` will flag as poor, along with alternatives suggested by `worduse`, are

poor phrase	**alternative phrase/word**
in accordance with your request	as you requested
a great deal of	much
a large number of	many
at the present time	currently, now

3. `prose`

Program `prose` takes the tabular information produced by `style` and describes it in prose. `wwb` prints the output of both `style` and `prose`.

3.1 `style`

`style` analyzes a document and prints a summary of information such as readability indices, sentence length and word use. This information can be used to improve document style. Readability indices are low for documents with short sentences and short words; they are high for documents with long sentences and multisyllabic words [Cherry 1981]. If a document is very technical, then it may be a good idea to make its readability index moderately low so that a reader can concentrate on the technical content instead of being distracted by long sentences and specialized vocabulary.

4. Example

To illustrate the output produced by `wwb`, I took some text from the raw version of a book on Ada I wrote [Gehani 1983] and analyzed it using `wwb`. Here is a partial listing of the raw text:

```
.H 1 "The Development of Ada"
The high level programming language Ada
is named in honor of Augusta Ada Byron,
the Countess of Lovelace
and the daughter of the English poet Lord Byron.
She was the assistant, associate and
supporter of Charles Babbage, the mathematician
and inventor of a calculating machine called the
Analytical Engine.
With the help of Babbage she wrote a nearly
complete program for the Analytical Engine to
compute the Bernoulli numbers circa 1830 [HUS80].
Because of this effort, the Countess may be said
to have been the world's first computer
programmer.
.P
To dispel exaggerated ideas about the powers of
the Analytical Engine, e.g., that the Analytical
Engine could think and feel, Ada wrote the
following assessment of its capabilities [MOO77]:
.DS CB
\s-1The Analytical Engine has no pretensions whatever
to \fIoriginate\fR anything. It can do whatever
\fIwe know how to order it to perform\fR. It can
\fIfollow\fR analyses; but it has no power of
anticipating any analytical relations or truths.
Its province is to assist us in making \fIavailable\fR
what we are already acquainted with.\s+1
.DE
.P
This assessment ...
```

The `wwb` program should be run only on raw documents because the `wwb` components rely on the formatting commands for some information; otherwise `wwb` may produce erroneous information.

The above text, which was stored in file **`EXAMPLE`**, was analyzed by the WRITER'S WORKBENCH tools using the command

```
wwb EXAMPLE
```

The output produced by `wwb` is[42]

```
******************** SPELLING ********************

Possible spelling errors in EXAMPLE are:

DoD            MCC79          Strawman
FIS78          MOO77          WAS80
HUS80          Steelman       Woodenman
Ironman

If any of these words are spelled correctly, later type

        spelladd word1 word2 ... wordn

to have them added to your spelldict file.

******************* PUNCTUATION *******************

The punctuation in EXAMPLE is first described.

0 double quotes and 0 single quotes
4 apostrophes
3 left parentheses and 3 right ones

The program next prints any sentence that it thinks is incorrectly punctuated and
follows it by its correction.

No errors found in EXAMPLE

******************* DOUBLE WORDS ******************

For file EXAMPLE:

No double words found
```

42. The `wwb` output format was changed slightly for presentation reasons.

******************* **WORD CHOICE** *******************

Sentences with possibly wordy or misused phrases are listed next,
followed by suggested revisions.

For file `EXAMPLE`

beginning line 23 `EXAMPLE`
It can do whatever \fIwe know how to order it to *[perform]*\fR.

beginning line 35 `EXAMPLE`
Indeed the Countess' statement is still quoted in modern debates on *[the nature]*
and scope of artificial intelligence [MCC79].

beginning line 37 `EXAMPLE`
Ada, the language *[which]* bears the Countess' name, was designed at the initiative
and under the auspices of the United States Department of Defense (DoD).

beginning line 42 `EXAMPLE`
DoD studies in the early and middle 1970s *[indicate]*d that enormous savings
in software costs (about $24 billion between 1983 and 1999)
might be achieved if the DoD used one common programming language for all
its applications instead of the over 450 programming languages and incompatible
dialects used by its programmers.

beginning line 56 `EXAMPLE`
Starting with Strawman (a jocular name), these requirements were progressively
refined *[by means]* of wide and public consultation, both domestic and
international.

file `EXAMPLE`: number of lines 67 number of phrases found 5

Please wait for the substitution phrases

------------------ **Table of Substitutions** -------------------

PHRASE SUBSTITUTION

by means: use "with, by, through" for " by means of"
indicate: use " indicate" for " give an indication of"

indicate: use "show, suggest" for " indicate"
perform: use "do" for " perform"
perform: use "measure, etc." for " perform a/the measurement, etc."
the nature: use "OMIT" for " the nature"
which: use ""that" when clause is restrictive" for " which"
which: use "of which" for " of that"
which: use "when" for " at which time"

----

* Not all the revisions will be appropriate for your document.
* When there is more than one suggestion for just one bracketed word, you will have to choose the case that fits your use.
* Capitalized words are instructions, not suggestions.
* To find out more about each phrase, type "worduse phrase."

NOTE: If you want this program to look for additional phrases or to stop looking for some, for instance to stop flagging "impact," type the command `dictadd`.

**************** SPLIT INFINITIVES ****************

For file `EXAMPLE`:

No split infinitives found

BECAUSE YOUR TEXT IS SHORT (< 2000 WORDS & < 100 SENTENCES), THE FOLLOWING ANALYSIS MAY BE MISLEADING.

READABILITY

The Kincaid readability formula predicts that your text can be read by someone with 16 or more years of schooling, which is rather high for this type of document. Good technical documents average close to 13th grade level, even though the audience has more education than that.

VARIATION

You have an appropriate distribution of sentence types.

The longest sentence, however, is 54 words long. Sentences this long are frequently lists, which will be easier to follow if you convert them into a list format. To find all your sentences over 50 words, type the following command after this program is done.

```
style -gt 50 filename
```

SENTENCE STRUCTURE

Passives

This text contains a much higher percentage of passive verbs (45.0%) than is common in good documents of this type. The score for passive verbs should be below 28.6%. A sentence is in the passive voice when its grammatical subject is the receiver of the action.

PASSIVE: The ball was hit by the boy.

When the doer of the action in a sentence is the subject, the sentence is in the active voice.

ACTIVE: The boy hit the ball.

The passive voice is sometimes needed

1. to emphasize the object of the sentence,
2. to vary the rhythm of the text, or
3. to avoid naming an unimportant actor.

EXAMPLE: The appropriations were approved.

Although passive sentences are sometimes needed, psychological research has shown that they are harder to comprehend than active sentences. Because of this you should transform as many of your passives to actives as possible. You can use the `style` program to find all your sentences with passive verbs in them, by typing the following command when this program is finished.

```
style -p filename
```

Nominalizations

You have appropriately limited your nominalizations (nouns made from verbs, e.g., "description").

PROSE OUTPUTS

Options

You can request that your document be compared against different standards; typing `-t` with the `prose` command, e.g.,

`prose -t` *filename*

will compare your text against training documents.

A `-s` option will provide a very short version of the `prose` output.

`prose -s` *filename*

If you already have a style table in a file, you can save time by using it as the input to `prose` rather than the textfile. To do this, precede the style table filename with a `-f`, e.g.,

`prose -f` *styletable-filename*

All the options can be selected at the same time and listed in any order.

`prose -f` *styletable-filename* `-s -t`

Statistics

The table of statistics generated by the program `style` can be found in your file `styl.tmp`. If you want to look at it type:

```
cat styl.tmp
```

You can also use the `match` program, which provides a better format, type:

```
match styl.tmp
```

If you are not interested in the file, remove it by typing:

```
rm styl.tmp
```

ORGANIZATION

The `prose` program cannot check the content or organization of your text. One way to look at the overall structure of your text is to use `grep` to list all the headings that were specified for the mm formatter. To do this, type:

```
grep '^\.H' filename
```

You can also use the organization program, `org`, to look at the structure of your text. `org` will format your paper with all the headings and paragraph divisions intact, but will only print the first and last sentence of each paragraph in your text so you can check your flow of ideas.

```
org filename
```

There are no spelling mistakes in the example document. An examination of spelling errors printed by `spellwwb` shows that they are not real mistakes; the words are bibliographic citations in the text and proper names. All `spellwwb` is saying is that it did not find these words in its dictionary. Printing of these words as possible spelling errors in the future can be suppressed by adding these words to the user's local dictionary using the program `spelladd`.

There are no punctuation mistakes, double words or split infinitives; `wwb` suggests some alternative ways of writing some words and phrases in the text, and says that the document is hard to read. Words and phrases flagged by `wwb` may be replaced with the alternatives it suggests in cases when it seems appropriate. The author should do something about the document being hard to read (e.g., use smaller sentences). As pointed out by `wwb`, this document was rather small; analysis of the complete document may give a different analysis of the document's readability.

The output produced by `wwb` for large documents, such as this book, is voluminous. In the case of file `EXAMPLE`, which contained 68 lines of text and formatting commands, it produced over 200 lines of input. The experienced `wwb` user might find it beneficial to instruct `wwb` to produce a shortened output or to analyze the document separately with some or all of the components of `wwb`.

5. Conclusions

The WRITER'S WORKBENCH tools are based on research results and/or expert consensus. These help the user with the mechanical aspects of copy editing and proofreading but not with the writing semantics and document content—this is still the writer's responsibility. The WRITER'S WORKBENCH software has been in use at AT&T Bell Laboratories for over four years. Users have responded quite favorably to the WRITER'S WORKBENCH software, many of them believing that it has helped them improve their writing skills [Frase 1983].

Chapter 8

Example Document Templates

This chapter contains example `mm` templates that I use to produce a variety of documents.[43] To avoid remembering the instructions needed for producing documents, their format and the order in which they should be given, I make templates for the documents I write often and store them. When I prepare a document, I copy the corresponding template and tailor it to suit my needs by adding, deleting and changing items in the template. I then fill in the text and other formatting instructions.

I will give templates for three kinds of documents:

- letters
- papers and
- books.

I am giving these templates primarily for your convenience; you can take these templates and tailor them for your own documents.

1. Letters

I will give templates for several kinds of letters: an internal or intra-company letter template, and two external letter templates. The first external letter template is for letters that will be printed on stationery preprinted with the company logo and address; the second external letter template is for printing letters on plain paper.

At the end of this section, I will also suggest a technique for printing a long letter on one-page.

1.1 Internal Letters

The template I use for writing internal letters has the form

---

43. For ease of presentation, I will show you slightly modified versions of the templates used by me.

```
.PH ""
.SA 1
.ND "m d, y"
.TL
title
.AU "N. Gehani" initials location dept ext room
.MT 0
.DS
.SP 3
name of receiver:
.DE
.P
message ...
.SP 2
.SG
.NS
list of persons getting copies
.NE
.NS 6
enclosures
.NE
```

Internal Letter Template

A letter produced using the internal letter template will have the form

Company Logo/Name

subject: *title*

date: *m d, y*

from: **N. Gehani**
location dept
room x*ext*

name of receiver:

message ...

N. Gehani

Copy to
persons getting copies

Encs.
enclosures

Internal Letter

1.2 External Letters

1.2.1 External Letters On Preprinted Company Stationery: I use the following external letter template when I use stationery preprinted with the company logo and address.[44]

```
.PH ""
.SA 1
.ND "m d, y"
.AU "N. Gehani"
.MT 5
.DS
name of receiver
address of receiver
.SP 3
salutation
.DE
.P
message ...
.SP 2
.FC Sincerely,
.SG
.NS
list of persons getting copies
.NE
.NS 6
enclosures
.NE
```

External Letter (Preprinted Stationery) Template

A letter produced using the external letter template will have the form

44. Some printing devices provide a mechanism for simultaneously using two types of paper. For example, such a mechanism would allow the simultaneous use of both letterhead and plain paper; the letterhead can then be used for the first page of a letter and the plain paper for the remaining pages. On the other hand, some printing devices require specially treated paper for printing and will not accept letterheads that are printed on plain paper. Printing letters on plain paper may be an attractive proposition in some situations because it bypasses the limitations of the printing device.

Company Name/Logo
Address/Phone No.

name of receiver
address of receiver

salutation

message ...

Sincerely,

N. Gehani

Copy to
persons getting copies

Encs.
enclosures

External Letter (Preprinted Stationery)

1.2.2 External Letter On Plain Paper: I use the following external letter template for printing letters on plain paper:

```
.PH ""
.SA 1
.ND "m d, y"
.AU "N. Gehani"
.AT "\fRAT&T Bell Labs\fP" "\fRMurray Hill, NJ\fP"
.MT 5
.DS
name of receiver
address of receiver
.SP 3
salutation
.DE
.P
message ...
.SP 2
.FC Sincerely,
.SG
.NS
copies
.NE
.NS 6
enclosures
.NE
```

External Letter to be Printed on Plain-Paper Template

The author-title command is used for printing the writer's affiliation and address, just below the writer's name. A letter produced using the above external letter template will have the form *m d, y*

name of receiver
address of receiver

salutation

message ...

Sincerely,

N. Gehani
AT&T Bell Labs
Murray Hill, NJ

Copy to
copies

Encs.
enclosures

External Letter Printed on Plain-Paper

1.3 Forcing Output of a One-Page Letter

Consider a two-page document, such as a letter, that has only two or three lines on the second page. Suppose we want to print the whole document on one page by printing the second-page lines at the bottom of the first page; that is, we want to reduce the bottom margin size. Unfortunately, `mm` does not provide a facility for decreasing the bottom margin size. However, by increasing the page length, we can fit the second-page lines at the bottom of the first page; `mm` will now not skip to the next page when it reaches the normal bottom margin because it expects the bottom margin to come later. Lines that were previously printed on the second page will now be printed at the bottom of the first page. The mm command-line option -rL*k* can be used to increase the page length.

2. Writing Papers

2.1 Internal and External Papers With All Internal Authors

This template works for both internal and external papers:

```
.EQ
eqn definitions and environment specification
.EN
.SA 1
.FD 1
.ND "m, d, y"
.TL charging-number filing-number
Title of Paper
.AU "N. H. Gehani" NHG loc dept-no extension room-no
.TM technical-memo-number
.AS 1
Abstract. . .
.AE
.MT use ".MT 4 1" for external papers; ".MT" for internal memos
.H 1 Introduction
Text (including other headings) ...
.H 1 Conclusions
Conclusion. . .
.H 1 Acknowledgement
Acknowledgement. . .
.SG nhg
.NS 3
References
.NE
.SK
.H 1 References
.VL 1.5i 0.5i
.LI reference-mark
reference ...
.LE
.CS
```

Papers With All Internal Authors Template

An external paper produced using this template will have the form

Title of Paper

N. H. Gehani

AT&T Bell Laboratories
Murray Hill, New Jersey 07974

ABSTRACT

Abstract ...

External Paper Cover Sheet

Title of Paper

N. H. Gehani

AT&T Bell Laboratories
Murray Hill, New Jersey 07974

1. Introduction
Text ... (including other headings)

m. **Conclusions**
Conclusions ...

n. **Acknowledgment**
Acknowledgment ...

Body of the External Paper

-page no-

p. **References**
reference-mark reference ...

First Page of References

2.2 Papers With Some Outside Authors

The following template is for external papers:

```
.EQ
eqn definitions and environment specification
.EN
.SA 1
.FD 1
.ND "m, d, y"
.TL charging-number filing-number
Title of Paper
.AF "outside author affiliation"
.ds YY outside author address
.AU "outside author name" "" YY
.AF "AT&T Bell Laboratories"
.AU "N. H. Gehani" NHG loc dept-no extension room-no
.TM technical-memo-number
.AS 1
Abstract...
.AE
.MT use ".MT 4 1" for external papers; ".MT" for internal memos
.H 1 Introduction
Text ... (including other headings)
.H 1 Conclusions
Conclusion...
.H 1 Acknowledgement
Acknowledgement...
.SG nhg
.NS 3
References
.NE
.SK
.H 1 References
.VL 1.5i 0.5i
.LI reference-mark
reference ...
.LE
.CS
```

Documents With Some External Authors Template

The external paper produced using the template will have the form

Title of Paper

outside author name

outside author affiliation
outside author address

N. H. Gehani

AT&T Bell Laboratories
Murray Hill, New Jersey 07974

ABSTRACT

Abstract ...

Cover Sheet

Title of Paper

outside author name

outside author affiliation
outside author address

N. H. Gehani

AT&T Bell Laboratories
Murray Hill, New Jersey 07974

1. Introduction
Text ... (including other headings)

m. **Conclusions**
Conclusions ...

n. **Acknowledgment**
Acknowledgment ...

Body of the Technical Paper

```
                    -page no-



        p. References
           reference-mark reference ...
```

First Page of References

As mentioned earlier, the template given here is for external papers. For internal papers, I take the template designed for all internal authors (given in the previous section) and add another `.AU` instruction with just the author's name, along with an asterisk, which I use as a footnote mark. In the footnote, I specify the external author's affiliation:

```
.AU "external author*"
.FS *
external author's affiliation
.FE
```

3. Writing a Book

A book can be partitioned into three major logical parts [Chicago University Style 1969]:

1. Front or preliminary matter.
2. Chapters.
3. End or reference matter.

Few books have all these parts (e.g., many popular fiction books do not have *end matter*) and some books have additional parts. Front-matter pages are numbered in lower-case Roman numerals.

Here are the definitions of two terms that I will be using in the templates for the different parts of a book. A *recto* (right-hand) page is an odd-numbered page. A *verso* (left-hand) page is an even-numbered page.

3.1 Front Matter

The front-matter pages are organized as follows:

Organization of the Front-Matter	
Section	*Page Number*
Book half title	i*
Series Title or Blank Page	ii*
Title Page	iii*
Copyright notice, printing history (sometimes the publisher will insert this material for the author) iv*	
Dedication	v*
Blank Page	vi*
Table of Contents	v or vii (depending on whether or not a dedication has been included)
Foreword	recto**
Preface	recto**
Acknowledgements	recto**

3.2 Chapters

Each chapter starts on a recto (odd-numbered) page.

* Page numbers are not printed on these pages; if a book does not have a dedication, then the table of contents begins on page v.

3.3 End Matter

The end-matter pages are organized as follows:

Organization of the End-Matter	
Section	*Page Number*
Appendix(es)	recto**
Glossary	recto**
Bibliography	recto**
Index	recto**

3.4 Running Heads

A *running head* is information printed on the top of a page; this information indicates the reader's position in the book. The running head I use consists of the page number (*folio*) and the current book section (e.g., chapter) title. A folio is printed on the left side of a verso page and on the right side of a recto page; the folios are positioned to be flush with the outside of a page. The section title is printed on the right side of a verso page and on the left side of recto page. In the case of an opening page of a new section (e.g, a new chapter), the running head is omitted and the folio printed at the bottom of the page.

3.5 Templates for Different Parts of a Book

`mm` does not have any built-in knowledge about book format, that is, books are not a predefined document type. Consequently, I had to specify the format of the various components of a book explicitly; while doing this, I had to use many `troff` instructions.

3.5.1 Template for the Definitions used in the Book: File `header`, which I used for typesetting this book, contains the following `eqn` and `troff` definitions:

** The page number on the starting page of these sections should be at the bottom of the page.

```
.EQ
gfont R
delim $$
define 12th %\^%
define 6th %"\|"%
define star %size +1 \(**%
define square % \(sq %
define app %size +1 \(aa%
define lb %size +1 bold [ "\|"%
define rb %"\|" size +1 bold ]%
define lc %size +1 bold "{" "\|"%
define rc %"\|" size +1 bold "}"%
define alt %size +1 bold |%
define ra %size +2 bold ->%
define tab %\(rh%
.EN
.de cL \"macro to draw 5.0 inch centered line
.sp
.ce
\fB\l'5.0i'\fP
.sp
..
.de (P \"begin constant width font display macro
.DS
.ft CW
..
.de )P \"end constant width font display macro
.ft P
.DE
..
.ds HP 12 10 10 10 10 10 10 \"heading point sizes
.ds HF 3 3 2 2 2 2 2 \"heading fonts
.ds cW \&\f(CW \"string to avoid CW font problem
.SA 1    \"right adjust text
```

Definitions Template I Use for Writing a Book

The template consists of some `eqn` instructions (which consist of the specification of the global font and in-line delimiters, and some definitions), some `troff` macro and string definitions, and an `mm` instruction specifying that text is to be right adjusted. Note that I need not always use all the definitions given in the above template. Of course, I can change, add or delete some or all of the definitions given in the template.

3.5.2 Template for the Front Part of a Book:

```
.nr p 6 1
.af p i
.am TP
.PF ""
..
.PH ""
.rs
.sp 3.0i
.ce
\fB\s+3Book Title\s0\fP
.SK
.OP
.ce
\fB\s+5Book Title\s0\fP
.sp 15
.ce
\fB\s+5Author\s0\fP
.ce 2
\s+3Organization Name
City, State, Zipcode\s0
.sp 16
.ce 2
Publisher
Address
.SK
.OP
.rs
.sp 3.0i
.ce number-of-lines-in-dedication
Dedication
.SK
.OP
```

Template for The Front Part of a Book (continued on the next page)

```
.rs
.sp 4
.PF "''\\\\n+p''"
.EH "'\\\\n+p''Contents'"
.OH "'Contents''\\\\n+p'"
.ce
\fB\s+5Contents\s0\fP
.sp 5
.TS
center;
l l l.
Preface☛☛Page Number

Acknowledgment☛☛Page Number

Chapter 1☛Chapter 1 Title\a☛1
☛   1.   Section 1 Title☛Page Number
☛   2.   Section 2 Title☛Page Number
☛   3.   Section 3 Title☛Page Number
    ...
☛   m.   Section m Title☛Page Number
    .
    .
    .
Chapter n☛Chapter n Title\a☛Page Number
☛   1.   Section 1 Title☛Page Number
☛   2.   Section 2 Title☛Page Number
☛   3.   Section 3 Title☛Page Number
    ...
☛   p.   Section p Title☛Page Number

Appendix 1☛Appendix 1 Title\a☛Page Number
    ...
Appendix q☛Appendix q Title\a☛Page Number
Bibliography☛\&\a☛Page Number
Index☛\&\a☛Page Number
.TE
```

Template for the Front Part of a Book (continued on the next page)

```
.if o .nr p +1
.EH ""
.OH ""
.SK
.OP
.PF "''\\\\n+p''"
.EH "'\\\\n+p''Foreword'"
.OH "'Preface''\\\\n+p'"
.ce
\fB\s+5Foreword\s0\fP
.sp 5
.P
foreword
.if o .nr p +1
.EH ""
.OH ""
.SK
.OP
.PF "''\\\\n+p''"
.EH "'\\\\n+p''Preface'"
.OH "'Preface''\\\\n+p'"
.ce
\fB\s+5Preface\s0\fP
.sp 5
.P
preface
.if o .nr p +1
.EH ""
.OH ""
.SK
.OP
.PF "''\\\\n+p''"
.EH "'\\\\n+p''Acknowledgement'"
.OH "'Acknowledgement''\\\\n+p'"
.ce
\fB\s+5Acknowledgment\s0\fP
.sp 5
.P
acknowledgement
```

Template for The Front Part of a Book

3.5.3 Template for a Book Chapter:

```
.PH ""
.PF "''\\\\nP''"
.OP
.EH "'\\\\nP''\fB\s-1Chapter Title\s0\fP'"
.OH "'\fB\s-1Chapter Title\s0\fP''\\\\nP'"
.am TP
.PF ""
..
.ce
\s+5Chapter n
.sp
.ce
\fBChapter Title\fR\s0
.sp 5
.P
Chapter Contents
```

Template for a Book Chapter

3.5.4 Templates for a Book Appendix, Glossary, Bibliography or Index:

```
.PH ""
.PF "''\\\\nP''"
.OP
.EH "'\\\\nP''Title of After Chapter Part of a Book'"
.OH "'Title of After Chapter Part of a Book''\\\\nP'"
.am TP
.PF ""
..
.ce
\s+5\fBTitle of After Chapter Part of a Book\fR\s0
.sp 5
.P
Contents of After Chapter Part of a Book
```

Template for an Appendix, a Glossary, a Bibliography or an Index

3.6 Using the Templates to Produce the Book

I have designed the templates for the different parts of a book anticipating that each part will be typeset separately. As I said earlier, it is a good idea to typeset parts of a big document such as a book separately. By default, page numbers and footnote numbers start with 1. Consequently, each part of a book (except the front part) must be typeset with a file containing the appropriate starting page and footnote numbers. Suppose that the last page of chapter 1 was page 29 and the last footnote number used was 5. Then chapter 2 should be typeset with the `troff` instructions

```
.pn 30
.nr :p 5
```

which specify that the starting page number for chapter 2 is 30 and the last footnote number that was used is 5. Because each chapter begins on an odd page, specifying that chapter 2 should start at page 30 will lead, as a result of the instruction `.OP`, to the printing of a blank page with page number 30; chapter 2 will itself start at page 31.

I typeset each part of a book using the command `book` which is the *shell* script:

```
pic header $*|tbl|eqn|troff -mm -rB2 -rL9.25i -rW4.75i -
```

The input to `pic` is the file named `header` and the files supplied as arguments to the command `book` (denoted by `$*`). The output of `pic` is the input to `tbl`, the output of `tbl` is the input of `eqn` and the output of `eqn` is the input of `troff`. When I use the special `eqn` characters defined in `/usr/pub/eqnchar`, then I have to modify the command `book` slightly to include this file.

Command `book` is used as[45]

`book` *page-footnote-no-file file-containing-part-of-book >book-part-file*

The output of command `book`, which is stored in the file *book-part-file*, is sent to the printing device as

command-to-send-file-to-printer <book-part-file

3.7 Index Generation Macros

Generating a good book index is a difficult task; fortunately the mechanical aspects of this task can be simplied somewhat. To generate the index, I use a macro called `iX`:

---

45. There is no need to supply the *page-footnote-no-file* for the *front matter* explicitly because, by default, page and footnote numbers start with the value 1. Note that the page numbers in the *front matter* are in Roman numerals starting with page number i; chapter 1 starts with the page number 1.

```
.de iX \"index macro
.tm \\$1 \\$2 \\$3 \\$4 \\$5 \\$6 \\$7  \\n%
..
```

Macro `iX` takes up to seven arguments and prints these arguments along with the current page number (the value of the `troff` page-number register `%`) on the UNIX system standard error output; I insert calls to `iX` in appropriate places in the text.

Some examples of calls to this macro are

```
 .iX \fIcalculator\fR example
.iX example, \fIcalculator\fR
.iX main program
.iX program, main
.iX & operator
.iX character set, transliteration to the basic
.iX characters, replacements for unavailable
```

While producing the book, I redirect the standard error output so that I can manipulate it later, for example,

`book` *page-footnote-no-file raw-book-part-file >formatted-book-part-file* 2>*index-file*

The output of the `.iX` macro calls is collected in *index-file*. Here is some sample output produced by the above `.iX` macro calls:

```
\fIcalculator\fR example 1
example, \fIcalculator\fR 1
main program 2
program, main 2
& operator 2
transliteration into the basic character set 4
character set, transliteration to the basic 4
characters, replacements for unavailable 5
```

After the index has been generated, I sort and eliminate duplicates from *index-file*, (by using the UNIX system `sort` command), combine references to the same item, and further massage the file a bit to improve its appearance and readability.

4. Exercises

1. Write a template that prints an external letter on plain paper similar to the one given in this chapter but that also prints the information printed

on your organization's letterhead.

2. The strategy for forcing output of one-page letters is a "kludge" that cannot be used to force output of *n*-page letters, where *n* is greater than one. What is the reason for this?

3. In the example about book formatting, a page number is printed at the bottom of the first page of each chapter. This is accomplished in the chapter template by setting the page header to null, and the page footer to the page number. The page footer is set to null at the beginning of the next page by appending the instruction

   ```
   .PF ""
   ```

   to the body of the top-of-the-page instruction `.TP`, which is automatically invoked at the top of every page. Page numbers on succeeding pages are printed by using the even and odd page header instructions `.EH` and `.OH`, respectively.

   Can you print the page number at the bottom of the first page without using the `.PF` instruction? *Hint*: Use an `mm` command line option.

Appendix A
More Document Formatting Tools

I will now very briefly describe some other Unix document formatting tools. Many of the tools mentioned here are not available on the AT&T UNIX (System V) but are available on other versions of the UNIX system, for example, AT&T UNIX (7th Edition) and Berkeley UNIX systems. For more details about these tools, please see the appropriate documents cited in the descriptions.

1. `ideal`

The `ideal` preprocessor [Van Wyk 1981a, 1981b], like `pic`, is used for drawing figures in documents. Figures are drawn by using

1. complex numbers to specify positions and direction (all variables are of type complex),
2. simultaneous equations to specify the relationship between important points in a picture and
3. a set of instructions to draw figures with respect to the points specified using simultaneous equations.

Using the simultaneous equations and the coordinates of the explicitly specified points, `ideal` automatically determines the coordinates of other points (assuming enough information has been given). `ideal` has some facilities that `pic` does not have, for example, the ability to specify dashed circle, and facilities for shading regions.

2. `grap`

Graphs can be drawn using `grap`, a recent addition to the UNIX document formatting facilities. `grap` [Bentley and Kernighan 1984] is a `pic` preprocessor; that is, it produces `pic` instructions as output (instead of `troff` instructions as produced by `pic`, `tbl` and `eqn`). A graph specification has the form

```
.G1
grap statements, if appropriate
graph data_1
grap statements, if appropriate
graph data_2
  ⋮
grap statements, if appropriate
graph data_n
grap statements, if appropriate
.G2
```

`grap` provides facilities for specifying tick marks, type of line joining the plotted points, axes labels and range, etc.

3. `ms` Page-Layout Macros

The `ms` [Lesk 1978a] macro package is high-level document formatting facility similar to the `mm` macro package. I will give you a flavor `ms` by briefly describing some of its instructions:

`ms` Macro Package	
Instruction	**Explanation**
`.AB`	Begin abstract.
`.AE`	End abstract.
`.AI`	Author's institution.
`.AU`	Author's name.
`.B`	Embolden/switch to bold font.
`.B1`	Begin text to be enclosed in a box.
`.B2`	End boxed text and print it.
`.BX`	Print specified word in a box.
`.CM`	Put cut mark between pages.
`.CT`	Chapter title.
`.DA`	Print specified date at bottom of page.
`.DE`	End display.
`.DS`	Begin display with keep.
`.CD`	Centered display with no keep.
`.EN`	End `eqn` specification.
`.EQ`	Start `eqn` specification.
`.FE`	End footnote.

ms Macro Package	
Instruction	**Explanation**
.FS	Start footnote.
.I	Italicize/switch to italic font.
.ID	Indented display with no keep.
.IP	Indented paragraph, with hanging tag.
.KE	End keep of any kind.
.KF	Start floating keep.
.KS	Start keep.
.LD	Left display with no keep.
.LG	Increase point size by 2.
.LP	Left aligned block paragraph.
.MC	Multiple columns.
.ND	Change/cancel date.
.NH	Numbered header.
.NL	Set point size back to normal.
.R	Return to Roman font.
.RE	End level of relative indentation.
.RP	Released paper format.
.RS	Start level of relative indentation.
.SG	Print signature line.
.SH	Section header, in boldface.
.SM	Decrease point size by 2.
.TA	Set tabs.
.TC	Print table of contents at end.
.TE	End of a tbl specification.
.TH	End multi-page header of table.
.TL	Title in boldface and two points larger.
.TS	Begin a tbl specification.
.UL	Underline.
.1C	Begin one-column format.
.2C	Begin two-column format.

4. mv Viewgraph Macros

The Viewgraph Macros mv [DWB 1984b] are a collection of macros for making viewgraphs and slides in a variety of styles and sizes.

mv Macro Package	
Instruction	**Explanation**
.VS	Foil-start macro; foil size is to be 7″×7″.
.Vw	Same as .VS, except that foil size is 7″ ×5″.
.Vh	Same as .VS, except that foil size is 5″×7″.
.VW	Same as .VS, except that foil size is 7″×5.4″.
.VH	Same as .VS, except that foil size is 7″×9″.
.Sw	Same as .VS, except that foil size is 7″×5″.
.Sh	Same as .VS, except that foil size is 5″×7″.
.SW	Same as .VS, except that foil size is 7″×5.4″.
.SH	Same as .VS, except that foil size is 7″×9″.
.A	Place text that follows at the first indentation level.
.B	Place text that follows at the second indentation level; text is preceded by the specified mark (default is a large bullet).
.C	Same as .B, but for the third indentation level; default mark is a dash.
.D	Same as .B, but for the fourth indentation level; default mark is a small bullet.
.T	Print specified string as an over-size and centered title.
.I	Change the current text indent (does not affect titles).
.S	Set the point size and line length.
.DF	Define font positions.
.DV	Alter the vertical spacing between indentation levels.
.U	Underline the specified string.

The following naming convention is used for the first 9 instructions:

1. the first character of the instruction name indicates a view graph (V) or a slide (S) instruction.

2. The second character indicates whether the viewgraph or slide is square (S), small wide (w), small high (h), big wide (W), or big high (H)

Command mvt automatically invokes troff with the mv macros.

5. `refer`

`refer` [Lesk 1978b] is a `troff` preprocessor that finds and inserts literature references in documents. Given an incomplete citation with sufficiently precise keywords, `refer` will search a bibliographic database for references containing these keywords anywhere in the title, author, journal, etc.

A document is cited in the text by using a specification of the form

`.[`
keywords giving approximate but unique citation
`.]`

This citation will be replaced by information from the bibliographic database in a user-controlled format. (To be more precise, the reference data retrieved from the database is assigned to a set of `troff` strings that are used by macro packages such as `ms` to print an appropriate citation.) A complete list of references cited in the text is also printed out at the end of the document. If the approximate citation does not identify exactly one document in the citation database, then `refer` reports an error. Correctness or appropriateness of a `refer` citation may be verified by using an interactive tool, `lookbib`, that can be used to examine the citation specified by the keywords. The bibliographic database provided by the local implementation, if any, can be augmented by user-specified bibliographic databases.

Appendix B

Document Formatting Commands

In this appendix I will describe the document formatting commands available on AT&T UNIX System V and many other UNIX systems. These descriptions are modified versions of excerpts from the corresponding descriptions in the *UNIX System Reference Manual* [AT&T UNIX 1983a]. For complete details, please refer to the *UNIX System Reference Manual* where these functions are described in detail.

The commands described in this chapter are summarized in the following table:

command	use
`checkmm`	check for mm errors
`double`	check for identical pairs of words
`eqn` `neqn`	format mathematical text with `troff` and `nroff`, respectively
`mm`	use `nroff` to format documents that use the mm macro package
`mmt`	use `troff` to format documents that use the mm macro package
`mvt`	use `troff` to make viewgraphs specified using the mv macro package
`nroff`	format text for printing on a terminal
`pic`	format pictures (figures)
`spell`	check for spelling mistakes
`tbl`	format tables
`tc`	preview `troff` output on Tektronix 4014 and 4015 display terminals
`troff`	format text for printing on typesetter, laser printer or viewing on a bitmap display
`wwb`	analyze a document using the WRITER'S WORKBENCH program

1. `checkmm` (mm and `eqn` Error Checker)

The `checkmm` command detects mm errors such as instructions used in the wrong order, unbalanced `.DS/.DE` instructions and so on. The `checkmm` command has the form

`checkmm` [*files*]

`checkmm` also checks for `eqn/neqn` errors such as missing or unbalanced delimiters and unbalanced `.EQ/.EN` pairs.

If no *files* is specified, then `checkmm` reads from standard input.

2. `double` (Double Word Finder)

The `double` command is used to search for consecutive occurrence of identical words. It has the form

`double [-flags] [-ver]` [*files*]

The `double` command skips text contained in `tbl` tables and ignores consecutive occurrences of any single character except *a*. When `double` finds two words in a row, it prints them along with the line number of the first one. If no *files* are specified, then `double` reads from standard input.

Options `-flags` and `-ver` are used to retrieve information about the `double` command:

- `-flags` print the command synopsis line (shown above) showing command flags and options, then exit.
- `-ver` print the *Writer's Workbench* version number of the command, then exit.

The `double` command is one of the programs executed by `wwb` command.

3. `eqn` and `neqn` (Format Mathematical Text)

The `eqn` command is used for formatting mathematical text which is to be printed on a phototypesetter; `eqn` is a `troff` preprocessor. The `neqn` command is similar to the `eqn` command except that it is used when the mathematical text is to be printed on typewriter-like terminals; `neqn` is an `nroff` preprocessor. The commands `eqn` and `neqn` have the form

`eqn [-d`*xy*`] [-p`*n*`] [-s`*n*`] [-f`*n*`] [-T`*dest*`]` [*files*]
`neqn [-d`*xy*`] [-p`*n*`] [-s`*n*`] [-f`*n*`]` [*files*]

If no *files* are specified (or if `-` is specified as the last argument), then `eqn` and `neqn` read from standard input. The various options of the `eqn` commands are explained below:

- `-d`*xy* set the in-line delimiters to the characters *x* and *y*.
- `-p`*n* print subscripts in the current point size minus *n*.

- `-s`*n* the default (global) point size is set to *n*.
- `-f`*x* use font *x* as the default (global) font.
- `-T`*t* prepares output for the typesetter type *t* (used with `eqn`).

Usually, these preprocessors are invoked as

`eqn` *files* ¦ `troff`
`neqn` *files* ¦ `nroff`

or using some equivalent command (e.g., `mm -e` or `mmt -e`)

4. mm (Print Documents Formatted Using mm)

The mm command uses `nroff` to format and print documents specified using mm instructions. The mm command has the form

mm *options files*

Options in the mm command are used to specify preprocessing by `tbl` and/or `neqn` (`nroff` version of `eqn`) and postprocessing by various terminal-oriented output filters. The proper pipelines, and the required arguments and flags for `nroff` and mm are generated, depending on the options selected.

Options for mm are given below. Any other arguments or flags (e.g., `-rC3`) are passed to `nroff` or to mm as appropriate. Such options can occur in any order, but they must appear before the *files* arguments. If no arguments are given, mm prints a list of its options.

- `-T`*term* Specifies the type of output terminal;
- `-12` Indicates that the document is to be produced in 12-pitch.
- `-e` Causes mm to invoke `neqn`; also causes `neqn` to read the file `/usr/pub/eqnchar` which contains some special `neqn` definitions.
- `-t` Causes mm to invoke `tbl`
- `-` This option, which is used in place of file names instructs mm to get its input from the standard input. (Mentioning other files together with - leads to disaster.) This option allows mm to be used as a filter, e.g.:

  `cat` *files* ¦ mm -

See Section 3 for the arguments which may be passed on `nroff`.

4.1 Hints on Using mm

1. mm invokes nroff with the -h flag. With this flag, nroff assumes that the printer has tabs set every 8 character positions.
2. Use the -o*list* option of nroff to specify ranges of pages to be output. Note, however, that mm, if invoked with one or more of the -e, -t and - options, together with the -o*list* option, may cause nroff to print a "broken pipe" diagnostic if the last page of the document is not specified in *list*.
3. If you use the -s option of nroff (to stop between output pages), use line-feed (rather than return or new-line) to restart the output. The -s option of nroff does not work with the - option of mm.
4. If you lie to mm about the kind of terminal its output will be printed on, you'll get (often subtle) garbage; if you are redirecting output into a file, use the -T37 option, and then use an appropriate terminal filter when printing the file.

5. mmt and mvt (Format Documents, Viewgraphs and Slides)

The mmt command is used to format documents and the mvt command is used to format view graphs and slides. These commands have the form

mmt *options files*
mvt *options files*

These two commands are similar to mm, except that they use troff, instead of nroff, to format the document. Moreover, they produce intermediate code which must be processed by an appropriate filter prior to printing the document. mmt uses the mm macro package, while mvt uses the mv macro package (for view graphs and slides). These two commands have options to specify preprocessing by tbl, pic and eqn. The proper pipelines, and the required arguments and flags for troff and for the macro packages are automatically generated, depending on the options selected.

Options are given below. Any other arguments or flags (e.g., -rC3) are passed to troff or to the macro package, as appropriate. Such options can occur in any order, but they must appear before the *files* arguments. If no arguments are given, these commands print a list of their options.

-e	Invokes eqn; also causes eqn to read the file /usr/pub/eqnchar which contains some special eqn definitions.
-t	Invokes tbl.

`-p`	Invokes `pic`.
`-Taps`	Creates output for the Autologic APS-5 phototypesetter and sends it for printing.
`-Ti10`	Creates output for the Imagen Imprint-10 laser printer, and sends it to the default destination at this installation.
`-T4014`	Directs the output to a Tektronix 4014 terminal via the `tc` filter.
`-a`	Invokes the `-a` option of `troff`.
`-z`	Invokes no output filter to process or redirect the output of `troff`.
`-o`*list*	print only the pages listed (this is really a `troff` option).
`-`	This option, which is used in place of file names, specifies that input is to be read from the standard input. (Specifying other files together with - leads to disaster.)

6. `nroff` (Format Text)

The `nroff` command is used to format and print text on typewriter-like devices and line printers. It has the form

`nroff` *options* [*files*]

If no *files* are specified, then `nroff` reads the standard input. An argument equal to "`-`" is taken to be a file name corresponding to the standard input.

The *options*, which may appear in any order, but must appear before the *files*, are:

`-o`*list*	Print only pages whose page numbers appear in the *list* of numbers and ranges, separated by commas. A range *N*–*M* means pages *N* through *M*; an initial -*N* means from the beginning to page *N*; and a final *N*– means from *N* to the end.
`-n`*N*	Number the first page *N*.
`-s`*N*	Stop every *N* pages. `nroff` will halt after every *N* pages (default is 1) to allow paper loading or changing, and will resume upon receipt of a line-feed or new-line (new-lines do not work in pipelines). When `nroff` halts between pages, the *bel* character

	is sent to the terminal.
`-r`*aN*	Set register *a* (which must have a one-character name) to *N*.
`-i`	Read standard input after *files* are exhausted.
`-q`	Invoke the simultaneous input-output mode of the `.rd` request.
`-z`	Print only messages generated by `.tm` (terminal message) requests.
`-m`*name*	Prepend to the input *files* the macro file `/usr/lib/tmac/tmac.`*name*, e.g., `-mm`, `-ms` and `-mv`.
`-T`*name*	Prepare output for the specified terminal.
`-e`	Produce equally-spaced words in adjusted lines, using the full resolution of the terminal.
`-h`	Use output tabs during horizontal spacing to speed output and reduce output character count. Tab settings are assumed to be every 8 nominal character widths.
`-u`*n*	Set the emboldening factor (number of character overstrikes) for the third font position (bold) to *n* or to zero if *n* is missing.

Documents formatted with `nroff` should be processed with the UNIX system program `col` before they are printed if they contain two-column output or tables. `col` performs the line overlays implied by the reverse line feeds, and by the forward and reverse half-line feeds produced by `nroff` and `tbl` in the above documents.

7. `pic` (Draw Figures)

`pic` is a `troff` preprocessor for drawing simple figures on a typesetter. The basic objects are box, line, arrow, circle, ellipse, arc and text. The `pic` command has the form

`pic` [*files*]

If no *files* are specified, then `pic` reads from standard input.

New `pic` [Kerngihan 1984] produces typesetter independent output. However, old `pic` [Documenter's Workbench 1984d; Kernighan 1982a, 1982b] produces typesetter-dependent code; consequently, the command for using old `pic` provides an option for specifying the typesetter that is being used.

The old `pic` command has the form

`pic [-Tt] files`

where the optional argument `-Tt` is used to specify the typesetter *t*. Typesetters supported are `202` (Mergenthaler Linotron 202), `cat` (Wang CAT) and `aps` (Autologic APS-5). Default value of the `-T` option is `aps`.

8. `spell` (Find Spelling Errors)

The `spell` command collects words from the named *files* and looks them up in a spelling list. Words that neither occur among, nor are derivable (by applying certain inflections, prefixes and/or suffixes) from words in the spelling list are printed on the standard output. The `spell` command has the form

`spell [-v] [-b] [-x] [-l] [+local_file] [files]`

If no *files* are specified, then `spell` reads from standard input. `spell` ignores most `troff`, `tbl`, and `eqn` constructions.

The `spell` command options have the following effect:

`-v` all words not literally in the spelling list are to be printed, and plausible derivations from the words in the spelling list are indicated.

`-b` British spelling is checked. Besides preferring centre, colour, programme, speciality, travelled, etc., this option insists upon *ise* in words like standardise.

`-x` every plausible stem is printed with = for each word.

`-l` follow the chains of all included files; by default, `spell` follows chains of included files (`.so` and `.nx` `troff` instructions), unless their names begin with `/usr/lib`.

+*local_file* words found in *local_file* are removed from `spell`'s output; *local_file* is the name of a user-provided file that contains a sorted list of words, one per line. With this option, the user can specify, in addition to `spell`'s own spelling list, a set of words, such as proper names and jargon, that are correct spellings for each job.

The spelling list used by `spell` is based on many sources. Coverage of the specialized vocabularies of biology, medicine and chemistry is light.

9. `tbl` (Format Tables)

The `tbl` command invokes the `tbl` preprocessor that formats tables for the `nroff` and `troff` formatters. The `tbl` command has the form `tbl [-TX] [`*files*`]`

The `-TX` option forces `tbl` to use only full vertical line motions, making the output more suitable for line printer and other devices that cannot generate partial vertical line motions.

If no *files* are specified (or if - is specified as the last argument), `tbl` reads from standard input, so it may be used as a filter. When it is used with `eqn` or `neqn`, `tbl` should be used first to minimize the volume of data passed through pipes.

The `tbl` preprocessor copies input files to the standard output, except for the lines, between the `.TS` and the `.TE` instruction, i.e., the `tbl` instructions. `tbl` translate these instructions into `troff` instructions which construct the table.

10. `tc` (`troff` Output Interpreter)

The `tc` command is used to view the output of `troff` on a Tektronix 4014 and 4015 display terminals. The various typesetter sizes are mapped into the 4014's four sizes; the entire `troff` character set is drawn using the 4014's character generator, using overstruck combinations where necessary.

The `tc` command has the form

`tc [`*options*`]` *file*

If no *files* are specified, then `tc` reads from standard input. The command line options are:

- `-t` Don't wait between pages (for directing output into a file).
- `-o`*list* prints only the pages enumerated in *list*. The list consists of pages and page ranges (e.g., 5-17) separated by commas. The range *n*– goes from *n* to the end; the range –*n* goes up from the beginning to and including page *n*.
- `-a`*n* Set the aspect ratio to *n*; default is 1.5.
- `-e` Don't erase before each page.

Typical use of `tc` is

```
troff file | tc
```

At the end of each page `tc` waits for a newline (empty line) from the keyboard before continuing on to the next page. In this wait state, the following commands are recognized:

- `!`*cmd* Send *cmd* to the shell.

`e`	Invert state of the screen erase
`-`*n*	Skip backward *n* pages.
n	Print page *n*.
`a` *n*	Set the aspect ratio to *n*.
`?`	Print list of available options.

11. `troff` (Text Formatting and Typesetting)

The `troff` command is used for formating documents that will be typeset and printed on a device such as a phototypesetter or a laser printer.[46] The `troff` command has the form

`troff` *options* [*files*]

If no *files* are specified then standard input is read. An argument equal to "-" is taken to be a file name corresponding to the standard input.

The options, which may appear in any order so long as they appear before the files, are:

`-o`*list*	Print only pages whose page numbers appear in the comma-separated *list* of numbers and ranges. A range *N*-*M* means pages *N* through *M*; an initial -*N* means from the beginning to page *N*; and a final *N*- means from *N* to the end.
`-n`*N*	Number the first page *N*.
`-s`*N*	Generate output that makes the printing device stop every *N* pages.
`-m`*name*	Prepend file `/usr/lib/tmac/tmac.`*name* to the input *files* (`-mm` prepends the mm macros).
`-r`*aN*	Set register *a* (one character name) to *N*.
`-i`	Read standard input after the input files are exhausted.
`-q`	Invoke the simultaneous input-output mode of the `.rd` request.

46. As in the rest of the book, the new "device-independent" version of `troff` is described here.

`-z`	Print only messages generated by `.tm` requests.
`-a`	Send a printable ASCII approximation of the results to the standard output.
`-T`*dest*	Prepare output for typesetter *dest*.

12. `wwb` (WRITER'S WORKBENCH Software)

The `wwb` command invokes the WRITER'S WORKBENCH software, which is a set of programs designed to aid writers and editors in editing documents. The `wwb` command has the form[47]

`wwb [-mm | -ms] [-li | +li] [-tm | -t | -x` *standards-file*`]`
`[-s | -l]` *files*

The `wwb` command runs modified versions of two major programs, which in turn run other programs. The two major programs are:

`proofr`	automatic proofreading system that searches for spelling and punctuation errors, consecutive occurrences of words, wordy or misused phrases, and split infinitives.
`prose`	describes the writing style of a document, namely, readability and sentence characteristics, and suggests improvements.

`prose` compares a document with standards for one of several document types, according to the following flags:

`-tm`	compare input text with technical papers that have been judged to be good. (This is the default.)
`-t`	compare input text with some standard training documents.
`-x`*standards-file*	compare input text with standards contained in user-specified *standards-file*.
`-s`	produce short versions of `proofr` and `prose`.

47. To analyze a document with a `wwb` component such as `proofr punct` or `style`, please refer to your UNIX system reference manual for details about the component.

`-l`	produce long versions of `proofr` and `prose`. This is the default.
`-mm`	eliminate `mm` macros and associated text that is not part of sentences (e.g., headings), from the analysis. This is the default.
`-ms`	eliminate `ms` macros, and associated text that is not part of sentences from the analysis.
`-li`	eliminate list items, as defined by `mm` macros, from the analysis. This is the default.
`+li`	Include list items in the analysis. This flag should be used if the text contains lists of sentences, but not if the text contains many lists of non-sentences.

If you are using header files containing formatting commands, then include them with each document. This is necessary to enable `wwb` to strip non-sentence text from the input.

Appendix C
Some Font Samples

In this appendix, I will illustrate the differences between a variety of different fonts and point sizes. I will do this by printing, in each font, the digits, some special characters and some text (a limerick);[48] Fonts are referred to by one- or two-character names in `troff`. I will give the `troff` name of each font in parentheses following its full name.

The Times Roman, Times Italic and Times Bold are widely used font families. For these font styles, I will show you fonts of three different point sizes: 6, 10 and 14. For the each of the other font styles, I will just show you one font of point size 10.

48. The limerick used in illustrating the fonts was taken from *The Nonsense Books of Edward Lear* [Lear 1964].

Times Roman Font (R)

Point size 6

0123456789
+-/*=;,.?|

There was an Old man of the Hague,
Whose ideas were exceedingly vague;
He built a balloon to examine the moon,
That deluded Old man of the Hague.

Point size 10

0123456789
+-/*=;,.?|

There was an Old man of the Hague,
Whose ideas were exceedingly vague;
He built a balloon to examine the moon,
That deluded Old man of the Hague.

Point size 14

0123456789
+-/*=;,.?|

There was an Old man of the Hague,
Whose ideas were exceedingly vague;
He built a balloon to examine the moon,
That deluded Old man of the Hague.

Times Italic Font (I)

Point size 6

0123456789
+-/*=;,.?|

There was an Old man of the Hague,
Whose ideas were exceedingly vague;
He built a balloon to examine the moon,
That deluded Old man of the Hague.

Point size 10

0123456789
+-/*=;,.?|

There was an Old man of the Hague,
Whose ideas were exceedingly vague;
He built a balloon to examine the moon,
That deluded Old man of the Hague.

Point size 14

0123456789
+-/*=;,.?|

There was an Old man of the Hague,
Whose ideas were exceedingly vague;
He built a balloon to examine the moon,
That deluded Old man of the Hague.

Times Bold Font (B)

Point size 6

0123456789
+-/*=;,.?|

There was an Old man of the Hague,
Whose ideas were exceedingly vague;
He built a balloon to examine the moon,
That deluded Old man of the Hague.

Point size 10

0123456789
+-/*=;,.?|

There was an Old man of the Hague,
Whose ideas were exceedingly vague;
He built a balloon to examine the moon,
That deluded Old man of the Hague.

Point size 14

0123456789
+-/*=;,.?|

There was an Old man of the Hague,
Whose ideas were exceedingly vague;
He built a balloon to examine the moon,
That deluded Old man of the Hague.

Century Expanded Font (`CE`)

0123456789
+-/*=;,.?|

There was an Old man of the Hague,
Whose ideas were exceedingly vague;
He built a balloon to examine the moon,
That deluded Old man of the Hague.

Century Bold Italic Font (`CI`)

0123456789
+-/*=;,.?|

There was an Old man of the Hague,
Whose ideas were exceedingly vague;
He built a balloon to examine the moon,
That deluded Old man of the Hague.

Stymie Medium Font (`SM`)

0123456789
+-/*=;,.?|

There was an Old man of the Hague,
Whose ideas were exceedingly vague;
He built a balloon to examine the moon,
That deluded Old man of the Hague.

Palatino Font (PA)

0123456789
+-/*=;,.?|

There was an Old man of the Hague,
Whose ideas were exceedingly vague;
He built a balloon to examine the moon,
That deluded Old man of the Hague.

Palatino Italic Font (PI)

0123456789
+-/*=;,.?|

There was an Old man of the Hague,
Whose ideas were exceedingly vague;
He built a balloon to examine the moon,
That deluded Old man of the Hague.

Palatino Bold Font (PB)

0123456789
+-/*=;,.?|

There was an Old man of the Hague,
Whose ideas were exceedingly vague;
He built a balloon to examine the moon,
That deluded Old man of the Hague.

Helvetica Font (`H`)

0123456789
+-/*=;,.?|

There was an Old man of the Hague,
Whose ideas were exceedingly vague;
He built a balloon to examine the moon,
That deluded Old man of the Hague.

Helvetica Italic Font (`HI`)

0123456789
+-/=;,.?|*

There was an Old man of the Hague,
Whose ideas were exceedingly vague;
He built a balloon to examine the moon,
That deluded Old man of the Hague.

Helvetica Black Font (`HB`)

0123456789
+-/*=;,.?|

There was an Old man of the Hague,
Whose ideas were exceedingly vague;
He built a balloon to examine the moon,
That deluded Old man of the Hague.

Techno Bold Font (`TB`)

0123456789
+-/*=;,.?|

There was an Old man of the Hague,
Whose ideas were exceedingly vague;
He built a balloon to examine the moon,
That deluded Old man of the Hague.

News Gothic Condensed Font (`C`)

0123456789
+-/*=;,.?|

There was an Old man of the Hague,
Whose ideas were exceedingly vague;
He built a balloon to examine the moon,
That deluded Old man of the Hague.

Script Font (`SC`)

There was an Old man of the Hague,
Whose ideas were exceedingly vague;
He built a balloon to examine the moon,
That deluded Old man of the Hague.

The Script font on my UNIX system has only lower- and upper-case letters—Century Bold Italic font is used for digits and punctuation characters.

German Script Font (GS)

0123456789
+-/*=;,.?|

There was an Old man of the Hague,
Whose ideas were exceedingly vague;
He built a balloon to examine the moon,
That deluded Old man of the Hague.

Constant-Width Font (CW)

```
0123456789
+-/*=;,.?¦

There was an Old man of the Hague,
Whose ideas were exceedingly vague;
He built a balloon to examine the moon,
That deluded Old man of the Hague.
```

Courier Typewriter Font (CT)

```
0123456789
+-/*=;,.?|

There was an Old man of the Hague,
Whose ideas were exceedingly vague;
He built a balloon to examine the moon,
That deluded Old man of the Hague.
```

Glossary

Term	Explanation
ascender	Part of a lower case letter that rises above its main body (e.g., upper stem of the letter "h").
bold font	Heavy face type, as in **bold**.
camera-ready copy	Documentation ready to be photographed for reproduction, without any further changes.
caption	Title for a figure, table or equations.
copy editor	An editor who prepares a manuscript for printing.
descender	Part of a lower case letter that descends below its main body (e.g., lower stem of the letter "p").
drop folio	folio printed at the bottom of a page.
ellipsis	Three character sequence ". . ." indicating omission of items such as words.
em	Spacing equal to the point size of the font in question (approximately equal to width of the letter *m*). Ems are used mainly to describe character widths.
en	Half an em.
folio	Page number.
font	A collection of alphanumeric characters and special symbols all of one style and size, for example, 10 point Times Roman font.
formatted document	Document produced by processing the raw document; it consists of formatted text, equations, tables and figures described in some intermediate language; using appropriate programs (called postprocessors), the formatted document can be printed on devices such as a phototypesetter, a laser printer or a typewriter, or viewed on devices such as a bitmap display.

Term	Explanation
formatter	Computer program which formats text.
galley proofs	Copies of text after it is set into type (in manual typesetting); the text is not split into pages and figures are not included in the text.
gothic	Block letters in a sans-serif font.
italic font	Font whose characters slant to the right as in *italics*.
laser printer	A versatile device, with essentially the same capabilities as a phototypesetter, for printing documents on plain paper. Laser printers are cheaper and faster than phototypesetters and their output is of sufficiently good quality to be used for technical papers, letters and so forth. However, the output of most laser printers is generally not appropriate for documents where further high quality reproduction is essential, for example, books.
letterhead	Sheet of stationery printed or engraved (usually) with the name and address of an organization.
leading	Vertical distance between the base lines of two consecutive lines of text (pronounced as "ledding"); also called the "line space".
ligature	Character consisting of two or more letters or characters joined together, for example, ff and ffi.
page proofs	Page proofs come after galley proofs; the text is separated into pages and figures are inserted.
page offset	Left margin.
phototypeset	To produce a document using a phototypesetter.
phototypesetter	A device used for printing characters on photograhpic paper; on the newer and mores versatile devices, the characters in any font and size can be printed (assuming a description of the font is available).
pica	Printer's unit of measurement equal to 12 points.
point	Printer's unit of measurement equal to 0.0138 inches (1/72 inches).

Term	Explanation
point size	The point size of a font is the amount of vertical space separating the lowest descender and the maximum ascender of the characters in a font (the point size does not describe the height of either and upper- or lower-case letter [Seybold 1979]).
proofread	To read (a document) marking errors and suggesting corrections.
raw document	Document as entered into the computer; it consists of two components: text that is to be printed and formatting instructions specifying the text format, layout of equations, tables and figures. The text and the document formatting instructions are intermixed.
recto page	Right-hand page; recto folios are odd numbers.
Roman	Normal type style (distinguished from *italic* and **bold**).
running head	Heading at the top of a page that is a signpost for the readers indicating where they are in the book.
sans serif	Basic type style without adornments such as the short lines that appear at the ends of the strokes of a letter, for example, notice the absence of the short lines.
script	Imitation of handwriting.
serif	The short lines that appear at the ends of the strokes of a letter as in S.
type	Alphanumeric characters plus special symbols for printing.
typeset	To produce a document using a phototypesetter (same as phototypeset).
verso page	Left-hand page; verso folios are even numbers.
widow	The first or last line of a paragraph that occurs by itself at the end or beginning of a page.

Annotated Bibliography

Anderson, M. D. 1971. *Book Indexing. Cambridge Author's and Printer's Guide*—Volume 6, The University Press, Cambridge.

AT&T UNIX 1983a. *UNIX System V User Reference Manual.* AT&T Technologies.

AT&T UNIX 1983b. *UNIX System V Programmer Reference Manual.* AT&T Technologies.

AT&T UNIX 1983c. *UNIX Programmer's Manual (Seventh Edition), Volume 2.* AT&T Bell Telephone Laboratories, published by Holt, Rinehart and Winston. Contains papers describing the document preparation facilities on the UNIX system.

Bentley, J. L. and B. W. Kernighan 1984. `grap`—A Language for Typesetting Graphs: Tutorial and User Manual. Computing Science Technical Report no. 114, AT&T Bell Laboratories.

Berg, N. E. 1978. *Electronic Composition.* Graphics Arts Technical Foundation, Pittsburgh, 1978.

Berkeley UNIX 1983. *UNIX Programmer's Manual (4.2 BSD).* Computer Science Division, Department of Electrical Engineering and Computer Science, University of California, Berkeley, CA 94720.

Bourne, S. R. 1982. *The UNIX System.* Addison-Wesley. A detailed and comprehensive guide to the UNIX operating system and the facilities available on it. One chapter is devoted to the document preparation facilities on the UNIX system.

Business Week 1984. Compugraphic: Trying to Move Typesetting From the Shop to the Office (in the July 2 issue).

Carroll, L. *Through the Looking Glass.* In *The Annotated Alice*, Bramhall House, New York.

Cherry, L. 1981. Computer Aids for Writers. *Proceedings of the ACM SIGPLAN SIGOA Symposium on Text Manipulation* (June), pp. 62-67, Portland, Oregon.

Cherry, L. 1982. Writing Tools. Special Issue of the *IEEE Transactions on Communications* on *Communications in the Automated Office*, pp. 100-105, vCOM-30, no. 1 (January).

Chicago University Style 1969. *A Manual of Style* (Twelfth Edition, Revised). The University of Chicago Press. This excellent book deals with all aspects of writing and making a book. The first part deals with the fundamentals of book making: the logical organization of a book, preparation of the manuscript and the legal aspects of publishing such as copyrights and getting permission to republish copyrighted material. Part two deals with writing style; items covered include punctuation, spelling, tables, mathematical equations, footnotes, bibliographies and indexes. Part three deals with book design and typography, and contains a glossary of technical terms.

Christian, K. 1983. *The UNIX Operating System.* John Wiley.

Corbett, C. and I. H. Witten 1982. On The Inclusion and Placement of Documentation Graphics in Computer Typesetting. *Computer Journal*, v25, no. 2, pp. 272-3.

DWB 1984a. *UNIX DOCUMENTER'S WORKBENCH Software 1.0 Text Formatters Reference.* Select Code. 307-151, AT&T.

DWB 1984b. *UNIX DOCUMENTER'S WORKBENCH Software 1.0 Macro Package Reference.* Select Code. 307-152, AT&T.

DWB 1984c. *UNIX DOCUMENTER'S WORKBENCH Software 1.0 Preprocessor Reference.* Select Code. 307-153, AT&T.

Frase, L. T. 1983. The UNIX WRITER'S WORKBENCH Software: Philosophy. *BSTJ*, pp. 1883-1890, v62, no. 6, part 3, July-August 1983.

Furuta, R., J. Scofield, A. Shaw 1982. Document Formatting Systems: Survey, Concepts and Issues. *ACM Computing Surveys*, v14, no. 3 (September), pp. 417-472. Extensive survey of document formatting systems. Characterizes document formatting, describes and evaluates many document formatting systems, for example, the UNIX document formatting facilities, *TEX* and SCRIBE.

Gehani, Narain 1983. *Ada: An Advanced Introduction.* Prentice-Hall.

Gehani, N. H. and W. D. Roome 1984. Concurrent C. AT&T Bell Laboratories.

Gingrich, P. S. 1983. The UNIX WRITER'S WORKBENCH Software: Results of a Field Study. *BSTJ*, pp. 1909-1921, v62, no. 6, part 3, July-August 1983.

Kernighan, B. W. 1978. A `troff` Tutorial. In *UNIX Programmer's Manual (Seventh Edition, Volume 2)* [AT&T UNIX 1983c]. A must for those who insist on programming in `troff`.

Kernighan, B. W. 1981. `pic`—A Crude Graphics Language for Typesetting: User Manual. Computing Science Technical Report no. 85, AT&T Bell

Laboratories.

Kernighan, B. W. 1982a. pic—A Language for Typesetting Graphics. *Software—Practice and Experience*, v12, no. 1 (January), pp. 1-21.

Kernighan, B. W. 1982b. A Typesetter-Independent troff. Computing Science Technical Report no. 97, AT&T Bell Laboratories. The original troff was designed for the CAT typesetter. Early troff "compilers" produced output for the CAT, that is, device-dependent code. Kernighan has modified troff to improve it and changed the troff compiler to make it produce device-independent output (this book is based on the new troff). Using appropriate postprocessors, the output of the device-independent troff can be printed or viewed on a variety of devices.

Kernighan, B. W. 1984. pic—A Graphics Language for Typesetting: Revised User Manual. Computing Science Technical Report no. 116, AT&T Bell Laboratories. This manual describes the latest version of pic. Unlike the previous version [Kernighan 1982a], the new version of pic provides facilities such as trigonometric functions, a random number generator, loop and conditional statements; text strings are now treated as first class citizens.

Kernighan, B. W. and L. L. Cherry 1975. A System for Typesetting Mathematics. *CACM*, v18, no. 3 (March), pp. 151-157. Also in *UNIX Programmer's Manual (Seventh Edition, Volume 2)* [AT&T UNIX 1983c]. Describes the eqn preprocessor for typesetting equations—an important contribution that has had significant impact on mathematical typesetting.

Kernighan, B. W. and M. E. Lesk 1982. UNIX Document Preparation. In *Document Preparation Systems* [Nievergelt, Coray, Nicoud and Shaw 1982].

Kernighan, B. W., M. E. Lesk, and J. F. Ossanna, Jr. 1978. UNIX Time-Sharing System: Document Preparation. *Bell System Technical Journal*, Part 2, v57, no. 6 (July-August), pp. 2115-2135.

Kernighan, B. W. and R. Pike 1984. *The UNIX Programming Environment*. Prentice-Hall. One chapter is devoted to the document formatting facilities on the UNIX system.

Knuth, D. E. 1979. *TEX and METAFONT: New Directions in Typesetting*. Digital Press and American Mathematical Society.

Knuth, D. E. 1984. *The TEXbook*. Addison-Wesley.

Lear, E. 1964. *The Nonsense Books of Edward Lear*. The New American Library.

Lesk, M. E. 1976. `tbl`—A Program To Format Tables. Computing Science Technical Report no. 49, AT&T Bell Laboratories. Also in *UNIX Programmer's Manual (Seventh Edition, Volume 2)* [AT&T UNIX 1983c].

Lesk, M. E. 1978a. Typing Documents on the UNIX System—Using the `-ms` Macros with `troff` and `nroff`. In *UNIX Programmer's Manual (Seventh Edition, Volume 2)* [AT&T UNIX 1983c]. Contains a description of the `ms` macros.

Lesk, M. E. 1978b. Some Applications of Inverted Indices on the UNIX system. Computing Science Technical Report no. 69, AT&T Bell Laboratories. Contains a description of `refer`, the `troff` preprocessor that finds and inserts literature references in documents.

Lesk, M. E. and, B. W. Kernighan 1977. Computer Typesetting of Technical Journals on UNIX. *AFIPS National Comput. Conf. Expo. Proceedings*, v46, pp.879-888. Computer typesetting is faster and more cost effective than typewriter composition. This assertion is supported by experimental results.

Macdonald, N. H., L. T. Frase, P. S. Gingrich and S. A. Keenan 1982. The WRITER'S WORKBENCH: Computer Aids for Text Analysis. *IEEE Transactions on Communication*, v30, no. 1 (January), part 1, pp. 105-110.

Macdonald, N. H. 1983. The UNIX WRITER'S WORKBENCH Software: Rationale and Design. *BSTJ*, v62, no. 6 (July-August), part 3, pp. 1891-1908.

McIlroy, M. D. 1982. Development of a Spelling List. *IEEE Transactions on Communication*, v30, no. 1 (January), part 1, pp. 91-99.

Morison, S. 1967. *First Principles of Typography. Cambridge Author's and Printer's Guide* (Volume 1). Cambridge University Press.

Nievergelt, J., G. Coray, J. D. Nicoud, and A. C. Shaw (Editors) 1982. *Document Preparation Systems: A Collection of Survey Articles.* North-Holland, Amsterdam, Netherlands, 1982.

Ossanna, Jr., J. F. 1977. `nroff/troff` User's Manual. Computing Science Technical Report no. 54, AT&T Bell Laboratories. Also in *UNIX Programmer's Manual (Seventh Edition, Volume 2)* [AT&T UNIX 1983].

Reid, B. K. 1980. Scribe: A High-Level Approach to Computer Document Formatting. *Seventh Symposium on Principles of Programming Languages* (January), Las Vegas. Scribe is a high-level document formatting tool that provides the user with standard types of documents. Detailed information about these documents in contained in a database freeing the user from specifying low-level details such as margins, indenting, fonts and spacing.

Ritchie, D. M. 1979. The Evolution of the UNIX Time-Sharing System. *Proceedings of the Symposium on Language Design and Programming Methodology*, pp. 25-35, *Lecture Notes in Computer Science*, no. 79, Springer-Verlag.

Seybold, J. W. 1979. *Fundamentals of Modern Photocomposition.* Seybold Publications Inc, Box 644, Media, Pennsylvania.

Scrocca (L'Hommedieu), C. 1978. New Graphic Symbols for `eqn` and `neqn`. In Computing Science Technical Report no. 17, AT&T Bell Laboratories.

Spivak, M. 1982. *Joy of TEX: A Gourmet Guide to Typesetting Technical Text by Computer.* American Mathematical Society.

van Leunen, M. 1978. *A Handbook for Scholars.* Knopf, New York., N.Y. A guide to scholarly writing; discusses document format and style, and how to write citations, references, footnotes and bibliographies, and so on.

Van Uchelen, R. 1980. *Word Processing: A Guide to Typography, Taste, and In-House Graphics.* Van Nostrand Reinhold.

Van Wyk, C. J. 1981a. A Graphics Typesetting Language. *Proceedings of the ACM SIGPLAN SIGOA Symposium on Text Manipulation* (June), pp. 99-107, Portland, Oregon. Describes `ideal` which, like `pic`, is a `troff` preprocessor for specifying figures in documents; also see [Van Wyk 1981b].

Van Wyk, C. J. 1981b. `ideal` User's Manual. Computing Science Technical Report no. 103, AT&T Bell Laboratories.

Webster's Dictionary 1977. *Webster's New Collegiate Dictionary.* G. & C. Merriam Company, Springfield, MA.

Wiseman, N. E., C. I. O. Campbell and J. Harradine 1978. On Making Graphics Quality Output by Computer. *Computer Journal*, v21, no. 1 (February), pp. 2-6.

WRITER'S WORKBENCH 1982. UNIX WRITER'S WORKBENCH Software—User's Manual. AT&T Bell Laboratories. Detailed explanation of the analysis done by the WRITER'S WORKBENCH programs, a tutorial introduction to using these programs, and a reference manual for the WRITER'S WORKBENCH programs.

Index

A

B

C

D

F

G

H

M

N

O

P

Q

R

S

T

U

V

W

Z